£20.00

PAPERS AND CORRESPONDENCE
OF
WILLIAM STANLEY JEVONS

Volume III

PAPERS AND CORRESPONDENCE
OF
WILLIAM STANLEY JEVONS

Volume III
CORRESPONDENCE 1863–1872

EDITED BY
R. D. COLLISON BLACK

M

in association with the Royal Economic Society

First published 1977 by
THE MACMILLAN PRESS LTD
London and Basingstoke
Associated companies in New York
Dublin Melbourne Johannesburg and Madras

SBN 333 10253 3

Printed in Great Britain by
UNWIN BROTHERS LTD
Woking and London

CONTENTS

Letter

Letter

Letter

Letter

Letter

Letter

Letter

A complete index to the *Papers and Correspondence, Lectures,* and *Papers on Political Economy* will be contained in Volume VII.

PREFACE

In the Preface to Volume I of this series a plan for subsequent volumes was indicated. According to this, the whole of Jevons's correspondence was to be included in two volumes, Volume II comprising letters up to 1862 and Volume III those from 1863 until 1882. A fourth volume was to contain the complete transcript of the lectures on political economy given by Jevons at Owens College, Manchester, in 1875–6, the text of all Jevons's papers on economic subjects previously published but not collected together, and a number of other items selected to cast light on the development and reception of Jevons's economic ideas.

Volume II was published as planned in 1973, but two developments have since compelled changes in the arrangement of the later volumes. Firstly, the quantity of correspondence for the years 1863 to 1882 was increased by a number of discoveries of material outside the main collection originally made available to me by Mrs Könekamp, so that the number of letters became greater than could be contained even in one very large volume. Secondly, the great acceleration of rates of inflation since 1973 has produced rises in printing costs so large as to make it impossible for Macmillan to maintain the original size and format of the volumes. Hence it has proved necessary to divide the correspondence for the years 1863 to 1882 into three volumes, now numbered III, IV and V, while the material originally intended to constitute Volume IV has had to be divided over two further volumes, now numbered VI and VII.

I apologise to readers for this deviation from the plan originally published, but trust that they will recognise it as the result of circumstances largely outside my control. Although the form of the volumes has been altered, their content has not been reduced and all the material which it was originally intended to publish will now appear in this and succeeding volumes. The complete index which it was originally stated would appear in Volume IV will now be included at the end of Volume VII. Additional letters which have come to light since the publication of Volume II are numbered with a suffix, e.g. '279A'. This seemingly clumsy method of insertion has been preferred to the neater alternative of renumbering the whole sequence of correspondence, because to have done this would have upset cross-references which had already been published in Volumes I and II.

The present volume covers correspondence during the years 1863 to 1872, years which saw the foundation of Jevons's academic career and the beginnings of his national and international reputation as an economist. In the earlier part of the volume family letters still predominate, and reflect the hopes and fears about his appointment at Owens College which also found expression at this time in Jevons's personal journal.[1] Mixed with these are his feelings of elation and trepidation at finding himself almost overnight an authority being widely quoted in national controversies – and the contributions which Jevons made to the 'gold question' and the 'coal question' brought a 'public' element into his correspondence for the first time, as he began to exchange letters with such men as Gladstone, Bagehot and Sir John Herschel in and after 1866. There are also the beginnings of correspondence with foreign scholars, such as Etienne Laspeyres and Louis Wolowski; but from the point of view of economic theory perhaps the greatest interest attaches to the letters from Fleeming Jenkin on the theory of exchange, which stimulated Jevons to give the ideas which he had sketched out in 1862[2] full expression in *The Theory of Political Economy* in 1871.

In the Prefaces to Volumes I and II I have acknowledged some of the debts which I have accumulated for help in the process of editing these papers. Since that time their sum has been greatly increased, both by further help from those patient and helpful friends and colleagues who had often aided me before and by new help from many others. My Research Officer, Mrs J. Wright, has throughout been my main source of assistance in searching for material and locating references; without her expert knowledge and continuing interest what has proved a lengthy process must inevitably have been much longer. For much hard work in the process of typing the complex and varied manuscripts from which these volumes have been compiled I am grateful to Mrs P. Finn.

For help in locating and identifying material published in this and subsequent volumes my thanks are due particularly to Professor Craufurd D. Goodwin of Duke University and Miss Mary Canada, Reference Librarian of Duke University Library, who provided biographical information about D. M. Balfour and assisted with other American references, as did Dr Kenneth Carpenter, Librarian of the Kress Library at Harvard University; to Professor R. H. Tener, Department of English, University of Calgary, for information about the papers of R. H. Hutton; to the Director of the Central State Historical Archive at Riga, Latvian Soviet Socialist Republic, who supplied biographical information on Ernst Nauck and other information about the early history of the Riga

---

[1] See Vol. I, especially pp. 205–6.
[2] In 'A Brief Account of a General Mathematical Theory of Political Economy', *JRSS*, 29 (1866) 284–5.

Polytechnic, which was kindly translated for me by my colleague, Professor M. C. Wheeler; and to Mrs J. Percival, Archivist of University College London, who helped me to trace the details of the donation of Parliamentary Papers from that college to Owens College, Manchester, which Jevons negotiated, as well as to establish many other points about his connections with University College.

I should also like to record my gratitude to Dr G. Chandler and Miss Janet Smith, of the Liverpool Record Office, for locating information concerning Jevons's appointment to the staff of Queen's College, Liverpool; to Mr Barnes, of the Archive Section of the Bank of England, for allowing me access to the staff records of the Bank to trace the career of John Laing; and to Mr Colin Davis, Secretary of the Manchester and Salford Trades Council, for biographical information on William Macdonald. Similar information was kindly provided concerning Charles Upton by Rev. Brian Golland, General Secretary to the Assembly of the Unitarian and Free Christian Churches; concerning A. B. Hopkins by Mr W. A. Taylor, City Librarian of Birmingham; concerning George Whitehead by Mr D. J. Bryant, Chief Librarian, Kingston upon Hull City Libraries; and concerning B. W. Farey by Mr C. W. Ashton, Director, the Bryan Donkin Co. Ltd, Chesterfield, and Mr R. T. Everett, Librarian of the Institution of Mechanical Engineers, London. To all these I should like to express my thanks, as also to Mr P. Spiro, Librarian of the Institute of Bankers, London, who assisted with biographical information on H. W. Roberts and William McKewan; to the Librarian, Chetham's Library, Manchester, for information on papers read by J. C. Ollerenshaw and E. Langley to the Manchester Statistical Society; to my colleague Mr Alun Davies, of the Department of Economic and Social History, Queen's University Belfast, for information about the Paris Exhibition of 1867 and the Electrical Exhibition of 1881; and to Mrs Kathryn Green, who researched a number of Manchester references for me. For permission to make use of manuscript material of which they have custody, or in which they hold the copyright, my thanks are due to Sir William Gladstone, Bt, the Rt Hon. Patrick Jenkin, M.P., Dr Wolfe Mays, Dr M. A. T. Rogers, the Rt Hon. Norman St-John Stevas, M.P., Mrs R. T. Sneyd, the British Library Board, the Trustees of the British Library of Political and Economic Science, the Co-operative Union, Ltd, Manchester, the Librarian, University of Leicester, the Cultural Services Committee of the Corporation of the City of Manchester, Dr F. W. Ratcliffe, John Rylands Librarian of the University of Manchester, the Directors of the Macmillan Press Ltd, the Trustees of the National Library of Ireland, the Directors of the National Westminster Bank, the President and Council of the Royal Society, the President and Council of the Royal Statistical

Society, the Directors of *Times* Newspapers Ltd, the Council of University College London, and P. S. Laurie Esq., Archivist, the Royal Greenwich Observatory.

Queen's University   R. D. COLLISON BLACK
Belfast
November 1975

LIST OF ABBREVIATIONS
used throughout the volumes

Relating to Jevons material

LJ   *Letters and Journal of W. Stanley Jevons*, edited by his wife (1886).

LJN   Previously published in LJ; manuscript not now in Jevons Papers, or other known location.

LJP   Previously published in LJ, but only in part; fuller text now given from the orginal manuscript in the Jevons Papers or other indicated location.

WM   From a manuscript made available by Dr Wolfe Mays, University of Manchester.

Investigations   *Investigations in Currency and Finance*, by W. Stanley Jevons. Edited, with an Introduction, by H. S. Foxwell (1884). All page references to first edition.

Methods   *Methods of Social Reform and other papers*, by W. Stanley Jevons (1883).

T.P.E.   *The Theory of Political Economy* by W. Stanley Jevons (1st ed. 1871, 4th ed. 1911). All page references to fourth edition, unless otherwise stated.

Relating to other material

BM   British Museum, London (now British Library).

FW   Fonds Walras, Bibliothèque Cantonale de Lausanne.

HLRS   Herschel Letters, Royal Society, London.

JRSS   *Journal of the London* (later *Royal*) *Statistical Society*.

KCP   Palgrave Papers in the Library of King's College, Cambridge.

LSE   London School of Economics, British Library of Political and Economic Science.

MA   Archives of Macmillan & Co. Ltd.

NYPL   New York Public Library.

RDF   From a manuscript made available by Mr R. D. Freeman.

TLJM   Isabel Mills, *From Tinder Box to the 'Larger Light'. Threads from the Life of John Mills, Banker* (Manchester, 1899).

Walras Correspondence   *Correspondence of Léon Walras and Related Papers* edited by William Jaffé (3 vols, Amsterdam, 1965).

Figures following any of these abbreviations denote page numbers.

LETTERS

8 Porteus Road,
18th January 1863.

. . . We unfortunately missed the last mail, from not thinking of it at
the right moment – perhaps because Christmas was coming upon
us . . . Whether you get on well or ill, I should be sorry to think of your
always remaining away. In some years to come I hope we may all be
better placed. But what every one, and yourself, of course, included,
wants, is not so much comfortable living as a satisfactory occupation – in
short – work, and that is even more difficult to get sometimes than
anything else. If you could make yourself interested in work, whatever it
be, and go through with it successfully, that, according to philosophers
from Aristotle downwards, is happiness. I believe he is right, and that
happiness is inseparable from exertion, and is, in fact, hopeful exertion.
This is in direct contradiction to your doctrine, which excludes exertion
altogether, and lets things take their course.

I am still *in statu quo ante* in London. I am trying the scheme of agency at
the Museum, but as yet have only had one job, and that not of the right
sort. I am much inclined to fear it will not do. It is regarded as too dubious
and irregular an occupation, as is apparent from the notes of the few who
have applied to me; to say the truth, I am not so much set as I was upon
remaining in London. Its principal advantage is access to the
Museum – but this rather misleads one into trivial subjects, and I should,
perhaps, do better with fewer books.

At Christmas Harry Roscoe[1] proposed my going as tutor to Owens
College, where I might make perhaps £200 a year. I put the matter off till
the beginning of next session in October, when, if nothing better occurs in
the meantime, I shall probably go. 'Half a loaf is better than no bread,' as
they say; and I am not afraid that, because I begin with a rather humble
place, I shall never get a better. I require some years of quiet work to
bring out my theories in at all a presentable form, and I must have a
means of living in the meantime. And if I do not get on so fast in worldly
ways, I am quite satisfied with my own theories, which ever become
clearer and more perfect.

The diagrams, after all, have not lost me much money, as they will pay
back more than £20 of what I spent on them. Since you left they were

---

[1] See Vol. I, pp. 39–40.

praised in the *Exchange Magazine* – the editor of which has a fancy for diagrams. They were just mentioned in a *Times* money article, and also in the *Economist*,[2] and by these *opinions*, sent in a fresh circular, I continued to sell a good many more of them, and Stanford has sold altogether nearly two hundred, and at Liverpool three dozen were sold. I have been encouraged therefore to prepare a new set of small diagrams, to form a small atlas, and give numbers of prices, etc., for the several months of 1844 – 62. They are getting on pretty well, and will, I think, succeed. In the meantime I have been led to observe the great rise in prices of nearly all things since 1851, which is obviously due to a fall in the value of gold. This I am now trying to ascertain and prove in a conclusive manner, which will, of course, be a very important and startling fact. Supposing it to be proved, I do not yet know whether to publish it with my atlas or separately. . . .

170.   W. S. JEVONS TO J. SMITH[1]

8, Porteus Road W.
18 February, 1863.

Dear Dr. Smith,

As a couple of newspapers just arrived show that you have kindly remembered me I must make it an excuse for one of my annual letters.

My thoughts are especially directed to Sydney at this time because my brother[2] was there at the latest date, and I hope still remains. Miller[3] was so good as to procure him an appointment in the Bank of N.S.W. but as the business of buying gold – which he was to undertake – must require a peculiarly knowing and active person I cannot feel sure that he will ultimately hold the place. By ill health some years ago, and subsequently by an unfortunate expedition to America, his energies and natural abilities have been much impaired and wasted – and I must confess to some anxiety as to his having any success even in Australia. At the worst he has only to return, and I am glad he should have tried Australia where the fine cheerful warm weather will suit him and perhaps improve his spirits.

A late letter from Miller informed me that the observatory had been vacant some months and urged me to apply for the place of Observer. It would indeed be a comfortable berth and quite to my mind in most ways.

---

[2] For particulars of these reviews, see Vol. II, Letter 167, p. 459.

[1] See Vol. I, p. 25.

[2] Herbert Jevons, who had sailed for Australia in 1862. See Vol. I, pp. 9 – 10.

[3] F. B. Miller, the second assayer at the Royal Mint in Sydney, with whom Jevons resided during his stay there. See Vol. II, Letter 27, n. 6, p. 49.

I might have done the meteorological work pretty well, and learnt to regulate the *time* accurately enough, but there are quite enough contrary reasons to prevent my thinking of it at all. Probably a Cambridge mathematician and astronomer is appointed long since, and they ought I think to be able to get a good one.

However poor may seem my prospects here at present I cannot give up the notion that they will improve in time, and that there is a scope for work and success here in a very different way from a colonial observership. I went out to Sydney originally with the full intention of returning and chiefly went because it gave me an independent start and was convenient at the time to the rest of our family.

My cousin Dr. Roscoe is urgent with me to go as a tutor and kind of supernumerary lecturer to their college at Manchester, where they have sometime been wanting something of the sort. I shall probably go at the beginning of next session as apart from getting some money by it, I shall have the agreeable company of my cousin and of the Principal – Greenwood, and Prof. Clifton,[4] who were respectively a favourite schoolmaster, and a favourite college fellow 10 or 12 years ago.

I have been employed the last 2 months on some long inquiries into com. statistics and prices, from which as a collateral result I have proved beyond doubt the great depreciation of gold. The prices of 39 chief articles of commerce are now some 15 per cent above the average of 1845–50 which I assume as the natural price previous to the gold disc[overies]. I further show that prices now are considerably lower than they were in 1857 and from commercial and political causes, especially the American war, must be regarded as at a minimum. Sixty-two minor commodities being examined gave an average rise of price of $8\frac{1}{2}$ per cent. From the whole 101 articles, I deduce that 10 per cent is the very least depreciation of gold which can be admitted. Silver is also found to be depreciated 7 per cent or 3 less than the gold, which is accounted for by the overflow of the French silver currency. But I have some notion of briefly printing the results and in that case will send them to you.[5]

171. W. S. JEVONS TO HERBERT JEVONS
[LJN, 179]

8 Porteus Road, 19th February 1863.

. . . We are at present in London as for the last few years, but I am convinced I must get some more regular occupation as soon as

4 See Vol. I, p. 41.
5 This manuscript is incomplete and the letter was apparently never sent.

possible. . . . The notion of living in Manchester is not altogether an agreeable one; but I think it will be a step in the right direction. After some experience in teaching, and by degrees in lecturing, I shall be more ready to offer myself for any professorship that may happen – perhaps one at Owens College itself. There is no doubt, I think, that the professorial line is the one for me to take. I have given up all notion, for the present, of hack-writing, as it seems to me it must be destructive of any true thinking, and, unless to a person with a very ready and popular style, must be an occupation full of hardship and disappointment . . .

172.   W. S. JEVONS TO T. E. JEVONS

8 Porteus R^d   W.

12 Mar. 1863. [1]

Dear Tom

We are rather relieved here that the marriage affair is over. [2] Tuesday night was such as few of us will see again.

As the Dawsons [3] expressed their intention of going on foot to see the illums Henny asked them to stay the night here, & to meet Talfourd Ely [4] & ourselves here previously. Thus it was I became committed to taking Lucy & Mary Dawson & Henny the round of the streets, Talf. of course taking his intended. We got as far as Farringdon Street very agreably* by the underground. I objected strongly to going citywards but Mary Dawsons desire to see St Pauls ultimately lead us to try Ludgate Hill. Finding it apparently safe we proceeded up nearly as far as the Old Bailey, when there suddenly came down such a rush of 'Whitechapel roughs', about 8 abreast, in wild humour, as would terrify any mortal. These men were in the highest state of excitement making for the West End. Many of them wore masks as noses, or other signs that they intended a spree. The thieves thinking that no body could be so foolish as to bring out anything worth stealing were taking a holyday* & contented themselves with appropriating all the wedding favours of their neighbours which they pinned in large numbers on their own breasts.

We naturally desired to escape from such a hazardous mob, & after waiting a few minutes in the lee of a lamp post until the stream had passed plunged across the street & into a narrow entry. After various winding

[1] The original manuscript of this letter is incomplete.

[2] i.e. the marriage of Edward, Prince of Wales to Princess Alexandra of Denmark. See Journal entry for 8 March 1873, Vol. I, p. 172.

[3] See Vol. II, Letter 5, n. 1, p. 10.

[4] Talfourd Ely (d. 1922), a master at University College School, 1854–76; Secretary of University College London, 1876–86; author of *Catalogue of Works of Art in the Flaxman Gallery, University College, London* (1900).

passed Printing House Square, we got safely & easily into New Bridge Street – Talf. & Ada Dawson in the meantime not much desiring to follow us had separated & not very wisely proceeded through the city. Today I heard that after being dreadfully crushed they ran a narrow escape of their lives from a prancing horse, Tal. losing his hat in seizing the horses bridle & struggling with it.

We proceeded onto Blackfriars Bridge where there were comparatively few people, in order to see St Pauls. At diff^t heights upon the Dome were three rings of lights, composed of ships lanterns the middle being red lights, & some light was thrown on parts of the arch^e from electric lanterns. This was not a brilliant display but the size & shape of St Pauls are always so imposing that seen as it was indistinctly in the mist & glare of the great town, standing calmly out from the centre of struggling humanity, the sight was very interesting & grand. It was rendered more singular by a splendid electric lantern placed near the ball, the rays of which were thrown by a hyperbolic mirror in various directions. The great comet like beam of slightly diverging light, perhaps a mile long thus thrown over the city, or whisked about in a moment over miles of circumference had a very remarkable effect.

Avoiding Fleet street we dived through many back streets to the side gate of the Temple. We were disappointed in finding it closed but after waiting with other people a few minutes it was opened to let a carriage pass. Before the old porter could shut the gate again we all rushed in & proceeded calmly across the ancient locality. The calm here was only broken by occasional sounds of revelry in the halls where the templars were celebrating the day – & by the strains of God Save the Queen from a Volunteer band, probably attending one of the banquets. Reaching the other gate, we were again concerned at finding two huge policemen struggling to shut the gate against a crowd, & refusing to let anyone out. The notion of being caged was not agreable.* But before long a templar came wanting to get out, & the mob wanting to get in had dispersed, & thus we were let out. Ascending into the Strand through Essex Street we saw without inconvenience many illum^s especially Temple Bar covered with golden drapery, decorations & images & well lighted up. Thence through Wych Street to the Strand opposite Somerset house, which was brilliant with lines of light tracing the architecture. We coasted down the Strand avoiding crowded parts by diving into side streets. At one corner however we were again involved in a struggling moving mass of people of a very dangerous character – one person probably a boy quite near us got on to the ground & was trampled on more or less but how much injured I did not stay to learn. Devoting my best efforts to extricating the ladies, who were but half conscious of the danger, I still more carefully avoided crowded parts. Yet we managed to get into Charing Cross where there was plenty of room & the grand displays in many directions were visible. Parliament Street was like a blaze of light, the National Gallery bore an elaborate work in glass. The fountains looked pretty under the rays of electric lanterns, & the moving masses of people the waving flags, & the general sense of excitement made up a thrilling scene. At the bottom of the Haymarket we were again involved for a few minutes in a crush, but then got easily along the Mall, avoiding the lower part of Regent Street in spite of its brilliant appearance. The club houses showed only moderately well. St James Square was well lighted, splendid ill[s][5] were visible down even the side streets. Crossing Piccadilly which presented a long line of brilliant designs vanished into the misty red distance we cut across into the Quadrant. A line of gas ran long the cornice throughout the Quadrant & dozens of fine designs rendered it as light as day. The crowd was moderate & far more gentle than nearer the city. Passing a part of the way up Regent Street we turned down Conduit Street & through passages into Savile row where the Tailor of the P Wales had put up a splendid glass design at the cost of £1700, attracting a huge crowd opposite his shop. We lastly turned homewards up Bond Street which was brilliant from end to end, & by Brook Street, across the corner of Hyde Park & through quiet streets home. Even the remote squares however had some minor lights or designs. We had started about 8 & reached home perhaps at 11.30 p m. Even then carriages cabs & vans of people were arriving in the Bayswater Road taking their place at the end of the line towards[6] town! Moving at a rate that would get them there in a week at the earliest. Thousands & thousands spent the greater part of the night in almost stationary vehicles, seeing little or nothing & only catching a cold. It was better to run some little risk & see as well as we did. But I should certainly not do so foolish thing again as take 3 ladies to see London ill[s] Never was a more joyous but excited & restless & immense body of people brought together & it is a wonder that only seven people were killed. The numbers hurt more or less must I think be in hundreds.

Very rarely I think is a pop[n] wrought up to such unanimous feelings of rejoicing some by real interest in the event, others by the love of a little excitement at an appropriate moment, & by the contagion of feeling.

[5] i.e. illuminations.
[6] 'to end' in the original manuscript.

173. W. S. JEVONS TO MRS LUCY HUTTON[1]
[LJN, 179–81]

43 Richmond Grove, Manchester,
20th April 1863.

. . . I don't know whether I informed you that I was coming here to arrange or consider the tutorship affair.

. . . On Sunday afternoon Mr. Greenwood, Harry, Alfred Booth, and myself went a walk, in the course of which I talked the matter over with Mr. Greenwood. I have also gone into it pretty fully with Harry, and also with Professor Clifton, who has been very friendly.

Although there are, of course, many things to deter one from coming here, it becomes more and more obvious that it will, on the whole, be greatly to my advantage to come.

It is *quite possible* that I may make £200 the first session – at least probable I shall make £150, and there can be no doubt I shall make over a hundred at any rate.

Considering the less cost of houses and living, my income would in any case be equal to or greater than my expenditure. The teaching work may be considered drudgery, but it is a very proper preliminary to a better place, and such as almost all go through in the larger universities before getting to a professor's chair. Even Mr. Greenwood hinted that in the course of a few years I might fairly look forward to a professorship in Owens College.

And then I find that Manchester, although smoky, has still a distinguished literary position. I should see a great deal more of good society than I should in London, living there for a quarter of a century.

I have not lived twenty-eight years without being aware that, independent of any inward merits, there is a certain position necessary to make one known and recognised. This I have a far better chance of getting here than in London. . . . It is also not to be forgotten that the college is a very rising one, and although decidedly a shabby one at present, may grow, and in future and more prosperous years will probably be rebuilt, and rendered very important. I have been to-day to see the Cheetham* Library, of which I had heard not a little. I find it to be one of the most delightful old libraries I could conceive to exist, apparently hardly touched since the Middle Ages came to an end. Nor is it the only good library here.

My work here would consist in teaching small classes of six or eight students for some two or three hours per day, as well as giving my general

[1] i.e. Lucy Jevons, who had married John Hutton in January 1862. See Vol. I, p. 11.

assistance. I might also have, if I liked, some of the evening classes, attended by men from the town, which are at present taken by the professors or by other teachers, the profits of which would amount to some fifteen shillings each evening, or £15 per course. And it seems I might almost have a *carte blanche* to form courses of logic or political economy for these evening lectures – if students presented themselves in sufficient numbers. I should of course have some difficulty in beginning to teach, but it must be met sooner or later, and there cannot well be a better opportunity for practice. On all these accounts I am inclined to come here, the only contrary inclinations arising from the dull nature of the town, and the regret in leaving London and the Museum. I have been much more inclined to the scheme since I found that Mr. Greenwood's explanations of the subject were even more favourable than Harry's. You may, then, I think, conclude that I shall to-morrow agree with Mr. Greenwood about it, and the minor arrangements may then be considered matter of course. . . .

174.   WILLIAM JEVONS JUNIOR [1] TO W. S. JEVONS

Grant House,
Hayward's Heath,
Sussex.
May 2, 1863.

My dear Stanley,

You are now, I presume, again in London, and I want to hear something about your visit to Manchester, and to tell you of our having left Brighton for a time. You see by the date where we are, and you must know something of the locality from having passed it on the railway. Our lodgings are very pleasantly situated nearly at the highest point of the common, and commanding an extensive and charming view on all sides. We came here on Thursday with the intention of staying a month or six weeks, and I hope the bracing air of this eminence will restore us all to a better tone of health. Accept my best thanks for your book on the value of Gold, and for the letter which accompanied it. I have read as yet only a part of your treatise, and feel incompetent to give an opinion on it, as the subject is new to me, and foreign to my usual studies. But I understand enough to see the justice of your conclusion that the late gold discoveries have added nothing to the real wealth of the world. The only mistake I have noticed in your book is in p. 8, where you say that "social causes such as *wars*, civil disturbances, disputes among workmen, are incapable of

---

[1] For biographical details, see Vol. I, p. 183.

causing fluctuations of supply of any importance". Yet on the next page you state that "during the present blockade of the ports of the Southern United States cotton has risen to three or more times its natural value."

I am much obliged to you for the extract from Grote's history.[2] It is interesting; but it does not give me the information I wanted about the priestesses of Apollo speaking many different languages.

Do not hurry yourself in reading my dissertations: but take your own time. Only let me know when you have done with them, and then I will tell you in what way I wish you to return them.

Hoping soon to hear that you have succeeded in Manchester.

> I remain,
> My dear Stanley,
> Your affectionate Uncle
> W. Jevons.

175. WILLIAM JEVONS JUNIOR TO W. S. JEVONS

> Grant House,
> Hayward's Heath,
> May 8, 1863.

My dear Stanley,

I was very glad to receive your letter of the 4th and to learn from it that you have made satisfactory arrangements for your settlement as a tutor in Manchester. I have no doubt the college will benefit by your services as much as you will benefit by the employment thus afforded you.

I am gratified by what you say about my dissertations. It is very true that the title of my work would be unsuitable if it consisted *only* of these destructive criticisms, or if the negative *preponderated* over the positive matter. But my intention is to intermix with the Dissertations an equal number of Discourses,[1] the aim of which will be to recommend practical Christianity and to fortify its moral lessons with the matter of philosophical religion. I do not, however, wonder at your having the impression that the critical and destructive parts preponderate, as I gave you in the last instance only *Dissertations* to read. I should have given you at the same time the Discourses which are to accompany them. But you did not ask for them, and I thought they would not equally interest you.

It is not my intention, as you seem to suppose, to publish my work

[2] George Grote, *A History of Greece*, 12 vols (1846–56).

[1] William Jevons Junior did not publish any work with such a title as *Dissertations and Discourses*. The manuscript here referred to may have been that on 'Christianity without Miracles' which he was seeking to publish in October 1862 – cf. Volume I, p. 184. Again, no work with *this* title seems to have appeared, but it may have been a modified version which William Jevons published in 1870 under the title *The Claims of Christianity to the character of a divine revelation considered*.

anonymously. My name, I know, will not at all serve to recommend the work to public notice. But neither will it, on the other hand, damage the book's chance of success, and it seems to me a more manly course to avow myself as the author. To withhold my name would seem as if I was ashamed to encounter the clamour and obloquy it may provoke.

There are two ways of returning my M.S.S. namely by *sending* them, or by *bringing* them, and I would much rather that you would choose the latter, if you can do so without inconvenience. I should be very glad to see you, and I think you would enjoy a trip to this delightful neighbourhood. We cannot offer you a bed: but if you come by one of the earliest trains (at 6 a.m. or 8 a.m., from either station) and return by the latest train which passes here at 8.25 p.m., you can breakfast, dine and drink tea with us, and have ample time to walk about and see the beauties of the country. If you cannot do this, I must invoke you to send my M.S.S. in a parcel by train. But first let me request you to visit Dr. Williams's Library and ascertain whether any of the books, of which I subjoin a list, are to be found there. In case they are, I will send back three of the books I have, and then perhaps you will get for me two or three of those in the list, and send them and the M.S.S. in the same parcel.

I have seen the advertisement of your book on Gold in the Athenaeum, and I hope I shall soon see a favourable review of it in that or some other periodical. I now understand you better in what you say in Sec. iv about *Wars* as affecting supply. You mean that they do not much affect the supply of *metals*. But I demur to this statement: for surely our supply of gold would be much diminished if all our colonies where gold is found were to revolt and go to war with us.

I shall have something more to say about your book if you come to see us. At present I can only add that your aunt and cousin send their love, and that I am,

Your affectionate uncle,
W. Jevons.

176.   W. S. JEVONS TO T. E. JEVONS
[LJP, 183]

8 Porteus Rd W.
15 May 63

Dear Tom

If you dont go and look for lodgings soon I shall be going off somewhere else. Go & take notes of the kind & cost of lodgings, & on hearing the result I shall be able to tell you when I will come. It will be before the end of the month. Probably either next Saturday or the Saturday after.

The chief thing *is perfect quietness* for me to work during the day. If you could get a solitary cottage on the Sandhills it would do admirably. But there must be neither children nor cocks & hens near it. There must be a comfortable parlour & a good double bedded room, & at a very moderate cost. If near the sea all the better – I dont object to the noise of the waves.

A good walk to the ferry early every morning will do you good. We will get up at day break & bathe before breakfast & all that sort of thing.

I have got your BA. Cert. I am now a veritable MA having been presented to Granville.[1] I have also got my medal which is a good heavy lump of bullion; it sorely tempts me as a prof. Gold assayer to try what metal it is made of. If nothing happens to it you shall see it some day. UCL as usual showed up strongly at the presentation.

I am in rather good spirits as my logical system is at last clear from further doubt. It is the same as Boole's[2] in some ways but free from all his false mathematical dress which I show to be not only unnecessary but actually erroneous, & only giving true results by a kind of compromise really reducing it to my own form. On the other hand my methods reduce the most complicated sets of prop^s with great ease & *intuitively*. From one set for instance of 3 prop^s involving say 5 or 6 different terms I can easily deduce as many other prop^s containing relations between those terms. There would be many hundred prop^s between 5 or 6 terms. Boole can get these relations but only by laboriously working out each case by mathem^l processes. The Aristotelian logicians might perhaps deduce one or two of the results with difficulty. The essential part of my method however is to show that the prop^n is really an equation, analogous in most of its properties to an equation in quantity. Boole has confused the equation of quality & the equation of quantity together, and all the wild complexities of De Morgan & other logicians arise from confusing quality & quantity. My doctrine is that there is no quantity at all in logic. All terms are really universal, as Boole shows indeed, but then Boole spoils his system by introducing 1 & 0, & various symbols whose meaning is really derived from logic not contained in it.

I understand from Richard Hutton that there will be an article in the Spectator tomorrow on my Gold pamphlet[3] – He considers that the fall is conclusively proved. There begin to be some slight signs that the thing is noticed, but very slight.

[1] Granville George Leveson Gower, second Earl Granville (1815–91), leader of the Liberal party in the House of Lords from 1855; Foreign Secretary, 1851–2, 1870–4 and 1880–5; Colonial Secretary, 1868–70 and 1886; Chancellor of the University of London, 1856–91.

[2] George Boole (1815–64), Professor of Mathematics at Queen's College. Cork, from 1849 until his death; F.R.S. 1857; author of *Mathematical Analysis of Logic* (1847). Cf. Vol. I, pp. 40 and 201.

[3] 'Political Economy and the Gold Discoveries', *The Spectator*, 16 May 1863, p. 2013. In this article Hutton reviewed both Fawcett's *Manual of Political Economy* and Jevons's *A Serious Fall*, but confined himself to considering Fawcett's view of the effects of the gold discoveries and comparing it with that of Jevons.

I am extremely lazy at present, chiefly occupied in loafing about & visiting here & there. I have been twice to the Academy, which is chiefly full of absurd things but contains two or three pictures which do your eyes good to see them.

Our inspection takes place tomorrow when I expect we shall cut a splendid figure. Our battalion drill last Saturday was very encouraging. I cannot say that individually I have improved or make anything of a non com. off.

I am glad to find from what one sees on every side, & what is said in Parliament that the V Force far from declining is in a most flourishing condition. It seems to me the Government has no notion of giving it up now.

Ever yours
WSJ

177.   W. S. JEVONS TO HERBERT JEVONS
    [LJP, 183–5]

8 Porteus Rd W.
19 May 1863.

My dear Herbert

As the mail day is nearly come again I must tell you what little there is to interest you. I am still in London but closing up my affairs here & in a week more I expect to leave here for good. London is very lively just at this time of year & there are various meetings, Rifle affairs & so forth which detain one, but I am very anxious to have some time in the country this summer before going to Manchester. I am arranging with Tom that we shall go into lodgings together at Wallasey where he is in treaty for a couple of rooms.

I shall stay there a month or six weeks & then spend the rest of the 4 months at Beaumaris or any part where Lucy may be.

My arrangements with Mr Greenwood the Principal of Owens College are that I shall go there in October if some 20 or 25 pupils offer to pay 3 guineas each for the Session. There is little doubt he thinks that some 30 will offer, giving me £100 a year to begin with. There is also an evening class of logic which I am to have, but which will not pay more than a few pounds. Private teaching must make up the rest. For the second session if I desire it, I may probably have elementary evening classes of Latin & Greek which pay more. It must however be chiefly left to experience to show how much I shall do there.

Henny is still at Beaumaris & they are all well there so far as I know. John has had much anxiety about his business but I believe his prospects are now improving.

Tom is all right in Liverpool. He has started a debating society, called the Pnyx which meets at the Royal Institution, and I hope it may prosper.

Our Lit. & Phil. Society at College of which I am President[1] seems to have a long future before it. At first many of the older students held aloof from it, & predicted its ill success, but a few dull meetings having been survived, many of the old students including distinguished graduates are joining & many of the papers are interesting. This day week we are to have a show meeting at which a Professor is to preside.

Rifle matters are in a very favourable position – The Force on the average is scarcely less than it was, & is probably better trained & managed. Our corps in their inspection last Saturday brought up 908 men of all ranks which is more than they presented last year by 15 per cent, & most of the manœvres were fairly done. Parliament have not only voted addit[1] allowances of money to support the corps but have readily passed a new Act[2] consolidating the law & giving various facilities & regulations tending to make the Institution permanent – & it is now regarded as such on all hands.

I shall be sorry to leave my Corps the Queens, but I shall be sure to join a Manchester Corps if I remain there any time.

I am forwarding some copies of my pamphlet on the value of Gold to Miller and he will I hope send one or two on to you. It has as yet sold very badly, & has not been noticed by more than one or two papers. R. Hutton has given me an article or part of an article, & warmly adopts my view of the question[3] I have had acknowledgement of copies which I sent to various persons, among whom Mr Newmarch[4] the chief Authority on the opposite side of the question does not agree to all my conclusions but says he has carefully read the whole & seems to regard it favourably. I also have a brief acknowledgement in the handwriting of Gladstone,[5] who is now regarded as the leading man in the country.

I shall not I think go on with these statistical matters much at present, but I have plenty of other work going on, & besides have to prepare for my College work at Manchester.

Your accounts of your Australian life are always interesting but as you will probably be in N Zealand before you get this it is needless to refer much to them. I am glad to hear that the 2 fields are proving so rich as it will increase the importance of your employment.

I hope you will stick to your Bank as long as practicable & no other

---

[1] Cf. the entry in Jevons's Journal for 31 December 1862, Vol. I, p. 187.

[2] 26 & 27 Vict. c. lxv, an Act to consolidate and amend the Acts relating to the Volunteer Force in Great Britain.

[3] See above, Letter 176, n. 3, p. 13.

[4] See Vol. I. pp. 180–1.

[5] Neither this note from Gladstone nor Newmarch's letter is now among the Jevons Papers.

really better place offers. I have requested Miller to send a copy of my pamphlet to Mr Woodhouse of the Bank.

I shall be glad when you are so settled that I may know where to direct to you straight, & I wish I could tell you the same as to my direction. For the present you had better write only to Liverpool.

You will be interested by the late American news. The utter failure of the boasted Monitors to take Charleston & the sinking or damaging of several, is the most important fact. The advance of General Hooker just begun is yet a matter of uncertainty. In spite of the great slaughter it is impossible to suppose that he will make any head against Stonewall Jackson.[6] It must be allowed that it is utterly impossible to say when the war will end, and if they go on much longer we shall become gradually indifferent to the result. With the exception of part of Lancashire, this country cannot now be said to suffer from the war.

We shall all be glad to have further news of your success, & your proceedings in New Zealand. Please write at length & say what you can cheerful for we are not always here so cheerful in England as to need anything uncheerful from Australia.

As soon as possible tell us how to direct straight to you so that it may not be needful to trouble Miller. Or should we direct to the Bank at Sydney.

Ever your affec. Brother
W. S. Jevons.

178.   J. E. CAIRNES[1] TO W. S. JEVONS

Stameen
Drogheda,
May, 28, 1863.

Dear Sir,

I have to thank you very much for your pamphlet on the "Fall in the Value of Gold", which you have done me the favour to send me. I have read it with very great interest – the more as it corroborates in what seems to me a very remarkable manner some opinions which I myself advanced upon the same subject some four or five years ago.

---

[6] The Northern and Confederate forces met at Chancellorsville, Virginia, early in May 1863. During the advance, the Army of the Potomac, under the command of General Joseph Hooker (1814–79), suffered a surprise attack by the Confederate General Thomas 'Stonewall' Jackson, who was killed during the battle. Hooker failed to recover sufficiently to win a decisive victory, despite vastly superior numbers. Cf. Vol. II, Letter 165, n. 7, p. 454.

[1] John Elliott Cairnes (1823–75), Professor of Political Economy at Trinity College, Dublin, 1856–61, Queen's College, Galway, 1859–70, University College London, 1866–72. Author of *Character and Logical Method of Political Economy* (1857), *The Slave Power* (1862), *Some Leading Principles of Political Economy Newly Expounded* (1874). Now generally regarded as 'the last of the classical economists', his influence at this time was second only to that of J. S. Mill. Cf. Vol. I, p. 192 and references there cited.

Indeed, considering the entirely distinct methods of inquiry we have pursued, and our complete mutual independence, I have thought the coincidence of sufficient importance to call attention to it in the columns of the *Economist*: I have accordingly written to that paper a letter which will probably appear about Saturday week (I fear it will be late for the next issue), and from which you will see that your conclusions receive from what I have written whatever confirmation can be given to them by a coincidence, almost complete, with those reached by an independent inquirer pursuing a perfectly distinct path.

The speculations to which I refer have been distributed through several different essays; but the portion of them which comes most directly into contact with the views advanced in your pamphlet is contained in a paper published in the journal of the Dublin Statistical Society for Jan. 1859, of which I hope to send you a copy by this post. I will refer you also to the other papers in which I have treated this subject: two appeared in *Fraser's Magazine* in the numbers respectively for September, 1859, and January, 1860, and a third formed a review of Chevalier's work and appeared in the *Edinburgh Review* for July, 1860.[2]

I may mention that the authorship of the last – though I am under no obligation to conceal it – I do not wish for the present to be *publicly* stated.

If you will do me the favour to read the above, I think you will find that our views of the whole subject jump very closely together; one aspect of the question, which you will find treated in the second of the *Fraser's* essays – the effect of the discoveries on the distribution of wealth in the world – you have not touched on, but I venture to think on consideration you will not deny its importance.

You have remarked very properly on the utter fallaciousness of silver as a criterion of the fluctuations in the value of gold, and observe, with reference to M. Chevalier's metaphor of the parachute, that "the French currency . . . cannot prevent either gold or silver from falling in value".[3] This is most true; but it appears to me also true (and I am not certain whether you mean *also* to deny this point) that the French currency – or we may say more generally that capability of mutual substitution which the two metals possess – has retarded, and does still retard, the fall of gold. In fact, as I regard the matter, the effect of this circumstance is that an increased supply of either metal operates not simply upon the metal of

[2] Cf. J. E. Cairnes, 'Laws according to which a Depreciation of the Precious Metals consequent upon an Increase of Supply takes place, considered in connection with the Recent Gold Discoveries', *Journal of the Dublin Statistical Society*, ii (1859) 236-69. The other essays listed here by Cairnes were all reprinted, under the general title 'Essays towards a Solution of the Gold Question' in his *Essays in Political Economy, Theoretical and Applied* (1873).

[3] Jevons, *A Serious Fall in the Value of Gold* (1863) p. 35. When the paper was reprinted in *Investigations in Currency and Finance*, Jevons altered this sentence to read 'cannot prevent both gold and silver from falling in value' (cf. 1909 edition, p. 56).

which the supply is increased, but upon the aggregate mass of the two; and this, I think, goes far to account for what has caused so much surprise to superficial observers – the slow progress of the decline – the relation in which the two metals stand to each other at once retards the depreciation of gold and conceals it. With reference to this point perhaps you will allow me to refer you to what I have said in a note to one of the *Fraser's* essays – Jan. 1860, p. 14.

The only point on which I feel inclined to differ from you seriously is that which you develop at pp. 31 – 32 – the explanation which you give of the phenomena disclosed by your tables; but this is a question of theoretic importance only.

With many thanks for the satisfaction you have afforded me by your valuable contribution to this important discussion.

I am, dear Sir,

faithfully yours

J. E. Cairnes

179.   W. S. JEVONS TO MRS LUCY HUTTON
[LJN, 185–6]

Wallasey, 31st May 1863

... I am at last out of London, and find the quiet of the country delightful. Our lodgings are just on the edge of the sandhills, and I shall never be tired of wandering on to the open shore. In the morning, too, we bathe with great convenience. . . .

I pretty well closed up my London business, and went to a few exhibitions, theatres, etc., before leaving the gay world. I have brought abundance of books here, and am looking forward to some quiet work, chiefly in preparation for October. . . .

We went to church this morning! There was a good musical service, which was as pleasant as could be expected, considering I was at Westminster Abbey last Sunday, where the organ-playing is perfection itself.

Just before leaving London I had a pleasing letter from Professor Cairnes, a political economist, who is thought a good deal of now, thanking me for a copy of the pamphlet, which he said strongly confirmed some conclusions of his own, arrived at in a different manner, and published in various essays in 1859 and 1860. He says he has written a letter to the *Economist*,[1] drawing attention to the fact. This will probably

---

[1] Cairnes's letter to *The Economist* had in fact appeared in the issue of 30 May 1863, but Jevons did not see it until 2nd or 3rd June. See below. Letter 181, and R. D. Collison Black, 'Jevons and Cairnes', *Economica*, 27 (1960) 214–32.

sell many a copy for me, and perhaps induce Mr. Bagehot[2] to take the subject up in the paper, as I have already heard he was reading the pamphlet. . . .

180.   W. S. JEVONS TO J. E. CAIRNES

Near Lpool
(letters to care of
Mess[rs] Rathbone Bro[s]
Liverpool
2 June 1863[1]

Dear Sir

I cannot but be highly gratified by your approval of most parts of my Essay. The only work of yours which I had read previously to getting your letter was "The Character & Logical Method &c" That work was quite sufficient to render me desirous of bringing my essay to your notice, in hope of having your opinion, & in this I have been gratified beyond hope. But I was quite unaware of your having already treated the subject so fully as to anticipate most of the points which I supposed to be new in my essay. I can only account for my ignorance of your previous essays by my[2] too great neglect of the periodical pub[s]. & by my failure to meet any reference to your papers in Newmarch's & other writings where I might have expected to meet it. Your essays were also published just in the year when I was returning from Australia & out of the way of English Lit.

I have now had the pleasure of reading in a Lpool Library all the essays to which you referred, as well as the paper in the Stat. Soc. Journal which you have so kindly forwarded.

Of the Essay on the course of things in Australia let me say that as far as I can judge from casual experience there, the accuracy of the facts, & their explanation leaves little or no thing to be desired. I was often struck by the apparent anomalies, of which it was not always easy on the spot to see the reason. The import of preserved meats & other food into the very towns where a few years previously flocks were daily driven into the boiling down houses, was one of these anomalies. To see waggon loads of timber felled & sawn in some part of N. America laboriously dragged up

---

[2] Walter Bagehot (1826–77), journalist, economist and political theorist, author of *The English Constitution* (1867) and *Lombard Street* (1873). Bagehot was editor of *The Economist* from 1859 until his death, and as such presumably had his attention drawn to Jevons's *A Serious Fall* through R. H. Hutton's review of it in the issue of 15 November 1862, p. 1267. Cf. Vol. I, p. 192 and Vol. II, Letters 164 and 167, pp. 450 and 459.

[1] The original manuscript of this letter is now in the Cairnes Papers, MS 8954, National Library of Ireland. On it, the date has been added by another hand.

[2] 'almost' is deleted in the original manuscript.

the country through dense forests of gum trees was still more singular. On one occasion getting a meal in a settler's hut in a peculiarly fertile district, Illawarra, where the soil was a rich black mould, I remarked upon the goodness of the bread, and was assured it was of the best *Chilian* flour.[3] I could hardly help laughing at the notion of bringing the staff of life itself across the Pacific to such a spot. The settler said he had cleared some of his land, but had since found it more profitable to return to his old trade of cobbling shoes for the neighbouring town of Wollongong. This town was chiefly supported by raising butter & dairy produce which is sent by sea some 50 miles to Sydney, which again is supported of course by the gold digging & wool growing.

I was perhaps most amused by the alarm of the old Governor Sir W. Dennison at the rise in the price of meat, which led him to suppose that a scarcity of food was rapidly approaching, in the greatest stock and wool[4] producing country in the world, where butchers meat had previously been unsaleable refuse!

But as regards the gold question I have arrived, I think, at an understanding of your theory of the successive disturbance of prices by the flow of bullion, a point which had not occurred to me at all. If I understand you rightly, it is only when a country is *absorbing* bullion, bartering gold (& silver?) against other produce, that it sells this produce at a low rate, & it is only a country which is giving out bullion to such an *absorbing* country that buys the produce at an advantage.

It is only a transaction in which bullion forms the one part that comes under your theory; for the absolute abundance of bullion in a country, although governing the prices in that country, make them vary proportionately, so that the relative prices or values of any two other articles remain unaffected and on this of course international trade depends. If then we suppose of the countries A, B, C, D, E, &c. for instance Australia, England, France, Mediterranean, India, China, &c. – that A is first saturated, then saturates B, B saturates C and so on. A, *to the extent of its bullion trade with B,* has the advantage of the low prices of B, then A & B have a similar advantage over C, A, B, C over D and so on.

Since reading your paper I cannot doubt that this disturbance does take place, but *it must be a matter of some difficulty to estimate its importance and the rapidity or inequality with which the diffusion of bullion* takes place. I perceive that the striking fact of the fall in prices of many kinds of oriental & tropical produce is what supports your theory, while I thought I had explained the fact by a general balance of demand in favour of English manufactures. This is the part of my conclusions (pp. 31 & 32) to which

---

[3] It seems probable that this incident took place in the settler's hut described in the Journal; see Vol. I, p. 168.

[4] 'and wool' is inserted in the original manuscript.

you object, but though I think the fact may be partly due to the causes you suggest, I am not at once inclined to give up my view altogether. There is this criterion; on your view the difference of prices should decrease as the equilibrium of the precious metals is attained; on my view it should continue and increase.

As regards the substitution of silver by gold, you are no doubt right in considering that the process is not confined to France, and it had not occured to me to consider more than France. Yet the price of silver must as yet be governed by France, & your views will serve well should the price of silver not rise rapidly after the French currency is exhausted.

I am not inclined to say that the silver[5] currency much retards the fall of value, although I now see that as prices rise in silver partly as they do in gold, the silver currency, as much as remains unreplaced by gold, must *swell* proportionately. This effect can hardly come under the consumption of gold and silver which I advert to at the top of p. 36.

You will I think see from an exam. of my tables & the first diagram that in selecting the three years 1849–51 as a standard you were mislead [*sic*] by the statements of Tooke and Newmarch quoted on pp. 265, &c. These were years of very low prices but little relieved by the very slight rise of 1850. I have learnt by this time that nothing in Tooke's History is to be accepted without exam. except the mere numbers & historical facts. And I may perhaps express to you what I have felt very disagreably* in this subject, viz., that the reckless statements of such leading writers as McCulloch, Newmarch and others made in utter contempt of obvious facts, tend very little to the credit of this country or of Statistical Science. I am greatly disturbed especially when I find the elaborate conclusions of Tooke concerning the currency of England during the wars, *quoted all over the world*, as an unquestionable authority, though I believe them to be *entirely mistaken*.

On the numerous points in which you anticipate me I have the satisfaction of feeling that I have been able to reach the truth independently. Of course, had I occasion to write on the subject again I should not fail to defer to your previous writings.

I am glad you see the fallacy of the prevalent notion that the extension of trade and demand occasion high prices. Apart from the gold discoveries, it would have just the opposite effect, & has had previous to 1848–51!

D.r Soetbeer's tables contain just the comparison of 1831–40 with 1841–50 which I desired in writing Note C.[6]

[5] replaces 'French' deleted in the original manuscript.

[6] Cairnes's Dublin Statistical Society paper 'Depreciation of the Precious Metals' contained (at p. 261) an 'Abstract of D.r Soetbeer's Tables' showing in index form the change in prices of 44 commodities at Hamburg between 1831 and 1857. The average of the years 1831–40 was used as a base, and compared with the average of the years 1841–50 and with single years from 1851 to 1857.

I presume that you intend me to keep this copy of the Journal which will be useful.

Very faithfully yours

W. S. Jevons.

181.   W. S. JEVONS TO J. E. CAIRNES

Wallasey near
Lpool
3 June 1863[1]

My dear Sir

Since posting my letter yesterday (addressed Drogheda) I have received a copy of the *Economist*, in which I find your letter duly inserted, earlier than you expected.

Again thanking you for the favourable opinion, I have to add that I cannot find my use of the word *value* to be faulty or against the authority of many good writers. I have however long had a horror of the word[2] & doubt whether it should not be altogether excluded from the theory of Economy. *Exchange value* merely means, as I take it, *the ratio of exchange of any two articles* in given units.

You look rather to production which may be regarded as an exchange of labour & use of capital for the commodity produced, & which ultimately rules the exchange of one com. against another. As regards the *supply of gold* this is what we have to look to, & what you look to. I look to the more complex relation of gold to other commodities, & I guard myself in several places especially p. 5 & p. 33 against the supposition that the alteration in the ratio of exchange is a measure of the effects of the gold discoveries.

I quite agree that these effects on the supply of gold are not limited to the rise of price but comprise a fall of price prevented.

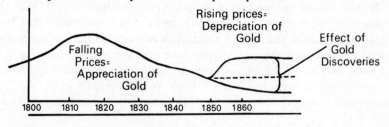

This abstract was taken from Soetbeer's *Beitrage zur Statistik der Preise* (Hamburg, 1858). (Cf. below, Letter 230, n. 3, p. 82.

In *A Serious Fall* Jevons used the average of prices for the years 1845–50 as a base, and Note C dealt with the question of extending the inquiry further back.

[1] The original manuscript of this letter is in the Cairnes Papers, MS 8954, National Library of Ireland.

[2] 'altogether' is deleted here in the original manuscript.

I must allow that when I worked out the result of the minor com^s I was puzzled & rather disappointed at finding the rise so much less than in the chief art. The remarkable distinction of home & foreign or tropical, of animal & vegetable arts somewhat compensated my disappointment. You will find the same distinction recognised but less clearly made out in some of Mr Newmarch's articles in Stat. Journal 1859, 60, or 61, or in the History of Prices.

Your theory, it now seems to me, amounts to saying that the prices of articles from a country will be low if the value of gold is *falling* in that country by the importation of bullion. You regard the fall in the value of gold as successive in different countries, not simultaneous. If the alteration of value, i.e. the import of bullion is either accomplished or not begun – your theory does not apply.

Yours very faithfully
W S Jevons

Prof. Cairnes.

182.   J. E. CAIRNES TO W. S. JEVONS

74 Ebury St.
Pimlico,
London.
4 June 1863.

Dear Sir,

Your letter has just reached me from Ireland, and I hasten to thank you for your liberal recognition of my labours in the same field of enquiry with yourself.

It was plain to me in reading your essay that you had not seen what I had written on the same subject; and it is fortunate that you had not. The common position is indefinitely strengthened by the entire independence of our efforts in its support. I have endeavoured, as you have probably seen, to bring this point out strongly in my letter to the Economist which appeared in Saturday's issue, and which I hope you will think satisfactory.

The testimony which you bear to the coincidence of my speculations on the local effects of the gold discoveries with your experience in Australia is very valuable: perhaps I might make bold to say – considering that they were the speculations of one who had never visited that country – that it adds something to our grounds for confidence in the essential soundness of economic science as it is cultivated in the U.Kingdom.I am glad also to find that you are disposed to acquiesce in my view as to the principles which govern the distribution of loss and gain incident to the diffusion of the new gold. It is quite true, no doubt, that it w^d. be a matter of much difficulty – if not impossibility – to estimate with anything like accuracy, the quantum of effect produced by these principles in an actual case: this results partly from the nature of economic theory, partly from the number and complexity of the agencies in operation: nevertheless I apprehend it is still important that our ideas as to the *character* of the effects incident to the movement should be in accordance with the facts.

With regard to our respective theories of the phenomena with the following explanation, I should be content to[1] acquiesce in the criterion which you suggest. My notion is that the elevation of English and U. States prices and, at an interval, those of Europe, above the prices of Tropical countries is due partly to the more immediate contact of the new supplies with our products and partly to the greater sensibility of our currencies. The deviation, however, need not attain its maximum at one: probably it has done so now; and on this assumption your criterion w^d. be applicable. As I have referred to my dissent from your theory of the case I may as well perhaps state briefly the grounds of it. If I apprehend it correctly it is to this effect: the materials of British manufacture have risen most rapidly because British skill has made these to be desired in all parts of the world by the useful and attractive forms with which it invests them: on the other hand, foreign articles of food and luxury do not offer the same inducement to extended purchase; and foreigners therefore in order to satisfy their desires as to our products must offer theirs on less advantageous terms. Now, first, this obviously goes much beyond the immediate problem; and, were it sound, would[2] have operated before the gold discoveries as effectually as since, and would continue to operate after these have run their course: in fact (and this I understand you to admit by the criterion you have suggested) the causes in question if real would[2] result in a constantly increasing divergence of prices in the commodities to which the theory applies. That any such continuous divergence has taken place is so far as I know without proof, and, according to my ideas, is not consistent with the known laws of value. But secondly the theory does not meet the actual case, since it wholly fails to account for its most prominent feature the marked rise in *animal* products, which, except in a few instances, do not enter into manufactures at all. Again it assumes, what I apprehend is not borne out by facts, that the demand throughout the world for British manufactures has increased more rapidly than the demand for, say, tea and sugar. As between England & America on the one hand, and India and China on the other,

---

[1] In the original manuscript after the words 'respective theories of the phenomena' Cairnes had at first written 'I am not quite certain that I should' but crossed this out and replaced it with the phrase given in the text here.

[2] Cairnes at first wrote 'should' but crossed this out and wrote 'would' above it.

the proportion is certainly the other way, of which the conclusive proof is furnished by the augmented dimensions during the last ten years of the Eastern drain, and if we have regard to the kind of commodities on which the surplus expenditure of the classes who have most profited by the gold discoveries w^d fall, I think there can be little doubt that few commodities w^d feel this more than tea and sugar. So far I venture to go in the way of objection.

I think it very likely I may have been mistaken as to the average character of the period – 1849–51 – which I took as my standard, and this of course could give an exaggerated view of the advance which followed.

In all you say as to the unreliability of Newmarch and McCulloch's statistics I entirely concur: whenever I have had an opportunity of testing them I have found them untrustworthy. I should not, however, be disposed to extend this observation to that portion of the History of Prices – the first 4 volumes – which were the work of Mr. Tooke himself. I have very great faith in Mr. Tooke's conscientiousness and accuracy, but in his later years he left the compilation of his statistics to Mr. Newmarch and others who performed the task in a very different spirit from his own.

I had proposed continuing the discussion in the *Economist* in a further notice of your pamphlet, but I have rather unexpectedly had occasion to leave for the continent, from which I shall not return till the second week in July. Meantime if I can find time I shall probably send another letter.

You are quite welcome to the D. S. Journal[3] which I had intended you to keep.

I am, dear Sir,
Yours truly,
J. E. Cairnes

In case you should have occasion to write, my address during June will be Aix les Bains,
Savoie.

[3] *Journal of the Dublin Statistical Society.* Cf. above, Letter 178, n. 2, p. 17.

183.   T. LEACH[1] TO W. S. JEVONS

Thornton Vicarage,
June, 20, 1863.

My dear Sir,

Now that I know through Mr. Hutton[2] where to address you, accept one line of thanks for your very kind present to me of a treatise[3] the reading of which has been to me, albeit not much given to reading of that class, most interesting, while its reasoning has seemed to me very conclusive. Out of the thought and labour that have evidently gone to the making of your little book, most men I suspect would have had a portly volume, for these are not days of such conscientious compression – and your charitable attempt to *console* that unfortunate body of men who have fixed income calculated according to the national standard of value after you have shown them that their sovereign is worth only some 17/-s and will by and by decline another three shillings, is not only very kindly meant but is, I must say, as successful as such an attempt could possibly be expected to be. I have no doubt that the book has already experienced a large circulation – its author we shall be very happy to see again in Yorkshire, and Mr. Hutton tells me that you will join his family party here during the latter half of July. In the meanwhile, believe me to be

My dear Sir,
Very sincerely yours,
Thos. Leach.

Wm. Stanley Jevons Esqr.

---

[1] Thomas Leach (1818–75) of Trinity College, Cambridge; B.A., and Senior Optime, 1846; Vicar of Thornton in Lonsdale, 1848–75. See *Crockford's Clerical Directory* (1858) p. 392; Rouse Ball & Venn, *Admissions to Trinity College, Cambridge*, IV, 524.

[2] John Hutton: Jevons stayed with John and Lucy Hutton at Newton in Cartmel, Lancashire, during July 1863.

[3] *A Serious Fall in the Value of Gold.* Leach's comments relate to chap. iii, § xxiv, 'Of the Probable Ultimate Fall of Value', where Jevons wrote: 'From a general view of the facts and arguments already presented, I am inclined to think the fall will be arrested at, perhaps, 30 per cent. As I think it not improbable that a depreciation of some 15 per cent has already occurred (though I do not positively assert it), it will follow that the more serious and sudden part of the fall is already felt.'

See also chap. iv, § xxvi, 'How the Effects will be Apparent'. In the reprint of the paper in *Investigations in Currency and Finance* these references occur on pp. 69, 74 and 75 (of the second edition).

184. WILLIAM JEVONS JUNIOR TO W. S. JEVONS

21 Cannon Place,
Brighton,
June 22, 1863.[1]

My dear Stanley,

I am much obliged to you for sending me Prof. Cairnes's letter,[2] and I am glad to find that your Treatise is so highly appreciated by so competent a judge. It appears to me, as well as to yourself, that he has not correctly represented your use of the word 'value', in saying that you speak of alterations in the value of gold *without reference to the cause of those alterations*. I am quite at a loss, indeed, to understand how he can make such an assertion, when the whole drift of your treatise is to discriminate between the several causes which affect the value of gold, and to ascertain the relative amount of their operation. But it must be gratifying to you that he so fully agrees with you as to your facts.

Are you acquainted with Eisdell's "Treatise on the Industry of Nations"?[3] In his chapter on Money he has a section "On the value of money, and the causes and effects of a change in that value", which I think you would read with interest, if you have not read it. It bears on the subject of your pamphlet, though, of course, without referring to that extraordinary increase in the supply of gold which has arisen from the late discoveries subsequently to the publication of the book. The whole work is an able exposition of the principles of Political Economy, and if you are not acquainted with it, and would like to see it, my copy of it is at your service.

I am glad to hear that you are to be something more than a *tutor* in connexion with Owen's College – that you are also to be employed as a *lecturer* on political economy and logic to a more extensive audience than the regular students of the college. You will have much to do in preparing your lecture, and if I can aid you in the way of books, I shall be glad to do so. Besides the treatise I have mentioned, I have Say's Political Economy translated by Prinsep,[4] Wade's History of the Middle and Working Classes,[5] which contains a good deal about money, wages, rent & and Burton's Political and Social Economy, published by W. & R. Chambers.[6] I can also lend you Mills' Logic, though not the latest edition. It is

---

[1] The original manuscript of this letter is incomplete.

[2] The context makes clear that Jevons must have sent his uncle a copy of the letter by Cairnes to the editor of *The Economist* which was published in that journal on 30 May 1863, p. 593.

[3] The full bibliographical reference for the work is given by William Jevons in his letter of 8 July 1863. See below, Letter 186, p. 31.

[4] Jean-Baptiste Say, *A Treatise on Political Economy; or, The Production, Distribution and Consumption of Wealth . . . translated from the 4th edition of the French by C. R. Prinsep, M.A.* (1823).

[5] John Wade, *History of the middle and Working Classes; with a popular exposition of the economical and political principles which have influenced the past and present condition of the industrious orders* (1833).

[6] John Hill Burton, *Political and Social Economy; its practical applications* (Edinburgh, 1849).

among my books at George's[7] house, and then you can get it whenever you like to call and ask for it. All the other books I have mentioned are there, but if you wish to see them, I can send them to you in a parcel or bring them with me when I visit Liverpool, if I do so. As to your mathematical logic, I question whether it will suit a popular audience such as you will have to address. Indeed, I question whether mathematical symbols can be employed with any advantage on such a subject.

185.   W. S. JEVONS TO HERBERT JEVONS
[LJP, 186]

(Direct to Care of Rathbone Bro.[s]
Liverpool)
Leasowe Hotel.
22 June 1863.

Dear Herbert,

We have now received your letter written when you were temporarily in Sydney. Everything then looked well with you and I cannot doubt that you have got on all right in your new position at Nelson or Otago. There is certainly some responsibility in being a bank agent, but I think the responsibility of acting honestly to them is the chief part, & that in which they know they can trust you. The price of the Nelson Gold is I suppose known, or a price agreed upon by the various buyers there. Otherwise you would have to send some parcels for assay somewhere. Doubtless however, the Bank have given you pretty full instructions.

Tom & I have been rather puzzled to know in what form you carried the money with you, or the power of raising money. We came to the conclusion that you must draw bills or some sort of thing upon the Sydney Bank & sell them on the diggings to traders, or diggers, who require to forward money to N S W. It will give us all great gratification to hear about the business with all its particulars.

I hope that when you are more settled at some of the N Z. diggings you will give us longer letters with some account of the place & your mode of life. Of course I know pretty well what sort of a place you must be in, but I should like to know how you manage to place yourself. You will I should think have a room in an Inn or store for the office, & lodge at the same place perhaps, but when you are settled some time I should hope you would get a comfortable berth for your office & yourself. The Inns at the diggings are very miscellaneous kinds of resorts, & there is little choice either of bed or board.

----

[7] See Vol. II, Letter 139, n. 16, p. 391.

Perhaps however you will be better pleased to hear of home affairs than to hear me prose about your affairs, of which I can know nothing certain. I have now been more than three weeks in country lodgings with Tom. We first went to Wallasey & lodged in a small neat cottage close to the Sandhills. The young landlady made us very comfortable, but unfortunately the rooms were taken for the whole summer by a new married couple, & we had to turn out. We could not find other suitable lodgings but in this out of the way Hotel, where we get a capital parlour and a double bedded room for 30ˢ per week. It is rather much to pay, but we cannot just at present resist the cheerfulness & country aspect of the rooms. Tom goes into business every day, starting about $8\frac{1}{4}$ or $8\frac{1}{2}$ & getting to the office at 10 am. He gets back here about 6.30 or 7. pm. He has a good deal of exercise altogether but for a time it will be good for him.

I have brought plenty of books with me, & spend nearly the whole day from 9 am to 6 pm in logical & other work then we have tea & stroll in the evening, going early to bed. I find the quiet of the country extremely delightful after so long living in the noise of London. But the long days of unbroken solitude & work are apt to become very tedious unless I now & then have a change. Most days indeed I get a bathe which freshens me up, & occasionally I go to Liverpool.

I am engaged partly in practising up my mathematics Greek & Latin for my tutoring work at Manchester, but just at present I am chiefly working at my logical system. It has only of late taken a definite form, but I have been more or less upon it for some two years. I think I shall have a paper ready in the course of a few weeks, of a very complete character, but I am afraid it will be hard to get it accepted because there are not half a dozen men who as far as I know occupy themselves with logical speculation and these are too much occupied with their own systems to tolerate an antagonist one.

About a week since I paid a visit of a day or two to Manchester both to see Mr Greenwood and to make some arrangement with Aunt Henry[1] concerning my future abode there. Harry is to be married on the 4ᵗʰ of next month[2] and goes into a new house. Aunt H is to take a small but agreable* house & let me a couple of rooms during the winter which I shall furnish for my own use. Henny will probably visit me during the winter especially while Aunt H is away & will thus have an opportunity of becoming acquainted with Manchester before definitely agreeing to take a house with me. Were my occupation to become permanent I

---

[1] See Vol. I, pp. 42 and 74, n. 1.

[2] On 4 July 1863 Henry Enfield Roscoe married Lucy (1840–1910), youngest daughter of Edmund Potter, F.R.S., for many years Member of Parliament for Carlisle. See *Life and Experiences*, p. 131.

should probably have a house at the beginning of the second session.

I feel rather relieved at having got away from London. It is an inhospitable place, and as I was placed made my life rather dreary. It got worse the longer I stayed. As yet I do not miss the Museum library, for I have far more books with me in a single trunk than I can read, & the Library is only useful now & then to look up out of the way books. A large library almost prevents thorough reading. There is too at Manchester besides the Free Public Library, & various half public ones, the fine old Cheetham's* Library, where I have no doubt I shall spend much of my time.

Henny is just about to go on a visit to Swansea, the Woods,[3] & then to Alfred Barhams[4] at Bridgewater. She has not been very well according to Lucy's accts but I believe it arises from the want of proper occupation of which she has none. Now I fancy she does not like staying very long with Lucy owing to the noise & trouble of the children & the household generally. It is hard to know what she is to do but visit about. This she enjoys whereas she is seldom well if she stays very long in one place. What we intend to do as soon as possible is to take a small house near Aunt Henry's house in Manchester so that Henny may have Aunt H's assistance & society when desirable without having too much of it. But Lucy thinks Henny is not quite able to set up house at once with me, nor do I want to go to the expense at first. Hence my temporary arrangement with Aunt H.

Lucy seems well – at least I do not hear to the contrary. John's business is much in the same precarious state that it has been for some time but the future prospects are said to be much better & there is some mention of more than one considerable contract. They have let their Beaumaris house for some 5 weeks and are going to Silverdale near Morecambe Bay, where Tom & I may perhaps join them for a time. I believe they will also make a brief visit to Thornton.

Some 2 weeks ago I visited Roscoe, finding him about as usual. They have a new Doctor at the Asylum, whom I like as far as I have seen him. He seems as satisfactorily placed as could be.

You inquired lately concerning your balance in Henry's[5] hands. He requested me to tell you that there was, if I recollect aright about £23 now to your credit (after subtracting a small sum which Mr Sage gave you.) By the end of the year he expected there would be £40 to your credit. It must be satisfactory to you to have a balance thus growing for you. We can also if you like invest some of it in any articles you may

---

[3] Cousins of Jevons's father. See Vol. II, Letter 43, n. 6, p. 89.

[4] Alfred Garrett Foster-Barham, husband of Jevons's first cousin, Eliza. See Vol. II, Letter 46, n. 5, p. 103.

[5] See Vol. II, Letter 21, n. 2, p. 38.

require when settled, & we shall be glad to send you out a small box before long.

I was interested to hear of your fishing excursion with Miller. I do not wonder at your thinking the Harbour a pretty place.

I have occupied myself so little of late with politics & general news, that I have nothing to say. The American war drags on in a very unsatisfactory condition. Home affairs are very quiet.

Hoping you will not omit any of your monthly letters.

I am

Your affec. Brother

W S Jevons.

186. WILLIAM JEVONS JUNIOR TO W. S. JEVONS

21 Cannon Place,
Brighton,
July, 8 [1863]

My dear Stanley,

Thank you for your kind letter of the 2nd inst., in reply to which I have only to say that if you desire to see Eisdell's Treatise on the Industry of Nations, I will bring it with me when I go to Liverpool, which will probably be this day or to-morrow week. The full title of the work is as follows – A Treatise on the Industry of Nations, or the Principles of National Economy and Taxation by J. S. Eisdell, Esq., in two volumes. Vol I on Production, Vol II on Distribution, Consumption & Taxation, Whitaker & Co., 1839.[1]

It is a long time since I read the work: indeed I have never read the whole of it: but my impression from what I did read was, that it is a very able and well written work, and on looking into it, I see I have marked many passages where I approved the sentiment.

Many years ago I wrote for the use of some of my pupils an Essay on the Faculties of Judgement and Reasoning. It is an unfinished and very imperfect work; but it might perhaps furnish you with some useful hints for your lectures on logic, and I will bring it with me, if you would like to see it. But you must let me know your wishes both about this M.S., and the work before mentioned, early next week.

I shall go first to William's[2] at Wavertree, and may stay there probably

---

[1] Eisdell's work is now almost completely forgotten. It is one of the few works of its time to contain a specific treatment of the problem of 'Want of Employment.' Viner lists Eisdell among minor contributors to the development of the theory of comparative costs – *Studies in the Theory of International Trade* (1937) pp. 494, 507.

[2] See Vol. II, Letter 143, n. 5, p. 405.

three weeks, after which I shall visit George and Elizabeth, if at that time they have returned from New Brighton, where they are now. I hope you will come over to Wavertree some day while I am there. Or, if I go to New Brighton to see Elizabeth, as I probably shall do soon after my arrival, we may perhaps meet there.

I am glad to hear what you tell me of Herbert. Pray give my love to him when you write. We all unite in love to yourself and Tom. Henrietta, I suppose, is still at Beaumaris-

Looking forward, as I do, to the pleasure of soon meeting you in person, I need not say more at present than that

I remain,

as ever,

Yours very affectionately,

W. Jevons.

I hope you were not overcharged for the large letter I sent last. I should have followed your example in putting on two stamps; but the clerk at the post office weighed it and told me it needed only one.

In Fraser's Magazine for last May, there is a curious article on the Principles of Currency by Bonamy Price,[3] which I think would interest you, though it maintains a doctrine which appears to me at variance with yours. The writer says that "each particular country has its own special amount of work to be performed by coin, & that when it possesses coin enough for carrying on that work, it is absolutely incapable of using any more." . . "When a currency is full, – that is, when every Banker, every shopkeeper, every gentleman, every traveller, every housekeeper, has as many sovereigns as they require, each for his own use, the arrival of a million of coined sovereigns from Australia would not bring a single additional one into circulation; they must go into store, just as every other commodity of which there is an excess beyond the demand for it." Again, "we thus arrive at the fundamental principle that coin is needed for a certain definite work, and that when there is enough for this specific use, the surplus must either lie idle, a pure waste, or else, – which is its most rational employment – it must be sent away to some other land." Does not this imply that prices are not affected by a redundancy of gold?

[3] Bonamy Price, 'The Principles of Currency', *Fraser's Magazine*, 67 (1863) 581–99.

Bonamy Price (1807–88) was at this time engaged in business in London; in 1868 he succeeded Thorold Rogers in the Drummond Professorship of Political Economy at Oxford, which he held until his death.

187.   W. S. JEVONS TO HERBERT JEVONS
       [LJN, 188–9]

Newton in Cartmel, Lancashire,
24th July 1863.

. . . Since posting my letter through Tom's hands we have got your first letter from Nelson, and we all greatly rejoice in its cheerful character.

It seems to me that a *warmer England* is what any one might desire for his adopted country. I hope that you may be able to stay at the Nelson side, by a good development of the diggings there. The Otago country, I should imagine, is somewhat wilder and more inclement. In any case I don't think the bank and you will wish to part for the present, and the longer you stay the more will be your salary.

Your photograph, taken by my old photographic friends the Freemans, has given great satisfaction here. It is really well done. It seems also to show that the voyage, the southern climate, or something else, have made you look fatter and better in a great degree.

I have just received the bill for my pamphlet on Gold. The total cost of printing, advertising, etc., is £43, and the offset by sales only £10: only seventy-four copies seem to have been sold as yet, which is a singularly small number. On the other hand, my diagrams still continue to sell, thirty copies having been sold by Stanford during the last half year, so that only ten of the 'English funds' now remain in their hands. This sale returns me some £3 : 10s. The superior success of the funds over the bank diagram makes me think that a single diagram well fitted for an office, and rather less costly than either of these, might sell well. By getting these diagrams spread about it spreads one's name, and might enable me at a future time to publish larger works successfully . . .

188.   W. S. JEVONS TO HERBERT JEVONS
       [LJN, 189–90]

Beaumaris, 23d August 1863.

. . . Our long-contemplated visit to Beaumaris is at last begun, and Henny and I are very agreeably settled here in a small house of our own, expecting Tom to join us at the beginning of September. You will be surprised at hearing *a house of our own,* but Lucy has managed very cleverly, as she usually does in these matters, to find a small house which was to let for the required period. We have only as yet been about four days here, but our visit promises to be a very pleasant one, as well as favourable to my work. I have indeed only a small bedroom to do my work in, but it is pretty quiet; and the cheerful life of Beaumaris, with daily visits to Lucy's house, will tend to relieve the tedium of working at home. . . .

Your letter is a great satisfaction to all of us. It makes us feel that the star of our family has passed its Nadir and is rising. We have none of us yet attained any permanent success or place in society; but I hope that in time we shall all have it. Some people may have thought that we had a wrongness in us which made us continually refuse the goods the gods provide us, and you and I especially may seem to have done so; but I trust we shall both be soon well enough off, even in the way society takes the meaning of this. I have no fear but that Tom will find a place suitable and profitable in due time, because his more peculiar qualities are so well tempered by sociability and sense. . . .

My own affairs are *in statu quo ante*. I am still reading up subjects for my tutoring, and writing a set of forty lectures on logic and political economy for my evening lessons. The latter is no light job, and I cannot finish them quite before the session begins. Nor can I do more than make them up roughly with great aid and copious extracts from books. It would require several years' practice in lecturing, and plenty of labour, to form a good set of lectures; but this of course is not to be expected in a mere evening class.

My work will at first be very novel and hard to me, and most inadequately paid; but it would be absurd to despise a small beginning. In fact, I could hardly venture to take a professorship, if I could get one, without some previous practice in lecturing. I have all my life had the strongest possible horror of public speaking, and I used to think myself absolutely incapable of it. But the last session at college I found it not impossible, and, after getting over a few failures and breakdowns, I have no longer an insuperable objection to it. After the practice which teaching will give me, I think I may become quite expert at it, and perhaps the fonder of it as I formerly so much disliked it. . . . I am inclined to think I only need practice myself to make a lecturer, though I should never make a rhetorical speaker or debater, the two things being quite distinct. It is a well-known fact that there is nothing to which practice is more essential than public speaking.

Since my last I have finished my first paper on logic and sent it to De Morgan,[1] who agreed to read it and give me some opinion on it. But he has not yet had it long, and has not yet sent any answer. I have written on the subject to Professor Boole, on whose logical system mine is an improvement. In his answer he does not explain away an objection I had

[1] See Vol. I, p. 15.

raised against his system. He seems to think that my paper probably does not contain more than he himself knows, this being a common failing of philosophers and others; but still he tells me very civilly that if I think still that there is anything new in my paper I ought to publish, which of course I shall do one way or another before long . . .

189. W. S. JEVONS TO T. E. JEVONS
[LJP, 190 – 1]

Beaumaris
Aug 30. 1863

Dear Tom

I think your notions on Logic are partially right. Every logical term must be either Unity or plurality, or o = a contradiction. It can hardly however be said that unity is a magnitude, but magnitudes or numbers are made up of units which are logically contrary terms – each of which is distinguished from the rest by some attribute.

Three apples are represented by *apple* $(1+1+1)$ where the units $1 +$ represent *unknown* logical characters by which one apple may be known from another. For unless we could by logical character know one apple from another we could not say there were three apples. And if we should by mistake count one apple twice – as $A' + A'' + A'' + A'''$ the two terms $A'' + A''$ not being logically distinct sink into one term by the Law of Unity that in logic $A + A = A$.

It is thus that number arises out of logic, but I do not like your expression that there are two factors. Number or magnitude may be something more than logic but never drops its logical character. As to continuous magnitude that of space degree &c, it can only be connected with logic by receding at once to infinitely small components. Each of which is logically distinct from every other & thus an unit.

I have just thought of a point which will remove a difficulty in the Primary Logic. I said there that every term *means* one or more qualities, known or unknown. I now see that every term must mean an indefinite or rather infinite collection of qualities of which only one is necessarily known viz the fact of being indicated by a certain sign, & of the rest some may or may not be known.

It is obvious in short that *anything* either must or must not have any property that you like to name. Every term also taken *in extent*, must be considered infinite for we can never tell how many things may exist of any kind in this world or in other worlds to which universal truths must extend *ad infinitum*. The only possible definition which is not unlimited, is that of things within your feeling at a time, as *this pen, this point, this world*.

Every universal term therefore contains a double infinity.

It is a pity you cannot sooner come to us. You did not lose much last week indeed as the rain was nearly constant. We have but a poor bedroom for you here but otherwise you will like our small cottage.

Hennys love & she desires notice of the day you are coming.

Ever yours

W S Jevons

Newspaper Controversy on the Value of Gold,
September-October 1863

The ensuing letter constitutes Jevons's first contribution to a controversy which he partly explains in the letter to his brother Herbert dated 15 September 1863 (Letter 192 below, p. 42).[1]

On 31 August 1863 *The Times* reported at length a paper read by Henry Fawcett at the British Association meeting at Newcastle, on the effects of the discovery of gold. Fawcett quoted from Jevons's *Serious Fall* and stressed 'the many serious consequences which would result from a depreciation in the value of gold'.

Editorial comment came from *The Times* on 1 September. In the article Jevons's estimate of a 10 per cent rise of prices was quoted in support of the view that 'gold has not fallen nearly as much as upon abstract principles it ought to have done'. This drew from Jevons the letter of 2 September here reproduced. On the same date a letter signed 'F.C.' appeared, drawing attention to the fact that the price level was influenced by the quantity of money, including bank notes and deposits, as well as gold.

In a further leader on 5 September *The Times* showed no alteration in its view: 'Whatever may be the case hereafter, no material depreciation has occurred yet. Some inquirers, such as Mr. Stanley Jevons, whose letter we published yesterday, conceive that an effect is visible, but, as a broad matter of fact, it is both certain and evident that the influx of the precious metal during the last fifteen years has occasioned no material derangement.'

On 9 September *The Times* published a letter from J. E. Cairnes strongly supporting Jevons's view, and another from John Crawfurd equally strongly concluding that there had been no fall in the value of gold. In a letter published on 12 September Fawcett reiterated his opinion that 'if the export of specie to the East should greatly diminish it certainly seems improbable that the present yield of gold can be absorbed

---

[1] See also Vol. I, pp. 191–2.

without a considerable depreciation in its value'. On the same date a correspondent, 'W.M.J.', who in a letter on 3 September had argued that other countries might feel the effects of the new gold more than Britain, nevertheless admitted that 'Mr. Jevons is substantially right in saying that the rise in prices has hitherto been 10 per cent in England'.

On the other hand John Crawfurd on 19 September declared himself 'thoroughly satisfied that Mr. Jevons has come to erroneous conclusions from his own data, the accuracy of which I do not at all dispute'. A further *Times* leader of 23 September declared 'that either a Depreciation of gold has not occurred, or, if it has occurred, it is not the depreciation which we were taught to apprehend'.

This drew a reply from Cairnes on 1 October, together with the letter from Jevons reprinted below. John Crawfurd replied on 6 October: 'I continue to be of opinion that Mr. Jevons's figures are correct, and his conclusions from them vicious and illusory'.

The final letter in the correspondence, published on 8 October, came from John Ruskin, who alone of the writers drew attention to the fact that the new money could be spent or saved, hoarded or invested: 'these agencies of daily economy have so much more power over the market than the supply from the mine that no statistics of which we are yet in possession are (at least in their existing form) sufficient to prove the dependence of any given phenomena of the market on the rate of metallic supply'.

190.   W. S. JEVONS TO THE EDITOR OF *THE TIMES*[1]

Sir, In Mr. Fawcett's[2] important communication to the British Association concerning the depreciation of gold he quoted a statistical conclusion of mine to the effect that prices have advanced only 10 per cent since the gold discoveries, and the fact is noticed in your article on the subject (Sept. 1).

However literally correct the statement may be with regard to the last three years, 1860–2, its real meaning is liable to be underestimated. One of the chief purposes of my statistical tables was to show with accuracy that flux and reflux of trade and prices, that "tide in the affairs of men" which has so long been a matter of vague remark. Without allowing for the point of the tide at which we make our observations, we cannot draw

---

[1] Published in the issue of 4 September 1863.

[2] Henry Fawcett (1833–84), Professor of Political Economy at Cambridge from 1863 until his death; M.P. for Brighton, 1865–74, and for Hackney, 1874–84; Postmaster-General, 1880–4. As a result of a shooting accident in 1858 Fawcett was totally blind.

any sure deduction. Now, after 1857 there was a considerable ebb of prices following the very great rise between the years 1852 and 1857. Since that ebb there has been no appreciable rise. Hence the last few years have been years of *minimum* prices – of commercial low water. And the fact that prices at their *minimum* still stand 10 per cent above the mean level of the commercial tide preceding the gold discoveries seems to me a proof of very extensive depreciation.

Obediently yours,
W. Stanley Jevons.

Sept. 2.

191.   HERBERT JEVONS TO W. S. JEVONS

address {
Bank of New South Wales

Dunedin N.Z.
Clifton Villa Sunday 13 Sept. 63

My dear Stanley,

Ere this reaches you you should have received my letter via Marseilles. I write this chiefly to enclose the within cutting from the Melbourne Argus by which you will see that your work on the value of Gold has received some attention out in the Colonies. The Sydney Morning Herald has also, in its issue of July 29 I believe, devoted a leading article to your work.[1] I am not surprized to hear of its not receiving much attention at home. Tho' you may sell but few copies, and lose some pounds by its publication, it may not be right to put it down as a failure, or a loss of time. You are making a beginning and clearing a way for more important and more successful publications in the future. Miller has not sent me a copy, or I have not received it. The belief that Gold has fallen in value relatively with other articles of commerce can hardly be resisted, without going deeply into the subject: but your statistics of prices clinches & settles the matter and cannot be answered. Cairnes' letter[2] is written nicely and will be of some service to you. A cousin of his is in our branch here, a young Irishman with a strong brogue. He is well connected however & yesterday shewed me a photograph of a lady cousin whom he told me was a Marchioness. I have lately received a good many letters from home. I have one or two letters from Lucy, Henny, Tom, & yourself. The news they contain is as good as I can or should expect. You have all

---

[1] *The Argus*, Melbourne, 10 and 17 August 1863; *Sydney Morning Herald*, 29 July 1863.

[2] Presumably Jevons had also sent his brother a copy of the letter by Cairnes in *The Economist* of 30 May 1863.

got your troubles, which you had before I left England. I should like to hear that Henny was getting better & stronger in health. If New Zealand was not such a great distance away a trip here might be good for her & pleasant to me, but the distance excludes the idea, & unfortunately there are few places out of England fit for English ladies to live in. I suppose you will be in Manchester by the time this reaches you, and in the congenial society of Harry, Greenwood, & others. The worst part of the colonies is the absence of company calculated to preserve a proper tone of mind & manners. There is an individual at present lodging in the same house with me, who is an intense admirer of Emerson. He is always breaking out into sayings of his, and is always ready to argue in an excited manner upon theoretic and metaphysical subjects. He reminds me of old times when I used to think there was something very wonderful in his writings; but this individual, Bremner by name, who is of a Manchester family, tells me my vigour of mind is leaving me & that I am dropping into old conservatism. I feel flattered with the idea, and certainly do think that I am getting more into the ways of common sense. I have ceased to have any interest in metaphysical subtilties*, not caring a pin whether fate or freewill has the better of the argument or whether there is a mixture of the two. My chief anxiety now is to bring my assays out correct and bring out clear pretty bars of Gold: & this leads me to my new occupation. Ryder remained only a month instructing me in my work and gave me up the keys, and care of the Gold about the 26th August. I am getting quicker & more handy, but I am somewhat anxious at the result of the meltings & assays. The melting room is very open to the public & the other clerks are rather fond of coming to look on & light their pipes. These are however only slight troubles. I and our Scotch messenger melted oz. 7000 Gold dust last Wednesday & Thursday then there is the numbering weighing & clipping of them. I have got 15 double assays to take this week, and one sent from the Union Bank. I am sending clips of these 15 assays to Sydney in order that my assays may be checked by the folks at Head Office. I am therefore anxious to bring this batch out well by which I shall get a good name, and lay the foundation for a further rise in my screw. Since the 1st August I have been allowed £50 extra, as a sort of gold fields' allowance making my rate per annum £250. This is so far satisfactory, & I shall be able while paying sufficient attention to my outward appearance to lay by a few pounds as a reserve for contingencies. From what Henry informs you I shall have at the end of this about £40 to my credit in his hands, and you suggest the desirability of sending me out a box of clothes and other articles. I have been revolving the subject in my mind, and have come to the conclusion to ask you to do something of the sort for me, not immediately, but as you may have time or opportunity. I expect you will have your time very much taken up in Manchester. Before you do

anything in the matter I should like to give you full & particular instructions and as I have not yet made up my mind what to ask you to get or at any rate all that I may ask for I should not like you to do the thing hasty and without my instructions. The fact is it is impossible to get some things good here, & what you do get are very dear. Therefore for economy & for quality I should like a box of things out. First of all my trunk has got very shabby having been knocked about in its travels to America & back & not being a strong one originally. I want therefore to replace it with a *wooden box* which is the first thing I wish you to get for me. I want a really strong good *neat looking* box. It will do to send the things out in, but I want it to keep my clothes in after its arrival. I want it to look pretty well outside, I dont mean anything very extravagant. You can get my name painted neatly on the front or top, also the direction
Bank New So. Wales
Dunedin, New Zealand
will require to be put on it. I should like two pieces of wood on the bottom to raise it slightly from the floor. & I should say it would be desirable to line it with zinc inside. The size would be somewhere about $2\frac{1}{2} \times 1\frac{1}{2} \times 1\frac{1}{2}$ with a good lock and key. These boxes are ready made in outfitting shops, made for parties going to India & Australia; but unless you are satisfied that the box is a strong one, with a good lock and key, perhaps you could meet with a joiner that could for a little more money make a better article. This is the first thing I want & I give you two months to get it or three if you require it. Next mail I hope to give you particular instructions what to get to fill this box with but until I give you my instructions I hope you will not move in the matter. I shall want about two suits of clothes, some woollen shirts, paper collars, boots, paper, envelopes, maybe a few books, but as I say I will give you particular instructions about them. When I left England it was understood that the chancery suit of the Moss Estate[3] would lessen the dividends that Lucy & Henny would receive for one or two years. It would not be prudent in me to let very much money go out of my hands, but I should wish to assist Henny to a small extent, should she find herself straitened in her means. I calculate the box, and contents & expenses upon it would reach £30 there would remain £10 yet to my credit with Henry to the end of the year. That £10 might come in handy to Henny for pocket money. I do not know exactly how she is situated moneytarily* but you will probably know & I authorize you to receive from Henry as per enclosed note £50 of my money as it may become due, and you can give Henny such of it as she may require. A new dress, a new pair of gloves, or a few extra shillings in one's pocket, has sometimes a beneficial influence upon the health. I dont

---

[3] For details of the Moss legacy, see Vol. II, Letter 30, n. 1, p. 56.

wish any money to be used needlessly, but I expect you will understand what I mean & act discreetly in the matter. This morning it is warm spring weather. The spring seems to be making some advance at last the new grass is springing green and fresh. & the roads are drying a good deal. I shall endeavour after a while to find some more suitable lodgings, may be in the country: but they are very difficult to find, and the charges are very high I pay £2 bo^d & lodging, but for a good place 50/-, is generally asked, but £2 with washing & other &c's comes to a good deal. By fellow lodgers leaving I am now in my third choice of a bedroom, which is a great improvement upon the two first. I had a very small window in my first looking out upon a dark wall of rock, with never no daylight. In the second I had the third part of a good window, which I accordingly could not open or shut, but which gave me some more light than the first, I have now the other two thirds of the same window which I can partly open & shut as I desire to endeavour to air the room & keep it sweet but the landlady & her two daughters are slovenly & allow the house to remain in a disagreeable state of dirt & dust.

I post this pr Omeo tomorrow but shall probably write a short note to post on the 18th and go via Marseilles. I hope before long to have another month's news from you. I have said nothing about politics of New Zealand, of home, or of America. The war in the North Island is a serious business, and there is no knowing how much it will cost before it is concluded. The small number of men on the side of the white, & the difficult nature of the country together with the skill & pluck of the Maories will make it a tedious affair particularly for so young a colony – I do not think the Duke of Newcastle has treated us fairly.[4]

Your affectionate brother
Herbert Jevons

When I commenced this note I did not intend to make it so long. I think it will have to go as my principle* production for this mail.

---

[4] The war in the North Island had begun on 17 July 1863, when General Cameron invaded the Waikato; it continued until the middle of 1864. The expenses of the war were much greater than estimated, and the Imperial Government (in which the Duke of Newcastle was then Colonial Secretary) refused to sanction the wholesale confiscation of Waikato lands, by the sale and settlement of which the New Zealand government had hoped to defray part of the cost. See *Cambridge History of the British Empire*, Vol. VII, part II, pp. 108 and 137. Cf. Vol. II, Letter 146, n. 3, p. 420.

192.   W. S. JEVONS TO HERBERT JEVONS
        [LJN, 191–3]

Beaumaris, 15th September 1863.

. . . I have myself been rather in luck lately concerning the pamphlet on Gold. Mr. Fawcett, a blind M.A. of Cambridge, to whom I sent my pamphlet, he having written on the subject before, was convinced by my figures, and delivered an address on the subject to the British Association lately, quoting my figures. The *Times* reported his speech, and took the subject up in *a leader,* also quoting me, and then there followed a discussion of the subject in many letters, as well as articles in other papers. Professor Cairnes also again wrote on the subject to the *Times*, and almost challenged people to disprove the conclusions of my pamphlet. Lastly, the *Economist* has been induced to notice the subject in a cautious manner, and, though attributing to me some exaggeration of the matter, comes over to my conclusion substantially. Thus it may almost be considered that the matter is settled as regards a certain depreciation. All that the papers admit, however, is the lowest possible estimate of 10 per cent, whereas, though this is the result given by my tables, as it happens, I believe the real depreciation to be nearer 20 per cent.

In the last few days I have been thinking of applying the method of my pamphlet to prices extending some centuries back – in fact, of trying to determine the general variation of prices from the earliest times of English history for which any data exist. The result, consisting in a simple curve of the value of gold, would be one of the most important and interesting statistical conclusions that could be got. The method I should use would enable me to bring into one general induction the most scattered and various data of prices, which are of little or no use for any other purpose. If I could get such an inquiry done in two or three years when prices are again rising and attention is drawn to the continued depreciation, the publication would be probably very successful. I have already so much work upon my hands that such a serious addition is no joke. I think, however, it is well, having had a first success in this subject, to draw that line well, and it is one in which a name is rather easily made. I am better in theory than I am in fact; but theorists have a bad odour until their soundness is established by the slowest possible process. Hence it is a good thing to begin by diagrams, tables of prices, and such things, so that you can never be charged with arguing without a reference to or knowledge of facts.

I am now within about two weeks of the time when I must set out on my Manchester business. I have been engaged lately in writing lectures on logic and political economy – a rather dreary occupation – and in working up some subjects for my tutoring. At first my work will be by no means easy, but perhaps the same might be said of any other new occupation. I think it probable that I shall not desire to take additional private pupils to any great extent, but rather to use my spare time on private work, which will ultimately make a better return. . . .

193.   W. S. JEVONS TO THE EDITOR OF *THE TIMES*[1]

Sir,

Mr. Crawfurd's letter in *The Times* of Saturday, the 17th inst.,[2] has by chance become known to me only to-day. What I find in it chiefly requiring answer is the initial statement, that "the whole of Mr. Fawcett's theory of the depreciation of gold . . . is founded on the pamphlet of Mr. Jevons." This is so far from being true, in the sense in which it is liable to be read, that it is well to explain in what sense alone it is true. Theory is necessarily founded on fact, since it consists in a comparison of fact with fact, to show some sameness of cause or character between them. Mr. Fawcett argued from a multitude of *data* concerning the demand and supply of gold – *data* certainly not derived from my pamphlet, since they were not in it. He compared the rise of prices which might, by analogy, have been expected with that which is believed to have occurred; hence his quotation of my statistical conclusion. All concerned in this discussion are highly indebted to Mr. Fawcett for the complete manner in which he has brought it forward. Those who have heard his discourses will not easily forget or undervalue the profound, lucid, and yet agreeable manner in which he is able to state and discuss the most difficult, dry, and intricate scientific arguments. His discourses, in fact, are quite a thing of their own kind. And if anything were needed to show the value of powers of discussion, it may be found in the lively attention he succeeded in drawing to the gold question – a question infinitely more important than it is attractive to most readers.

As to Mr. Crawfurd's views and objections, they were most of them

[1] Published in the issue of 1 October 1863.

[2] This was an error on Jevons's part. Crawfurd's letter had been published on Saturday, 19 September, although dated 17 September (a Thursday).

John Crawfurd had presented a paper entitled 'On the Effects of the Gold of Australia and California' to the Dublin meeting of the British Association in 1857. In this he argued that 'the enormous quantities of gold and silver suddenly thrown upon the market during the last nine years have not produced a proportionate depreciation in the price of these metals'. See *Report of the Twenty-Seventh Meeting of the British Association, held at Dublin . . . 1857*, Transactions of Sections, p. 160.

The author of this paper and the letters to *The Times* may possibly have been John Crawfurd (1783–1868), who wrote a number of works on the trade of India and the Far East between 1828 and 1843.

answered before they were stated, being chiefly such as I anticipated. Mr. Crawfurd will discover this by a more careful reading.

I fully agree both with Professor Cairnes and your late article that no distress, disturbance, or serious inconvenience need be apprehended from the slow change in the value of gold which must go on. The most sudden and serious part of the fall has already occurred, I fully believe, and in fact occurred during the prosperous commercial period preceding 1857. And it is a curious point about this subject that the fall of value *manifests* itself during those periods of active trade and speculation when prices rise rapidly, and most persons at least think that they are better off than before.

I have only further to request that those who are interested in the subject will turn to the writings of Professor Cairnes in the *Journal of the Dublin Statistical Society* for January, 1859; in *Frazer's Magazine* for September, 1859, and January, 1860; and in the *Economist* of the 30th of May last.

W. Stanley Jevons

Owen's College, Manchester, Sept. 24.

194.   H. FAWCETT TO W. S. JEVONS

Bodenham,
Salisbury.
Oct. 1st, 1863.

My dear Sir,

I cannot sufficiently thank you for your most kind and handsome letter which I have just read in today's Times – I fear you have been too complimentary to me, but I cannot help feeling deeply grateful to you because I know you have expressed your sincere feelings.

I think you have most properly replied to Craufurd* – I know sufficiently of his qualifications to discuss the gold-question that I really did not regard his letter as worth replying to. I should however have done so, had I not feared that I might be dragged into a personal controversy and this I was most anxious to avoid.

Your letter combined with Cairnes most able remarks makes the reply complete – I candidly tell you as I told the people at Newcastle that your pamphlet convinced me that the opinions I had previously expressed on the subject were erroneous, and the chief object I had in view in bringing forward the question at Newcastle was to make this avowal. I certainly think that the discussion which has resulted must have been satisfactory to you, as it has done much to strengthen and confirm the conclusions at which you have arrived.

I hope you will undertake the comparison of prices which you speak of. I am sure there is no one better qualified than yourself to carry out such an important work.

When I return to London I hope to have the pleasure of making your acquaintance.

Again thanking you.
Believe me to be,
My Dear Sir,
Yours very truly,
Henry Fawcett.

W. S. Jevons, Esq.,

195.   WILLIAM JEVONS JUNIOR TO W. S. JEVONS

Brighton, Nov. 17 1863.

My dear Stanley,

Many thanks to you for your long and interesting letter which I was very glad to receive. I have long been wishing to hear from you and wondering you did not write, though I thought it likely that you were prevented from writing by your multiplied occupations. I was much inclined to write to you to ask how you were going on; but knew not how to direct. It gives me great pleasure to hear how well you are employed and how much you like your employments. Never fear that you will not "get to lecture well". By your own account you do already lecture well for how could you otherwise so deeply engage the attention of your logic class and make them "quite absorbed in the subject". I only wish your labours were more remunerative. But that I trust will come in due time—

I was glad to see how much notice your pamphlet has gained and how your name figured in the Times. It astonishes me to hear that with all your onerous college duties, you can find time to extend your statistical researches as far back as data can be got. In those researches I am afraid you will miss the advantages lately afforded you at the British Museum. I am glad to hear that your paper on Logic is nearly printed, and I anticipate much pleasure and instruction in reading it when it comes out. You need not hurry yourself to return the books and MS. I lent you. I am glad you found them occasionally useful. I have found your book (Livermore's Commentary on the Gospels[1]) exceedingly useful and I have less scruple in keeping it, so long as you keep books of mine. As for Williams book, though I do not think he is likely to want it, you had

[1] Abiel A. Livermore, *The Four Gospels; with a Commentary* (1850).

better return it to him next time you go to Liverpool, and I hope you will see him when you do so, as he was much disappointed that he did not see you when you were in Liverpool last summer. I am glad to hear that dear Henny likes Manchester, and finds there so much good society and so many evening entertainments. Manchester has always abounded in good society, and now that a college is established there its advantages in that respect must of course be increased. I am glad also to hear that you are so comfortably settled with your aunt in an agreeable locality. If your aunt should visit Brighton, I hope she will favour us with a call – we shd. be very glad to see her.—

Brighton is now very full and it is amusing to see the throng of fashionable people on the esplanade at certain hours and the stream of equipages and equestrians along King's Road. A new hotel of enormous size is now created opposite to the site of the battery,[2] and a new pier is to be constructed opposite Regency Square. The hotel is erected by a company, and, being nine storeys high, and elegant in its architecture, it forms a conspicuous ornament of the town.

I have very little to tell you respecting ourselves. We are going on in our usual quiet way. But now and then we see friends from a distance, and within the last few weeks we have had two very welcome visitors. The first was George who brought his wife and two youngest children to Hastings for the winter and came over thence to see us for part of a day. The other was J. H. Rowland, who, having occasion to visit London, ran down to spend a few hours with us—

I am going on with the revision of my work on Christianity, in which I find great room for improvement, and as my mind is very slow in maturing its ideas and often incapacitated for deep thought by physical ailments, I cannot look forward to a speedy completion of the work. Feeling, indeed, as I do, the infirmities of age coming upon me and being near the termination of my 70th year, I sometimes despair of ever accomplishing my task—

We all unite in best love to yourself and sister, and I remain,

My dear Stanley,

affectionately, yours,

W. Jevons.

I shall be glad to hear from you whenever you can find time to write, and a short letter will be better than none.

[2] The Grand Hotel, Brighton, was built on the site of the old Battery house in 1864. The West Pier, opposite Regency Square, was completed in 1866. See Clunn, *Famous South Coast Resorts* (1929) p. 61; *Baedeker's Great Britain*, second edition (1890) p. 50.

196.   J. E. THOROLD ROGERS[1] TO W. S. JEVONS

Oxford, Nov. 23
1863

My dear Sir,

I forward with this a copy of the paper read by me in 1861 at Manchester. The paper was printed in the proceedings of the Statistical Soc[y]. of London.[2]

I do not pretend to have arrived at any definite conclusions in this publication. At that time I was only just commencing my investigations into a history of prices, though since I have devoted almost all the time at my disposal to these researches, and have besides the services of a gentleman in the Record office whom the gov[t]. has placed at my disposal.

As my intended work begins at the year 1260 and as I have devoted most of my research as yet to the thirteenth fourteenth and fifteenth centuries, I cannot suggest much by way of inference about the sixteenth, though I have already a very large accumulation of facts about it. But I am convinced generally that the circumstances which led to the change in Money values at that time were so wholly distinct from any that do or could take place now, that I doubt the possibility of ever deriving a reasonable analogy from this part of economical history to the circumstances of our own time. But I feel that no part of this history is more interesting, and none which is less known than the real nature of the change of that period.

I hope to put out a volume of my work (from 1260 to 1376) in the course of next year. Another will occupy the period from 1377 to the close of the fifteenth century. My third volume will treat of the epoch to which you refer.[3]

I need hardly observe that the currency in England as well as the continent was almost wholly silver, and that the derangement such as it was was due to the change which was induced by the influx of silver from the new world.

Yours very faithfully,
James E. T. Rogers

[1] James Edwin Thorold Rogers (1823–90), Tooke Professor of Economic Science and Statistics at King's College, London, 1859–90; Drummond Professor of Political Economy at Oxford, 1862–7 and 1888–90. A friend and follower of Richard Cobden, he became active in politics and was M.P. for Southwark, 1880–5, and for Bermondsey, 1885–6. Academically he was one of the founders of economic history as a discipline in England.

[2] 'Facts and Observations on Wages and Prices in England during the Sixteenth and Seventeenth Centuries, and more particularly during the Thirty-Nine Years, 1582–1620, the data principally employed being the Fabric Rolls of York Minster and the Shuttleworth Household Books', *JRSS*, 24 (1861) 535–85.

[3] Thorold Rogers's *A History of Agriculture and Prices in England, 1259–1793,* appeared in six volumes between 1866 and 1887. Vols I and II appeared in 1866 and covered the period 1259–1400, vols III and IV (1882) dealt with the years 1401–1582 and vols V and VI (1887) with the years 1583–1702.

197.   W. S. JEVONS TO HERBERT JEVONS

Birch Grove,
Rusholme
19 December 1863

Dear Herbert

. . . I have just got my Logic book out, and will send you a copy in the box. I have not as yet had any opinion upon it having only received copies myself a few days.

We are now close at the end of the term. In the holydays* we are going to Beaumaris where we shall have a noisy time I dare say, but I get to like Beaumaris very well.

I find myself slightly used up at the end of this term, probably because my four evening lectures require considerable exertion after the days work. I am now getting quite accustomed to lecturing which presents no great difficulty to me.

I have a few private pupils from whom I shall receive a little but my tutoring work at the College does not progress much and my profits as a whole will be very small this year. But it is better than nothing & small beginnings may have larger endings. Prof Scott[1] whose class I have been holding as yet has come back & intends to recommence his class after Xmas. But he is not at all well, or at least acts as if he were not[2]. . . .

Ever yours
W. S. Jevons

198.   W. S. JEVONS TO MRS LUCY HUTTON
[LJN, 195]

Birch Grove, Rusholme,
10th January, 1864.

. . . I enclose a letter of Tom's, mentioning a review of my pamphlet among other works, which is quite as satisfactory as he says.[1] It also speaks of me as being master of every part of the subject. You will also, perhaps, like to hear, and I only tell you because I know you will like to hear, that

---

[1] See Vol. I, pp. 41–2, and Vol. II, Letter 110, n. 6, p. 305.

[2] The remaining parts of the letter are concerned with gold assaying technique, and details of the shipment of the box which Herbert Jevons had requested in his letter of 13 September 1863 (see above, Letter 191, p. 39).

[1] This letter has not been traced. The review may have been that which appeared in the *Westminster Review* for January 1864 (vol 81, 88–101). In this *A Serious Fall* was reviewed along with other works on the depreciation of gold by Chevalier, Fawcett and W. Nassau Lees; it referred to 'the unquestionable insight which he [Jevons] displays into every collateral branch of his subject'.

my pamphlet was mentioned in a report by one of the English delegates to the International Statistical Congress at Berlin on the progress of Statistical Science in England as in a certain degree a novelty.[2] Altogether the pamphlet has had an extraordinary degree of success but it brings no money and I don't seem likely to get money anywhere.

I have a note from De Morgan[3] pointing out a slight mistake in my logic, but saying he likes it well at first sight. He evidently takes some interest in it.

I find it somewhat dull and discouraging beginning here again after our cheerful time at Beaumaris. I think I shall need a holiday again at Easter with you if it can be managed, but it is rather soon to begin thinking about it. . . .

199.   W. S. JEVONS TO T. E. JEVONS

> Birch Grove
> Rusholme.
> Jan 17. 64.

Dear Tom

I should have liked to see the vessel explode in the Mersey.[1] I cannot think why they did not get the powder out or wet it or sink the ship. If there had been a plucky captain I should think it would have been done.

I am glad Will is coming home, & hope he will settle down somewhere here, & give up all Penang schemes.[2]

I have not heard much about my logic yet. I have indeed a note from De Morgan expressing some approval but pointing out that the § 146 about his prop^s. is wrong.[3]

Cairnes in acknowledging a copy, congratulated me concerning the

Report of Dr William Farr, F.R.S., F.S.S., one of the delegates from England at the meeting of the International Statistical Congress, Berlin, September 1863', *JRSS*, 26 (1863) 415–6:

'Prices have been investigated by Mr. Jevons, formerly of the Sydney Royal Mint, who, by the investigation of the prices of 118 commodities, shows that there has been a depreciation of the value both of gold and silver. There is a novelty in the methods which Mr. Jevons has employed, as well as great interest in his facts, collected from the best authorities.'

[3] Augustus de Morgan to W. S. Jevons, 4 January 1864. For the mistake to which De Morgan drew Jevons's attention, see below, Letter 199. n. 3.

[1] On 9 January 1864 the *Lotty Sleigh*, with $11\frac{1}{2}$ tons of gunpowder on board, caught fire in the Mersey. The crew had been taken off before the cargo exploded – with sufficient force to cause considerable damage and panic in Liverpool. See the *Annual Register* (1864) pp. 3–6.

[2] William Edgar (Will) Jevons returned home in May 1864 after three years' residence on a sugar estate at Jawee, Province Wellesley, Penang. See Vol. II, Letter 32, n. 1, p. 58.

[3] W. S. Jevons, *Pure Logic; or the Logic of Quality apart from Quantity* (1864) § 146: 'Two new propositions of De Morgan's system are thus expressed:

Everything is either A or B	$A = b$
Some things are neither A nor B	$a = b$'

Gold P – & said he knew of no P on such a subject that had been so well received for a long time back. I have seen the review in the West^r. [4]

Do you know whether Henry has sold our Ry shares or not. He wrote to ask whether I agreed to it, & I said not – at least as regards the L. & N W. I have not heard what he has done. I dont like speculating with them for though we have gained upon them it is no reason we should always gain. If there should be war shares would of course fall somewhat, but on the balance of probabilities I think they will rise rather than fall or at all events keep their value as a good investment with pretty good dividends.

I dont think there will be an European war, & so I told Henry. All the continentals will be too afraid of the Revolutionists & of France.

Your affec. Brother

W S Jevons

200.   FRAGMENT OF A LETTER FROM W. S. JEVONS TO HERBERT JEVONS

[January 1864]

. . . and hazardous and almost always cause a loss of some silver.

The method by reducing the chloride by iron or zinc before melting is far more sure & need not cost the loss of 1 per cent of silver. As I fully described the process in previous letters I need not repeat.

I do not think that acid can be used in the Union Bank to purify the gold. It might indeed be used in the full method of gold refining, but it could scarcely be done with profit in New Zealand, since we scarcely attempted it even in the Sydney Mint. Our melter Hunt however found out an easy way of curing brittleness.

Expose the gold to a strong melting keep the crucible lid open and occasionally throw a little *nitre* or (Saltpetre) on to the surface of the melted gold. It is still better to add a little copper, (a halfpenny piece – not a bronze coin,) for instance) but this you could hardly do in the first melting as it would increase the weight of the gold.

I am sorry to say the Chemical Dic^y. has not yet got on to my Article on Assaying, [1] but I hope to send you the contents of the article by next mail. It contains my improved process of assaying which you might at least try.

I have got nearly all the articles you required, or rather the share of them that I undertook to get. Tom undertook to get the box & some of the clothes in Liverpool & to pack them up & ship them.

---

[4] Cf. above, Letter 198, n. 1, p. 48.

[1] Jevons's article 'Gold Assaying' in Henry Watt's *Dictionary of Chemistry* was written in 1861 but not published until 1864. See Vol. I, pp. 20 and 35.

I have got the books you desired together with an excellent Manual of Assaying, which contains almost all the practical & scientific information you can require. The account of gold assaying in this book is however very poor & you need not mind it much.

The Dict^y of Chemistry is so elaborate an affair so full of organic chemistry, that I hardly think it would serve you much; I think I may as well keep it, being a very expensive work that I could never afford to buy.

In Sydney we used to weigh out equal portions of lead by casting small shots. I got you two bullet moulds, the smallest I could find thinking they might serve you, but afterwards found they were hardly so small as the mould for the revolver which I am sending. We used to flatten the bullets by the stroke of a hammer on the anvil; perhaps you might do this and afterwards cut them in two or reduce them. But you have not told me how you do your work; otherwise I should know much better how to give you hints to save labour or increase accuracy.

The French flasks  are cheap & easily got.

The range of gas burners would have to be made for you, and might cost £5 here. If you should adopt my way of assaying, the sand bath and a few large flasks would be quite suft. all you will require extra are rather larger flat bottomed flasks, & small punches to number the slips. I will try & procure the numeral punches & send them in the box, & you will then be able to try my way. This consists merely in marking one end of the slip of alloy or cornet with a number, & then putting several cornets together to boil in one flask, with as many quantities of acid. If the cornets are smooth & good this may be done with complete safety, & I carried on the work of the Mint thus for a year or two generally boiling 8 cornets in one flask. To decant the cornets put a flat piece of tile, for instance a piece of a muffle in the bottom of a basin of water.

Fill the flask with water, put your thumb over the top, upset it & let the cornets fall onto the tile. This is withdrawn the cornets separated gently & then annealed. You might try this beginning with two or three together if you have flasks large enough; but I will next month send you a copy of my article in the dictionary describing the process more fully.

I will send you the account of expenses for your clothes books etc. next month.

When your new Bank is built or nearly so I think you should persuade your Bank to send an order for a good set of apparatus. I would undertake to make you a list of things & perhaps order them.

My gold P has been very successful; there is a review of it among other books on a similar subject in the Westminster Review for Jan 1864, very complimentary to me on the whole. Prof Cairnes tells me that he does not think any pamphlet on an Economic subject has been so well received for a long time back. It may be said that I have made a fortunate beginning but there is still little in my position as yet . . .

201.   W. S. JEVONS TO HERBERT JEVONS
[LJP, 195]

Birch Grove
Rusholme
Febr. 18. 1864.

Dear Herbert,

I have your letter up to Dec. 17. about which time you seem to have had some rainy weather but nothing more to find fault with. . . .

. . . I have not much to tell you about my own affairs. I shall make this year nearly £100 from the College. Railway dividends also are improved up to 6 per cent, so that I shall have an income of about £170 which fully covers expenses. My work takes up a good deal of my time but after Easter the evening classes cease. I am going on with various work. I am nearly completing the full reduction of prices since 1782 which will show many things of interest I think. I am also about undertaking the Subject of the exhaustion of Coal in England which I believe is a very serious matter. A good publication on the subject would draw a good deal of attention. I am convinced that it is necessary for the present at any rate to write on popular subjects. My logic has made no noise although it is somewhat favourably regarded by De Morgan, Prof. Sandeman[1] here, & others who know what Logic is or should be . . .[2]

Ever yours
W S Jevons

[1] Archibald Sandeman (d. 1893), first Professor of Natural Philosophy at Owens College, Manchester, 1851–60; first Professor of Mathematics, 1851–65. Cf. Vol. I, p. 42.
[2] See above, Letters 198 and 199, pp. 48 and 49. The remainder of this letter is concerned only with details of the Jevons family's finances.

202. W. S. JEVONS TO J. E. CAIRNES

Owens College
Manchester
April 23rd 1864

My dear Sir

I am much obliged to you for the paper on the Confederate Rams,[1] which you have been so good as to send me. I have no doubt you are right in saying that there is no law for the case. Lawyers never seem to be aware that totally new & unforeseen combinations of things & events must occur from time to time which cannot be provided for in any law. Many of the most difficult law suits arise upon logical points and it is worst of all when the question is one of *degree* as it clearly is in this case. It is very difficult to know what can be done, but fortunately it does not lie upon me to decide.

I may add that I lately read your 'Slave Power' with great pleasure.[2] It seemed to me a nearly or quite irrefragible piece of reasoning. You did not seem to me to give quite sufficient evidence that slave agriculture is essentially exhaustive & must therefore demand new land. If cooped up in a definite area might they not alter their habits? Do the planters in Cuba & elsewhere similarly exhaust their soil? You are I dare say quite right, but do you give sufficient evidence in the work that Slave Culture can only be exhaustive? Though I greatly admire the 'Slave Power' as a piece of reasoning, I hardly go with you in your Northern Sympathies. I am strictly neutral.

I chiefly write now to enclose tracings from two curves representing part of the results of calculations which have occupied most of my spare time for 6 months past. I have been carrying out a reduction of the tables of prices in Tooke's Hist &c, so as to improve the inquiry very imperfectly begun in my pamphlet. One of the tracings shows the general average var^n of all the Com.^{s} It exhibits clearly the great rise of prices during the war, the several spec. rises of 1810, 1825, 1836–9, 1847, 1857 &c. It also shows that the permanent rise of prices since the gold disc^s though very distinct, especially in comparison with the previous downward course of prices, is not very serious in amount. Curiously enough it appears that for the last seven years prices have been on the average more steady than for at least 80 years before. But there is enough to indicate I think that a great speculative rise of prices may soon be expected.

[1] Two steam rams which were under construction at the Liverpool yard of Laird Brothers. Ostensibly ordered by a French firm, they were intended for use by the Confederate navy in breaking the blockade of southern ports. In September 1863 the Foreign Secretary, Earl Russell, ordered the seizure of the rams, a decision which gave rise to heated debate in Parliament on the issues of international law involved. Cf. the *Annual Register* (1864) pp. 123–30.

[2] J. E. Cairnes, *The Slave Power; its Character, Career and Probable Designs: being an attempt to explain the real issues involved in the American contest.* (1862; second edition, 1863). Cf. below, Letter 204, p. 56, for Cairnes's comments on Jevons's queries.

The other curve shows the variation of prices of tropical articles of food (sugar, coffee, tea, spices &c) *relatively* to the general mass of com! Thus the falling of the line indicates that tropical articles did not rise so much as the average by the ratio given by the logarithm. You will remark the great comparative fall about 1800 lasting till near the end of the war, as well as the recent comparative depression. The former marked fall may throw some light upon the question of the high war prices, which in spite of what Tooke has written seems to me wholly unsolved. But the more I go into the subject the more difficult it seems, & for the present at least I venture on no theories.

I am classifying com⁵ in all ways which occur to me as

animal	Food	and in
vegetable	clothing	groups
mineral	materials	

according to place of production &c, so that if there is anything to be learned I may find it I hope. If you know of any better ways of grouping commodities I should like to try them while the iron is hot.

I am thinking of giving the results at the Brit assoc, unless any better way of pubⁿ occurs to me.[3]

I remain my dear Sir
Yours very faithfly.
W. S. Jevons.

203.   D. M. BALFOUR[1] TO W. S. JEVONS

Boston, April 27, 1864.

Dear Sir,

I have perused with much pleasure your work, entitled, – "A serious fall in the value of gold", – in which you state, (p. 26) that it is ascertained beyond reasonable doubt, that prices between 1845 and 1862 (18 years) are greatly raised. No doubt that is the fact. But, had you have extended your comparison over a longer period, say forty years, (1821 to 1860), it would have shown a slight decline in prices. You will find a table of fourteen articles, during that period, in the American Almanac for 1861, p. 194.[2]

---

[3] The results were in fact incorporated in the paper 'The Variation of Prices and the Value of the Currency since 1782', read before the Statistical Society of London in May 1865 and published in *JRSS*, 28 (1865) 294–320; reprinted in *Investigations*, pp. 119–50, with the diagrams here described by Jevons appended.

[1] David Miller Balfour (1811–1902), of Charlestown and Boston, Mass., where he set up business as a broker in 1837; appears to have had interests in economic and historical questions.

[2] *The American Almanac and Repository of Useful Knowledge, for the year 1861* (Volume XXXII, fourth series,Volume II) (Boston, 1861) p. 194: 'Prices of Beef, Pork and Nine Other Articles for Forty Years. Prepared for the American Almanac by David M. Balfour.' Balfour's reference to a table of *fourteen* articles was presumably a slip of memory.

That an advance in prices has taken place since 1849, there can be no doubt. But it may, I think, be fairly attributable to two separate and distinct causes, – viz –

1. The double discovery of the California gold mines in 1848, and the Australia in 1851.
2. The repeal of the British Corn laws in 1849. [*sic*]

Since 1849, the foreign commerce of Great Britain, the United States, and France, have nearly doubled; the condition of the middle and lower classes in your country has greatly improved; owing to the greater demand for labor, and the consumption of manufactured articles, induced by the opening of the California and Australia markets, prices have been enhanced by the ability of consumers to purchase more extensively. Cheap bread has induced the increased consumption of other articles of necessity as well as luxury.

Taking this opportunity to express to you, the satisfaction I have derived from the perusal of your valuable work, and begging you to excuse me, for thus intruding myself upon your notice,

I remain, Yours truly,
David M. Balfour

Mr. W. Stanley Jevons, M.A.
    London

204. J. E. CAIRNES TO W. S. JEVONS

Delvin Lodge
Balbriggan
28 April 1864

My dear Sir,

Your interesting letter has followed me from Galway here; and I have to thank you very much for it as well as for the tracings which you kindly enclose.

The tracings set in a very striking light two features in the course of prices – the normal tendency to a fall, and the exceptional and on the whole steady rise since 1850. The most perplexing feature is the rise from 1832 to 1840; but I presume this w^d find its explanation in the – as well as I recollect at present – remarkable succession of unfavourable seasons which occurred in that interval. I was surprised to observe in your pamphlet (I think it was) the strong terms of disparagement which you apply to the speculations of Mr. Tooke respecting the war period, and which I perceive further study of this subject has not induced you to modify. I myself thought his explanation of the monetary phenomena of that time on the whole satisfactory. It is however some eight years since I have read the volumes of his work which deal with that time. You remark on the steadiness of prices during the last seven years: doubtless this is the result of our free trade regime. Increased steadiness of price with a progressive rise is what I should expect as the result of the combined influences of the new gold and free trade.

As to the question of classification the course which I should follow w^d be – indeed that which I have already followed – to consider the conditions of production, more particularly with reference to the facilities available for enlarging or contracting the supply. Cost being the fundamental principle in relation to price, it is only as cost is modified by special circumstances affecting it, that deviation from the natural level may be expected to occur.

Many thanks for what you so kindly say on the "Slave Power". I imagine from your criticism that you read it in the first edition which was brought out rather hurriedly. If this be so, and you will do me the favour, when an opportunity offers, to look at the passages in the second edition in which the subject of the exhaustive character of slave agriculture is discussed, I think you will find that the evidence on this point is tolerably full.[1] You ask "if cooped up in a definite area might they not alter their habits"? Yes certainly. That is precisely my point. It is an[2]

205.   W. S. JEVONS TO HERBERT JEVONS
       [LJP, 197]

Beaumaris
18 May 1864

Dear Herbert

I omitted to write last month, being much occupied & knowing that Tom was about to write to enclose a bill of lading for your box. I believe he will also write this month to enclose a second bill.

I am here for a weeks holyday* at Whitsun week during which our College is closed. It happens to be a period of splendid hot summer weather thus early in the year. The sun is so hot here that we can hardly go out in the middle of the day, and the season as yet has been such that the trees and all vegetation are growing with the utmost luxuriance.

As the tide happens to suit well I get up before breakfast and have a

---

[1] The second (1863) edition of *The Slave Power* contained a considerable volume of additional evidence on the character of slave economy, including examples taken from Brazil and Cuba, supporting Cairnes's thesis that only where a single crop could be cultivated extensively would slave labour be effective and profitable. Cf. pp. 51–63 of the second edition, and also W. L. J. E. Miller, 'Cairnes on the economics of American negro slavery', *Southern Economic Journal* (April 1864) pp. 333–41.

[2] The remaining sheet of the original letter is missing.

delightful bathe all the better perhaps because from the coldness of the water it must be brief, & I sometimes have a second bathe towards evening.

By the end of the week I think I shall be almost recovered from the fatigue of my first College session.

I here find John & Lucy quite recovered except that they are a little thinner than before. The children are all well and Grindal[1] quite flourishing and intelligent which is of course a great pleasure to Lucy. The business affairs are yet in *statu quo ante* and almost I am afraid likely to remain so. It is true that they are doing a fine business, & obliged even to refuse orders, but their capital is so deficient that many necessary improvements cannot be carried out. John has decided to leave Beaumaris & live near the works to urge them on a little, but there are some difficulties in getting a house, & I am afraid the summer may pass without his doing anything. Then again all the negotiations for forming a quarry Company, seem to come to nothing so that I am afraid lest present good opportunities of placing the affair upon a firmer foundation should be lost. Then there may come times when business will be slack again & more competition from other quarries felt. But you had perhaps better not allude to these matters in your letters. I want them very much to move into a healthier house than this at Beaumaris.

Henny is at Manchester now or rather I think visiting some of her friends there for a day or two. She gets on capitally in Manchester; has plenty of friends, & is much occupied with school teaching. At home too she is now generally mistress.

I have now only two weeks more work at College and after that intend to go up to London for some months of my vacation. In spite of my ill success this year I am inclined to think I shall succeed better next session & shall find it much easier & pleasanter work. In that case I might make an income of some £200 to £250 over all, and might begin to think of taking a house of my own & settling more comfortably with Henny.

Tom gets on well in L pool, but is very wavering as to his arrangements on leaving Rathbones as an apprentice. He may join Jevons, go out as foreign agent of Rathbone's or even remain with them with a fair salary. It is hard to know what is best. Jevons & Co may lose something I believe when the American Smash comes as it must come in a year or two at the furthest, and it might be well for Tom not to join them in too much of a hurry & yet not give up a good chance.

From your last letters I gather that things are not quite so busy in Otago, & that a certain degree of reaction had set in. This is always to be expected at Gold diggings. But no doubt you will be needed by your Bank

---

[1] The son of John and Lucy Hutton, born 26 December 1862. Cf. Vol. I, p. 11; Vol. II, Letter 168, n. 6, p. 462.

at one or other of its branches even if the Otago diggings should not get on so well as hitherto. And as you are equal or may make yourself equal to almost any part of the banking business in addition to the gold work, you will be valuable to any bank. I hope to see you manager or agent yet, but I should think you could hardly expect further advances of salary just at present.

I have at times overworked myself during the past session, and always feel it in subsequent depression; but I try to work to the best advantage by giving up night work and taking plenty of sleep, & occasional holydays*. And I hope then to get through the whole of the summer, & do a great deal of reading in connection with the question of the exhaustion of Coal, which I look upon as the coming question. At the same time I am going on with the gold question, & only slightly deferring further logical work.

I saw Roscoe on Saturday. He seemed so much recovered from his serious symptoms of weakness during the winter, that I dont suppose we need make any change at present.

You know I suppose that Eddy Hutton is going out to India in a few months. He likes[2] the notion, is very suitable for the undertaking and it is in almost every way a fortunate arrangement. He may easily make a fortune in the course of 20 years as editor of the "Friend of India".[3]

As Lucy is going to add a little more I will close—

Yours affectionately

W S Jevons.

206.   W. S. JEVONS TO HERBERT JEVONS
       [LJN, 201]

London, 18th July 1864.

. . . I have now been a full month in London, working at the Museum at this subject of coal exhaustion.

It is not at all easy work to grind up so extensive a subject, and get it all done in three months. London, too, is getting very hot, and I sometimes feel lazy and languid; perhaps I shall be too lazy to write to you next month or two. I don't know, but may be the others will write.

About a week ago the council of the college[1] elected me a fellow, with a

---

[2] 'like' in the original manuscript.

[3] Edward Malin Hutton (b. 1848), eldest son of John Hutton by his first wife, Eliza Malin.

The *Friend of India*, an English-language newspaper which took a reforming Christian standpoint, was published at Calcutta. Jevons's reference to it was probably prompted by the fact that R. H. Hutton's associate on the *Spectator*, Meredith Townsend, had edited the *Friend of India* until 1856. In fact, Eddie Hutton returned from India only two years later. Cf. below, Letter 277, p. 149.

[1] i.e. University College London.

share of proprietorship. This is the usual thing, sooner or later, to those who get M.A. honours. It is no profit and no honour, but still I like being permanently connected with the college. . . .

207.   W. S. JEVONS TO H. E. ROSCOE

Beaumaris
Care of J. Hutton.
27 Aug. 1864.

My dear Harry,

I have often been thinking how you were getting on with your great lecture. Thank goodness I have no such thing to do.

I should like to have some notion of how you have made it up and shall look anxiously for the report in the paper. I shall not be at Bath[1] having given up the notion of finishing my inquiry on Prices just at present. All summer I have been wholly engaged on the *Coal Question* which I have got into a very alarming position. How & when I shall finish it up I dont quite know just at present, being inclined for a few days air & pleasure before settling to work again.

I have had very little communication with Manchester – but look forward to the new session mostly with satisfaction.

I find that during last half year my logic has not sold at all, only to the extent of 4 copies. The diagrams & pamphlet on the other hand continue to go off pretty well & new impressions of the diagrams will probably be taken. Probably I shall make a new & improved edition.

You will be pleased to hear of Frank's[2] matrimonial success.

I have got pleasant small lodgings in a house here & board at Lucy's house. As it is tea time & near post time I must close today rather briefly and remain

Your affte Cousin
W. S. Jevons

I hope young Edmund[3] is doing as well as young Grindal here. Lucy here is strong & mostly well, & I hope your Lucy is even better.

[1] The British Association met at Bath in September 1864 and H. E. Roscoe read three papers before the Chemistry section of which the most important was probably 'Contributions towards the foundations of Quantitative Photography', *Annual Report of the British Association for the Advancement of Science*, Bath, 1864, Transactions of Sections, p. 40.

[2] A reference to the marriage of Francis James Roscoe to Letitia Le Breton; see Journal of W. S. Jevons, Vol. I, p. 193, n. 6.

[3] The son of H. E. Roscoe, born 6 June 1864; he died on 2 January 1885 while at Magdalen College, Oxford.

208.   W. S. JEVONS TO SIR JOHN F. W. HERSCHEL[1]
        [HLRS 320]

Owen's College,
Manchester,
Sept. 27, 1864.

Sir J. F. W. Herschel.

Dear Sir,

Permit me to express to you in a few words the extreme satisfaction with which I read your answer concerning the Theological Declaration of Scientific Men. Such an appropriate statement of the position of an inquirer in the present day strikes me as invaluable both to Science and True Religion. And I cannot sufficiently express my concurrence in your protest against a desire for freedom of inquiry being interpreted as a tendency to Irreligion.[2]

Is it worthy of Religion to assume that it must be discarded by all who freely seek after the Truth?

I am Dear Sir,
Yours with much respect,
W. S. Jevons.

[1] See Vol. II, Letter 151, n. 1, p. 432.

[2] Herschel had evidently been circularised by Professor John Stenhouse, F.R.S., with an invitation to join over two hundred other eminent scientists in a declaration regarding science and scripture. He declined to do so, in a letter dated 6 September 1864, reproduced with other relevant correspondence in *The Times*, 20 September 1864, p. 7.

The so-called Theological Declaration of Scientific Men expressed regret that 'researches into scientific truth are perverted by some in our own times into occasion for casting doubt upon the truth and authenticity of the Holy Scriptures. We conceive that it is impossible for the Word of God, as written in the book of nature, and God's Word written in Holy Scripture, to contradict one another. . . . We believe that it is the duty of every scientific student to investigate nature simply for the purpose of elucidating truth, and that if he finds that some of his results appear to be in contradiction to the Written Word . . . he should leave the two side by side till it shall please God to allow us to see the manner in which they may be reconciled. . . .'

Herschel had replied in strong terms that he considered 'the act of calling on me publicly to avow or disavow, to approve or disapprove, in writing any religious doctrine or statement, however carefully or cautiously drawn up (in other words, to append my name to a religious manifesto) to be an infringement of that social forbearance which guards the freedom of religious opinion in this country with especial sanctity'. He went on '. . . I protest against my refusal to sign your "Declaration" being construed into a profession of atheism or infidelity . . . I consider this movement simply mischievous, having a direct tendency (by putting forward a new shibboleth, a new verbal test of religious partizanship) to add a fresh element of discord to the already too discordant relations of the Christian world. . . .'

209. E. LASPEYRES[1] TO W. S. JEVONS

Basel 20 xi, 1864.

Sir,

I regret from all my heart, that I was not enabled to answer to your kind letter, I received seven months ago in Lübeck. This letter contained the prices from 1846 to 1865 for several of your minor articles, you will see that I have made use of them and I hope not a bad use.

As a little sign of my gratitude for your great kindness, I send you an exemplar of my little essay on the prices of Hamburg[2] compared with those of London from 1845 to 1863. I should have answered your kind letter long ago, if I had not hoped from day to day that I should quickly accomplish my little essay, and when it was accomplished, that it should be more quickly printed.

This hope is not fulfilled till this moment and now I haste to answer also on your demand whether we possess in Germany any think lyke your most excellent work of Tooke and Newmarch on the history of prices.

I regret to confess that we have nothing lyke this, but I hope that in ten or twenty years I shall have accomplished a history of prices etc. in Germany.

You wrote, Sir, that you are occupied with an essay on the prices from 1784 collected in the history of prices by Tooke and Newmarch.[3] I should be very thankful, if you might send it to me, when it is published. Lykewise I risk to beg you, that you may make some notice from my essay in the Economist or in one of your excellent reviews.

In the hope of a kind answer,

I am Sir your most obedient
Dr. Etienne Laspeyres
Professor of political economy at the
University of Basel.

Adr. Basel Switzerland.

[1] Etienne Laspeyres (1834–1913), now best remembered for his contributions to the techniques of index numbers, was at this time beginning the extensive researches into price statistics from which his index-number work developed. In 1864 he was appointed Professor of Political Economy at Basle, from whence he moved to Riga in 1866 (see below, Letter 263, p. 125), to Dorpat (now Tartu) in 1869 and Karlsruhe in 1873, before settling at the University of Giessen where he taught from 1874 until his retirement in 1900. Like Jevons, Laspeyres was a strong advocate for a quantitative science of economics designed to trace the regularities in economic phenomena.

[2] 'Hamburger Waarenpreise 1851–1863 und die Kalifornischaustralischen Goldentdeckung seit 1848', *Jahrbucher für Nationalökonomie und Statistik*, 3 (1864) 81–118, 209–36.

[3] W. S. Jevons, 'The Variation of Prices and the Value of the Currency since 1782', *JRSS*, 28 (1865) 294–320, reprinted as No. iii in *Investigations*, pp. 119–50.

210.   FRAGMENT OF A LETTER FROM W. S. JEVONS TO
HERBERT JEVONS

[November or December 1864]

. . . Logic & critique upon his, as he declined to see it until he had
finished a mathematical book he was engaged upon. I have received from
a German Professor an elaborate essay on Prices in Hamburg, containing
also a great deal of criticism of my pamphlet. It is unfortunately written in
very hard German which I cannot read but with the greatest labour. As
far as I have yet gathered from it he more than confirms the fact of a great
rise of prices though he disputes some of my theoretical parts which
however are probably right. [1]

I have been elected a Fellow of the Statistical Society [2] & have just paid
up the life membership fee of £21 a rather large haul out of my resources
but I put it down to the capital acct.

I shall be rather busy again at the beginning of the new term & may not
write again for a month or two but I will send newspapers & hope to have
letters in return. Frank has gone a month or two with his wife Letty. [3] He
has been very successful in buying up the rival ironmongers there on
favourable terms, & he & his partner will probably have a fine leading
business there. But he has had the bad luck to lose his wedding presents
furniture &c, by a ship foundering in which he had sent it round the
Horn.

Ever yours
W. S. Jevons.

211.   W. S. JEVONS TO MRS LUCY HUTTON
[LJN, 202-3]

Rusholme, 3d December 1864

. . . I am sorry not to have answered your letter sooner; I would gladly
write oftener, but that I have so much other writing and work to do, and it
is by no means a light work for me to write a letter. . . . I hear a doubtful
rumour through Aunt H. [1] that you are moving. I hope it may be so for
several reasons. If you do move before Christmas, I am convinced we

---

[1] See above, Letter 209, and notes thereto, p. 61.
[2] The London (later Royal) Statistical Society of which Jevons subsequently became a Vice-President.
[3] Cf. above, Letter 207, n. 2, p. 59.
[1] Mrs Henry (Maria) Roscoe. Cf. Vol. I, p. 42.

shall have a most merry Christmas. If there is snow on the ground, the country will be especially beautiful. I am in much want of a holiday; for the truth certainly is that I overworked myself during the summer altogether; I have consequently to take much rest now, and to go an excursion almost every week. Last session somewhat exhausted me; and then London and Beaumaris did not set me up; so that, when I got back here, I just felt as if a good long holiday were the thing for me, rather than a session's work. My anxiety at Beaumaris, with the further anxiety of setting my college classes to work again, and the *Coal Question* at its most difficult and tiresome point, were certainly rather too much. But now that I know what it is to be overworked I shall take care to avoid it for the future. I am now quite well . . .

212.   W. WHITAKER[1] TO W. S. JEVONS

Canterbury, Dec. 13, 1864

Dear Jevons

I shall be glad to do what little I can for you.

Hull[2] has some remarks in his book on that underground ridge, & he shows that if there be Coal Measures they are likely to be so on the "lucus a non lucendo" principle. You should look to this.

Would you like an introduction to Hull? or to Binney?[3]

Remember that Godwin-Austen[4] was the man who did the underground ridge business. However he gave no figure in his paper. I've tried to supply that want, not a very small one. Lyell told me that he was very pleased with said figure &c.

I've reason to think that there may be a review of my memoir[5] in the next No. of the Geological Magazine.

I shall be here for about a week longer, then home for a few days, &

[1] William Whitaker (1836–1925), F.R.S., F.G.S., served with the Geological Survey of England from 1857 to 1896, and afterwards as a consulting geologist. He was recognised as an authority on the geology of south-east England, particularly with reference to water supplies.

[2] Edward Hull, *The Coal Fields of Great Britain: their history, structure and duration* (1861). In the second edition of 1881 the passage referred to occurs on p. 349.

[3] Edward William Binney (1812–81), chief founder of the Manchester Geological Society and its first secretary in 1838. As a geologist he was reputed to possess the most exact knowledge of the coal fields of Lancashire and Cheshire.

[4] Robert Alfred Cloyne Godwin-Austen (1808–84), 'On the Possible Extension of the Coal Measures beneath the South-Eastern part of England', *Quarterly Journal of the Geological Society of London*, 11 (1855) 533–6.

[5] The memoir referred to was Whitaker's *The Geology of parts of Middlesex, Herts, Bucks, Berks and Surrey (Sheet 7 of the Map of the Geological Survey of Great Britain)* (1864). The review appeared under the title 'The Geology of London and Neighbouring Country' in the *Geological Magazine*, 2 (1865) 64–7.

then away to some friends elsewhere. The address Geological Survey Office, Jermyn St., S.W. is safe at any time.

I am yours very truly

W. Whitaker

213.   W. S. JEVONS TO J. E. CAIRNES[1]

Owens College
Manch[r]
5 Jan 64 [sic]

My dear Sir

I am about to apply for a small Professorship in Logic Mental & Moral Phil[y] which is now vacant at the Queens College Liverpool. As you have on several occasions expressed a favourable opinion of my small publications, I hope you will feel able now to favour me with some testimonial of my logical ability.[2] The subjects indeed are not quite those which we have previously discussed but if we may judge from many instances Pol. Phil[y], Pol. Econ. Logic, Mental & Moral Phil[y] are all subjects requiring very similar habits of thought.[3]

I have already had some experience here in reading with students in these subjects & lecturing to our evening students.

It occurred to me that a letter in a late *Economist* concerning the periodical occurrence of panics was from your hand. If so I can only say I cordially concur in your remarks about the common fallacy of *looking for uniformity*. Perhaps I am not quite free from the fallacy but it was far from my intention to assert any considerable uniformity of undulation. I say for instance in Sec XI p. 15 of the my [sic] gold pamphlet that Com[1] Fluctuations "are never so similar & well marked &c", & speak too of their having been interrupted by wars.

I must confess my expectation judging from the present prolonged activity of trade & *fixed investment* that a collapse will occur of serious magnitude not far from 10 years after 1857. The recent pressure was but of a temporary character, not unlike that of 1836 which was followed by the serious collapse of 1839, aided by American failures.

It is hardly possible now that the cotton trade of Liverpool should be restored to its normal state without a dreadful collapse; a fall in the price

---

[1] The original manuscript of this letter is in the Cairnes Papers, MS 8954, National Library of Ireland.

[2] The testimonial, dated 8 January 1865, is reproduced below along with others submitted by Jevons with his application for the Chair at Owens College. From its date and the context, it is clear that in dating this letter Jevons made the common error of putting the old year instead of the new.

[3] In the original manuscript the following sentence is deleted here: 'It is possible too that I might some time have to undertake lectures on Pol. Econ.'

of cotton if it should coincide by chance with a rise in the price of corn which may be anticipated, & renewed & intensified pressure in the money market must occasion a reverse. But though there is I believe *some tendency to a periodical recurrence* of *excessive fixed investment* & consequent scarcity of capital, all matters of trade are of course constantly liable to disturbance & reversal by political or natural events.

A matter which has been taking most of my attention lately is the possible exhaustion of our Coal Mines. I have lately completed an essay directed to clearing up the popular ideas on the subject, and showing that it is physically impossible for our industrial progress to be long continued (a few generations) at our present rate of geometrical increase. The consequences must be of a serious character.

I hope in a few days to read your essay on the methods of working Welsh Slate Quarries.[4]

Yours faithfully
W. S. Jevons

214. TESTIMONIAL FOR W. S. JEVONS FROM J. G. GREENWOOD[1]

Owens College,
Manchester.
20th Jan. 1865.

To the Council of Queen's College, Liverpool.

Gentlemen,

Mr. W. S. Jevons, M.A. and Gold Medalist of the University of London, and at the present time College Tutor in Owens College, informs me that he is a Candidate for the vacant Professorship of Logic and Mental and Moral Philosophy in Queen's College, Liverpool. I have great pleasure in offering my testimony to the high qualifications I believe Mr. Jevons to possess for the office he seeks. The success with which he has performed his duties as Tutor in Owens College gives ample proof that he has the general qualifications of a good *teacher* – patience, conscientiousness, learning, and that firm grasp of his knowledge which alone enables a man to impart knowledge to others. Evidence to this point alone the electors will, I am sure, deem valuable. To his possession of the special qualifications for the Professorship he aspires to fill Mr. Jevons will lay

[4] J. E. Cairnes, 'Co-Operation in the Slate Quarries of North Wales', *Macmillan's Magazine*, 11 (1865) 181–90, reprinted in *Essays in Political Economy, Theoretical and Applied* (1873) pp. 166–86.
[1] This testimonial was not included in the printed set submitted by Jevons to the Council of Owens College, Manchester, and reproduced below, Letter 256, pp. 103–20.

before you higher testimony from others: but I am able to speak to this also. Mr. Jevons has conducted evening classes in Owens College in Logic and Political Economy, and during the absence for a part of last session of our Professor of Logic Mr. Jevons conducted the ordinary classes of the College in that important subject. I have had very satisfactory and convincing evidence that he fulfilled the duties which thus fell upon him with signal success; and further that as Professor *locum tenens* he soon acquired and maintained the warm esteem and regard of his pupils. In his intercourse, official and private, with me and my colleagues he has enjoyed, no less, *our* hearty esteem and regard: and I should have had less satisfaction than I now have in writing this letter did I not believe that his appointment to Queen's College would not involve the resignation of his office in Owens College.

I have the honour to be,
Gentlemen,
Your obedient Servant,
J. G. Greenwood.
Principal.

215.   E. LASPEYRES TO W. S. JEVONS

Basel, 18th March, 1865.

My Dear Sir,

I am sorry that I have not yet answered your kind letter of 24 January. I will now no longer delay.

I am as little convinced by your arguments for the geometrical mean, as you are by the arguments of mine for the arithmetical.[1] However as you say yourself, it is of no great importance.

I regret that I make you so much trouble of reading my *german* essay. It is a great advantage of the German race, that the read very easy, the french and englisch books, though the are not enabled to write even so good.

But, because you have understood my former lettres you will also understand this and other lettres from my.

You write in your last letter, that a Mister Rogers Professor at Oxford is occupied with a history of English prices some centuries ago.

---

[1] See M. G. Kendall, 'Studies in the History of Probability and Statistics, xxi. The Early History of Index Numbers', *Review of the International Statistical Institute*, 37 (1969) especially §§ 32 and 35; Irving Fisher, *The Making of Index Numbers* (Boston, 1922) *Appendix* iv, pp. 458–60. Cf. Edgeworth, 'On the Method of ascertaining a Change in the Value of Gold', *JRSS*, 46 (1883) 714–18. Edgeworth conceded that 'the geometric mean constructed by Professor Jevons has not much ground to stand upon' but pointed out that while Laspeyres (in his criticism of Jevons in the *Jahrbucher für Nationalökonomie*, iii) gave a good account of the theory of the arithmetic mean, he did not follow this in practice, since he employed an unweighted arithmetic mean.

I permit me, to lead your and Mister Roger's attention to a very fine research of Mr. Mantellier [2] in the V volume of the Memoires de la société archéologique de l'Orleanais page 103–494, [3] Orleans 1862. I have the honour to send you two exemplares of the principal results which I have extracted from the inquiries of Mister Mantellier concerning the prices or the value of silver compared with many commodities. I hope you shall lead the attention of Mister Rogers on this Inquiry not much known either in Germany either in England. May I beg you, to send him, one of the two Tables which I am about to send you?

What you do write over your researches on the exhaustion of brittish coalmines, is of the highest interest for my. I regret, that you were not yet enabled, so as you have promitted in your last letter, to send my the essay. I should have been very glad to employ the results in my lessons over the mining-production. I am very curious on that matter.

Can you write me, Dear Sir, in which review the inquiry on prices by Mr. Rogers will be published?

I am Sir your very faithfull

Dr. E. Laspeyres.

216.   J. E. THOROLD ROGERS TO W. S. JEVONS

Mar 23 [1865]
Oxford

My dear Sir,

Pray acknowledge my obligations to your correspondent for the table which he has sent me. I have to thank you for referring me to his enquiries, I shall examine what he has stated.

My advertisement refers to two volumes only from 1259–1400. The second vol consisting wholly of evidence will be of about 800 pp of (generally) 5 columns to a page. In most of the articles I have an uninterrupted and abundant mass of evidence.

I shall have you to decide what the relations of the currency were to values in the time before me at present. In general there are so many counterpoising influences affecting any estimate as to the price of money determined by goods that I feel the question to be extremely eel-like. For instance I do not quite see my inference from the facts published in the *Economist* supplement. [1] But as I hope to meet you before long (I shall be

---

[2] Philippe Mantellier (1811–84), French judge and antiquary.

[3] 'Mémoire sur la Valeur des Principales Denrées et Marchandises qui se vendaient ou se consommaient en la ville d'Orléans, au cours des xive, xve, xvie, xviie, et xviiie siécles.'

[1] *The Economist,* 23 (1865), 'Commercial History and Review of 1864', Supplement to the issue of 11 March 1865. On pp. 5 and 6 of this supplement there appeared a table comparing the wholesale prices in London of 14 commodities as at 1 January 1865, with those for 1 July 1864, 1 January 1864,

examining the Manchester Grammar School in June) I will postpone this debate. I send you a few copies of my prospectus.

Yours faithfully,

James E. Thorold Rogers.

217.   W. S. JEVONS TO HERBERT JEVONS
       [LJN, 204–5]

9 Birch Grove, Rusholme,
Manchester, 25th May 1865

. . . The *Coal Question* has been out now for a month, and notices of it are beginning to drop in, but not so quickly as one might wish. However, I will give it a year or two for its trial. The reasoning in the book is, I think, almost unanswerable, except where I have left the question open; but not one in a hundred that look into the book will read it properly; and it is irritating to find that those who notice it usually represent your statements as far as possible from the truth, and overlook all the strong points of argument. However, the subject is one that must receive attention before long.

My appointment to the professorship at Liverpool has just been announced in various papers. I shall like having such a place in the old town and the old Mechanics', and it will no doubt repay me for all the trouble one way or another, but the pay will be small indeed.[1]

It is only this afternoon virtually decided by the trustees at Owens College that I am to be lecturer in political economy next session, getting £50 and the fees. I shall hold the tutorship very much as a nominal thing next year, as it does not pay in my hands proportionately to the great amount of the work.

---

1 January 1861, 1 July 1857, and their average price in the years 1845–50. On these figures *The Economist* commented: 'We read in Col. 9 of this table, the immense fall which has taken place in prices since July, 1857 and in Col. 7 the marked fall which has taken place since 1 January 1861. We find in Col. 3 very plain traces of the depression which occurred in the six months preceeding 1 January 1865. . . . The truth is, that with the present extended and growing commerce of the world, far more mischief and inconvenience will arise from the effect of what seems to be a continuous gradual decline in the new supplies of gold than from any effects which have flowed or may flow from the Californian and Australian discoveries.'

¹ On 8 May 1865 the Committee of Queen's College, Liverpool, had resolved to recommend to the Council that Jevons be appointed to the Professorship of Political Economy as well as that of Logic, and that, as to one lecture a week, to be given in the evening, he be guaranteed a minimum payment of five shillings per lecture.' . . . Mr. Jevons to be at liberty to open a day class also, if he be desirous of doing so, but without such guarantee. The students' fees to be apportioned in both cases, four-fifths to the Professor and one-fifth to the College' (Minutes of the College Committee, Liverpool Record Office, 373/INS/1/12/2). Cf. Vol. I, p. 198.

I have recently got over a piece of work that I was anxious about, namely, reading a paper before the Statistical Society on Prices, in continuation of the pamphlet.[2] I got through it pretty well, half reading and half lecturing, and shall perhaps be able to send you a copy in a month or two.

We have now only about a week more of the working session, and my college work is light, although I have other things to do. My newest job on hand is a reasoning machine, or logical abacus, adapted to show the working of Boole's Logic in a half mechanical manner. I got a rough model to work excellently the other night, and I think I can easily get it finished during the summer. It consists merely of a number of slips of wood with sets of letters or terms upon them, with little hooks by which they can be readily classified in any order. This classification represents the processes and results of reasoning; and by its means I can argue out in a minute or two problems that would be very puzzling otherwise. . . .

218. WILLIAM JEVONS JUNIOR TO W. S. JEVONS

Scrase Bridge, nr. Lindfield
Sussex — May 26, 1865.

My dear Stanley,

I heard yesterday that you are appointed to a professorship in Queen's College Liverpool. If so, I presume the change will be both agreeable and advantageous to you, and I beg to offer you my sincere congratulations, in which your aunt and cousin join. We are now, as you will see by the date, in country lodgings. Our present situation is very near that we had this time last year, but not so elevated. Then we were almost at the top of Hayward's Heath, and had an extensive view of the surrounding country. But now we are at its lower extremity, on the high road from the station to Lindfield, and see only trees from our windows. We are within easy reach, however, of the same beautiful views which we enjoyed last year, and our lodgings, though very small, are comfortable. Just before we left Brighton, we had the pleasure of seeing there George and his wife. They came thither from Bournemouth, and stayed just a week in lodgings very near us. They have since been staying at Tunbridge Wells, and we heard a few days ago of their safe return to Claughton, Elizabeth, I am glad to say, being much better for her travels. I have often been thinking of you since we came here, and was inclined to write, though I had not much to say. But the news of your appointment has brought me to the point, and I

[2] See above, Letter 202, n. 3, p. 54.

hope to have it confirmed by your own hand, and to learn more fully what new duties will devolve upon you in consequence. I am still engaged in my Dissertations on the history of Jesus: but have been much hindered of late by illness. I brought a bad cold with me from Brighton, in hopes of getting relieved from it by the change. But instead of getting better, I became worse, and am only now beginning to recover. Your aunt also has been suffering in a similar way. But the fine weather we now have, will do us both good, I hope, and enable us in a few weeks more to return to Brighton better than we came.

We all unite in love to yourself and sister, if she is with you, and I remain, Dear Stanley,

Yours very affectionately,
W. Jevons.

219.   E. J. BROADFIELD[1] TO W. S. JEVONS

Accrington,
May, 30th, 1865.

My dear friend,

I have been much interested in Mills letter, which I return with thanks.

I enjoyed your brief visit very much, and look forward to a future one with much pleasure. I have often considered your coming to Owens a fortunate thing for me, and am glad to be able to retain as a friend one who was so kind and encouraging as a tutor.

One of your Logic pupils was here on Monday (JA. Simmonds) you appear to have smoothed the steps in his flight up to B.A. for him.

I have been almost overdone with work since Sunday morning, and have only now a few minutes for this hurried note.

Yours very truly,

E. J. Broadfield

W. S. Jevons, Esq.

Don't put 'Rev' when you write to me. I am not ordained, nor likely to be. It seems a trifling thing but I never liked the title.

---

[1] Edward John Broadfield (1831–1913), journalist, well known for his public services to education in his native Manchester. One of the earliest students of Owens College, of which he became a life governor in 1876, he took a prominent part in the foundation of the Victoria University of Manchester. For many years associated with the management of the *Manchester Examiner,* he also contributed to the *Manchester Guardian.* Intensely interested in music, he sometimes wrote as a music critic and was chairman of the Hallé Concerts Society.

220.   S. A. BEAUMONT[1] TO W. S. JEVONS

144, Piccadilly London,
July 26th. 1865.

Sir,

I hope you will excuse the liberty I take in addressing you. I am reading with great interest your book "The Coal Question" – and have heard it spoken of as the best work on this important question.

I am one of the members of an International Commission for enquiring into the commercial relations between England and Austria with a view to a Commercial Treaty. One of the most frequent reasons given why Austria cannot compete with England and other countries is her inferior fuel. This I believe is a great error. Austria has fine coal-fields in Hungary, in Styria in Bohemia – of brown coal, not of steam coal. If her resources in coal could be made better known in this country and her resources in coal compared with the resources of Germany and of France a great public service would be rendered to Austria and to the Continent. It would be an impertinence on my part to solicit or urge you in any way to undertake this enquiry, but if you should happen to be inclined to extend your enquiry I am confident every possible facility would be given in Austria and great gratitude would be expressed by the Government and industrial classes. I enclose some "Notes" just published by my friend Mr. Bell of Newcastle[2] to give you an idea of the nature of the enquiry I should be so glad to see you undertake.

I am going to return to Austria very shortly,

Yours faithfully,
Somerset Beaumont

[1] Somerset Archibald Beaumont (1836–1921), M.P. for Newcastle, 1860–5; for Wakefield, 1868–74; one of the joint founders (with Messrs Glyn & Co.) of the Anglo-Austrian Bank. The commercial treaty between Britain and Austria which he promoted, was concluded on 16 December 1865. See S. Leone Levi, *History of British Commerce,* second edition (1880) p. 423.

[2] [Sir] Isaac Lowthian Bell (1816–1904), industrialist and metallurgical chemist; author of numerous papers on the blast furnace; F.R.S. 1875; M.P. for the Hartlepools, 1875–80; created a baronet, 1885; president of a number of professional bodies connected with the iron industry, including the Iron and Steel Institute (1873–5) and the British Iron Trade Association (1886). The publication referred to was probably *The Industrial Resources of the district of . . . the Tyne, Wear and Tees* (1864), edited by Bell and Sir W. G. Armstrong.

221.   E. J. BROADFIELD TO W. S. JEVONS

Accrington House.
July 27th, 1865.

My dear friend,

I am much obliged by your thoughtful kindness in forwarding your paper.[1] I shall read it with interest. I think it a great privilege to be able to speak to men as you can on such important subjects. When I think to what advantage you are using the capital you have acquired by study and think how little I am doing with my less extensive store I feel somewhat ashamed but I think also that the excitement of a public career would not be good for me. I have need of your coolness and calmness.

It is remarkable that I should receive your paper today. I was thinking of writing to you yesterday but I fancied you were in Holland or somewhere on the continent. I thought of asking you if you were going to the meeting of the British Association. I am not quite sure *when* it is but if you decided to go I would try to go for a day or two and I think you ought to read something in the Statistical Section.

I have to go to Bath in about ten days to stay a week & then intend to visit Cornwall & Devon for the first time.

Since I saw you I have been to Derby & Nottingham also to Matlock Haddon & Chatsworth. Haddon is a glorious old place I spent a few days also at Melbourne on the borders of Leicestershire & Derbyshire. there is a fine old Norman church there – and many antiquities in the neighbourhood.

What a splendid summer we have had! our garden here is a constant delight – the flowers are not to be despised – but the fruit is even more respected.

Hoping you are well
Believe me,
Yours very truly,
    E. J. Broadfield

222.   WILLIAM JEVONS JUNIOR TO W. S. JEVONS

84 Lodge Lane, July 27 [1865].

My dear Stanley,

I have just been reading your book on the Coal Question, which I could not procure at any library in Brighton, but which I have obtained

---

[1] Presumably 'On the Variation of Prices, and the Value of the Currency since 1782', the paper which Jevons read before the London Statistical Society in May 1865. See above, Letter 209, n. 3, p. 61.

from the Liverpool Library, and I cannot deny myself the pleasure of telling you how much I admire it. The subject, as you know, is not much in my line; but I have nevertheless been much interested by the facts and arguments you bring forward. You have shown very clearly how wide a bearing the Coal question has, and how closely it is connected with all the great problems of economical and social science. Your 8th, 9th and 10th chapters, which I have read twice over, are particularly interesting and important and I cannot but admire the large amount of statistical information which they contain, and the skill with which you analyse it and present it in the right aspect to your readers. I was glad to see your notices of your father's pamphlet in p. 187,[1] and I only wish he could have lived to see how much more his son has done to enlighten the world on the philosophy of trade, and what honours he has won both as an author and a professor.

I take this opportunity of mentioning that a friend of ours in Brighton, upon whom Annie[2] called a few days ago, told her of a young Prussian gentleman of the name of Schmidt,[3] a civil engineer, now living in Manchester, who is desirous of being introduced to you. He knows you, she says, by name through Professor Greenwood and your book, and would be very glad to know you personally. Annie accordingly wrote in her mother's name a letter of introduction to you and sent it to her friend Mrs. Fisher, who will forward it, I suppose, either to you or Mr. Schmidt. Soon afterwards this gentleman called on your aunt to thank her for this kindness and I have no doubt you will see him when you return to Manchester, and I can answer for it that any friend of Mrs. Fisher's will be found worthy of your acquaintance. I hope this letter will find you at your sisters after you have enjoyed your extended tour in Scotland, and I also hope that I shall have an opportunity of seeing you before I return to Brighton. I shall stay here till Wednesday, after which I shall be for a few weeks at George's house in Queen's Road, Southport, when I shall be glad to hear from you.

My love to John and Lucy. I had the pleasure of meeting the former here last week.

Very affectionately yours,
W. Jevons.

---

[1] Jevons had drawn attention to the fact that in *The Prosperity of the Landholders not dependent on the Corn Laws* (1840) Thomas Jevons had expressed a view similar to that of T. C. Banfield, that the farmers and landlords should have favoured repeal of the Corn Laws, as bound to increase demand for all other agricultural produce.

[2] Annie Jevons (1825–1905), second daughter of William Jevons Junior. Cf. Vol. II, Letter 70, p. 176.

[3] It has not proved possible to trace any biographical information about Schmidt.

223.   HERBERT JEVONS TO W. S. JEVONS

Bank of New South Wales
Weatherstone's Agency, 15th Sept^r.

1865.

Dear Stanley,

Weatherstones is the oldest gold field in this province, it is 20 minutes walk from Gabriel's Gully, where gold was first found, and from which a large amount of gold has been taken. [1] Weatherstones having been falling away for sometime in favour of Tuapeka $1\frac{1}{2}$ miles from it, our directors have built a permanent Bank at that place & Mr. Farrer who had charge of this agency has gone to the new place, leaving me for a short time in charge here. I hope to be at my old place again in Dunedin in a few days, as I find the gold fields very dull. Nothing but nobblers billiards & the like going on. The removal has given us something to do & I have seen something of the interior of the country. The change is also pleasant. I have also picked up a little more information, and shall have a little more importance in the eyes of my fellow clerks in consequence of having this little job given me. The work of the agency consists in receiving & paying deposits, current accounts issuing drafts & buying gold. I intend in a future letter to give you some account of the country up here & the gold diggings. Unfortunately, the weather is very wet this spring time & I cannot see as much as I should like to.

I have read your book all through & was very much interested in it. It is very well written, and ought to receive the attention of the learned public, & the unlearned also, as it is written very clearly. A similar event to what you foreshadow in England is shown very clearly in these gold fields. At first everything is cheery plenty of gold is got & people live freely but soon the claims get worked out & the place gradually declines in prosperity. I am afraid these gold fields will yield but poorly in future. They are at present being deserted wholesale in consequence of the attraction to the new west coast gold fields which have turned out very rich & are attracting a large population.

This is a queer country one mass of hills mountains and gullies, the hills very steep, the roads from place to place go along the tops of the ranges very often. Some quartz reefs are being opened & two copper reefs unless these latter turn out well it will be a hard case for Otago. Still Victoria continues to give a steady yield of gold & may be after a while Otago will do the same.

Canterbury is yielding a large amount of gold now. Let me know if you

---

[1] Gabriel's Gully was named after Gabriel Read (1824–94), who first found gold there on 23 May 1861. All the places named are in the Otago area of the South Island of New Zealand.

have received my £100. from Moss Estate, or if not what sort of document is wanted to enable you to draw it.

Your affec. brother

H. Jevons.

224.   TIMOTHY JEVONS [1] TO W. S. JEVONS

St Michael's Hamlet
Sept 23 [1865]

Dear Stanley

If I am rightly informed this will find you returned home from your tour with Tom; but I have not seen him yet. I have received an invitation from the Secretary, to be present at the opening of the session at the Queen's College, to hear the introductory address by Professor Jevons, which I hope to have the pleasure of accepting. [2]

I presume you do not think of returning to Manchester after delivering the address, (if indeed you can do so at all;) and therefore I write to say that I hope you will make this house your head quarters for the night, as we have a bed at your service, & shall be glad to have you to occupy it. And not on this one occasion only, but on your subsequent weekly visits to fulfil your duty at the College. You may consider this as a permanent invitation, without being repeated; and if it is at any time inconvenient to have you, (which I do not anticipate,) I will let you know. Before this you will have heard the news of Fred's engagement. [3] Henrietta was here last evening, she is now with Henry & Susan at Lodge Lane. I hope you have enjoyed your Swiss tour; indeed it c^d not be otherwise I think, if you have had as fine weather as we have had here.

Hoping to see you on or before the 2nd Oct., I am

Yours very truly
Tim^y Jevons

225.   J. G. GREENWOOD TO W. S. JEVONS

York Terrace,
Fallowfield,
25th. Septr 1865.

My dear Mr Jevons,

You have, I believe, already heard that Mr Scott is unfortunately again unable to meet his classes. [1] In effect he asks me to obtain leave of absence

[1] See Vol. I, p. 3, and Vol. II, Letter 21, n. 2, p. 38.

[2] The address, 'On Reading and Study', which W. S. Jevons delivered at Queen's College, Liverpool, on 2 October 1865. See Vol. I, p. 198, n. 2.

[3] See Vol. II, Letter 56, n. 20, p. 132.

[1] See above, Letter 197, p. 48.

for him until Christmas. When I meet the Trustees on Thursday may I state that you will once more act as his substitute in the logic and M. & M. Philosophy classes? I know that I am asking a good deal making this request at so short notice, but I hope that you will nevertheless be able to come to the rescue. Believe that I am

Most truly yours,

J. G. Greenwood

P.S. Will you give me the pleasure of dining here on Friday the 6th October to meet Prof^r Barker?[2] Dinner at 6.30.

226. W. S. JEVONS TO HERBERT JEVONS
    [LJN, 212–13]

9 Birch Grove, Rusholme,
18th October 1865.

. . . My prospects here are somewhat improved. Mr. Scott has not been well enough to come back, and has asked for leave of absence for a year. I have consequently been appointed his substitute in logic, for which I shall receive nearly £70. I have already Christie's political economy class – about £60. My evening political economy class met for the first time last Monday and is very large, probably on account of the scholarship in political economy which is to be awarded soon. I am resigning the tutorship here, which is tiresome and pays little.

I have now been three times to the Liverpool College, but the number of students are very small, and the prospect not good. I am, however, guaranteed £1 a day, which will leave me perhaps about £30 profit above cost of railway. As Uncle Timothy has asked me to sleep at the Hamlet once a week, the journey becomes a rather agreeable 'out'.

The introductory meeting with my address [on Reading and Study] was a stupid affair. I send you a partial report. The main point is my logical machine, on which I am working now. The one adapted to lecture-room use is now almost done, and I am thinking of a more complicated one adapted to extensive problems and arguments. . . .

[2] Thomas Barker (1838–1907), who had succeeded Sandeman as Professor of Mathematics at Owens College, Manchester, from 1865 to 1885. Educated at King's College, Aberdeen, and Trinity College, Cambridge, where he became a Fellow and assistant tutor in 1862, he was a follower of Boole and De Morgan. See Vol. I, p. 42.

227. SIR JOHN F. W. HERSCHEL TO W. S. JEVONS
[LJP, 216]

Collingwood, Hawkhurst,
Kent.
Nov. 23, 1865.

Dear Sir,

Pray accept my warmest thanks for the very valuable and important book you have been so good as to send me on the Coal question. It embodies in the most clear and luminous form of expression, and supported by the most telling statistical documents a mass of considerations that as I read them seemed an echo of what I have long thought and felt about our present commercial progress and the necessary decline of our commercial and manufacturing supremacy, and the transfer of it to America. *Longe absit* – but it *must* come – and *I think you have been merciful in giving us another century to run.*

Such a work as yours has been long wanted to dissipate *completely* the delusion which so large a majority of our own countrymen labour under, of the "inexhaustibility of our mineral resources" etc. etc. and the "probability amounting to certainty" that science will ere long put us in possession of a substitute for coal. A dim perception of the truth to be sure has dawned here and there, but after this let no man plead ignorance and say "who would have thought it?" Not that I suppose we shall take warning. In such a rush there is no pulling up.

I have read every word of it (received yesterday) with the avidity with which one devours a new novel and when I laid it down I could not help inscribing on the title page as a motto

Old experience doth attain

To something like prophetic strain [1]

and (not without a most melancholy feeling) under the words *The End* on p. 349 Dido's parting words Vixi, et quam cursum dedein fortuna peregi! Et nunc magna mei sub terra, ibit imago! [2]

It used to be a favourite notion of mine that the tides might be utilized to transmit power through air tubes up the country to any extent, till I made a calculation of what would be the available power so to be gained by laying under contribution the sea to 1000 feet distance from the shore by a vast construction extending all round England from Berwick on Tweed to Solway Firth – taking it at 1570 miles of coast, and supposing

---

[1] Milton, *Il Penseroso*, lines 173–4:
       'Till old experience do attain
       To something like Prophetic strain.'

[2] Virgil, *Aeneid*, Book IV, lines 653–4:
       'vixi et quem dederat cursum fortuna, peregi;
       et nunc magna mei sub terras ibit imago.'

the mean available fluctuation at each tide 6 feet and taking a bushel of coals at 84 lbs and 80,000,000 lbs raised one foot as the work of a bushel I found that about a million tons per annum or $\frac{1}{5}$ of the consumption of London would do the work which in fact would hardly do more than keep 10 Great Easterns constantly under [full] steam! – This of course put me out of conceit with my "notion".[3]

Once more repeating my thanks I beg to remain, Dear Sir,
Yours very truly,
J. F. W. Herschel

P.S.   May I venture on a request
There is no indication on the volume that I owe it to your kindness – would you favour me with a small slip of paper to that effect that I might paste into the first leaf.
I am sorry to see you attribute such weight to Liebig's criticisms on Bacon. We owe much to Bacon and it always grieves me to see him under rated (?)[4]

228.   T. E. JEVONS TO W. S. JEVONS

Brevoort House Hotel
28 November 1865.

Dear Stanley,
I daresay you will like to hear a little about my business position here which would not be quite so interesting to Lucy & Henny.
The agency business at present is on a very small scale, but it is now about to be enlarged & Busk[1] is going to do a general & commission merchants business here though entirely under the thumb of the Rathbones.[2] I take a position next to Busk & over the clerk who has been in the office for several years & who in Busks absence all this summer was all in himself. He is very pleasant & does not seem to mind being

---

[3] Herschel seems here to envisage some form of pneumatic transmission of power, rather than simple tidal mills, which had been known from as early as the twelfth century. But on this see his letter to Jevons of 30 June 1866 and notes thereto: below, Letter 261, p. 123.

[4] 'Great as was Bacon in many ways, we cannot regard him as more than an expounder of the scientific tendency of his age. And after the severe, and for the most part, the true exposure of his claims by Baron Liebig, it is to be hoped that we shall give up some of our absurd national fallacies concerning him' – Jevons, *The Coal Question*, first edition (1865) p. 70. See Justus von Liebig, 'Lord Bacon as natural philosopher', *Macmillan's Magazine*, 8 (1863) 237–49, 257–67.

In later years Karl Pearson also described Jevons as 'unreasonably contemptuous' of Bacon – *The Grammar of Science* (1892) p. 34.

[1] J. R. Busk, one of the New York agents of Rathbone Brothers and Co., with whom T. E. Jevons later went into partnership. See Vol. I, p. 10.

[2] See Vol. II, Letter 139, n. 17, p. 391. Rathbones' American trade was severely restricted during the Civil War owing to the instability of the currency and fluctuating exchange rates.

superseded at all. – Another young clerk completes our staff.—Until we actually receive some tea here which will not be for some months my peculiar province will not be opened to me, but I am gaining some insight into all the branches little by little.—My great difficulty is a shyness in meeting men which I do not think will ever quite wear off.—

The currency question is of course the great one at present. People are very nervous lest Government should set to work to fund the currency which they see plainly enough would nip all their fancied prosperity in the bud. Some 50,000,000 have already been converted into 5 – 20 bonds [3] but this 50,000,000 consisted principally of a particular kind of currency which bore compound interest up to a certain date & consequently was not much circulated but held as an investment. [4] Consequently no real contraction has yet taken place while the National Bks are pouring out some $3,000,000 weekly of fresh currency. A national bank is a splendid contrivance. A capital is subscribed with which government 6 p cent bonds are bought & then 90% of their value they may at once issue in their own notes redeemable on demand in government paper notes, a capital plan for floating government bonds isn't it,—

Nothing but funding some 200,000,000 can restore things to a proper basis. The paper dollar is not only depreciated because the prospect of it's being redeemed in gold is not an early one, but it is further depreciated because too many are issued. If they were all turned into gold tomorrow they would not keep their value at par unless a large portion was exported or melted down. Now as more paper money is issued the total amount becomes more excessive & prices of all articles creep up; but the premium on gold (which simply expresses the estimate of the probability of the redemption of the paper dollar) does not advance in equal ratio; consequently America is the dearest market to buy in & the best to sell in.

To bring prices to their proper ratio to gold the amount of currency must be reduced. This process will first appear as reducing the amount of floating capital. Rates of interest will go up, Govt. bonds will go down, the national Bank securities will no longer secure their issues, & the Bks must suspend payments even in paper.—

If there is the slightest hint at funding in the forthcoming report of the Secretary of the Treasury, money will tighten & there will be something like a panic I expect. [5]

[3] These were tax-exempt securities bearing 6% interest in gold, redeemable in not less than five nor more than twenty years.

[4] The Secretary of the U.S. Treasury, Hugh McCulloch (see Vol. IV, Letter 431, n. 6), whose policy was to retire the government legal-tender issues as soon as possible, had commenced by funding these interest-bearing notes soon after taking office in March 1865. See Patterson, *Federal Debt-Management Policies 1865–1879* (Durham, North Carolina, 1954) p. 62.

[5] In the report, issued on 4 December 1865, Secretary McCulloch sought the authority of Congress to retire the 'greenbacks' as a first step towards resumption of specie payments. Congress

I send you two specimens for your collection of paper currency; if you do not want them send them back if you want more I send them.

I want to hear about the logical machine.

Please forward the enclosed to Lucy.

Best love to Henny,

Ever your affect. brother
Thos E Jevons

I expect to get boarded including dinner comfortably at $15 p week equal £2.5.0 which is better than I expected at one time.

229.   W. S. JEVONS TO SIR JOHN F. W. HERSCHEL
[HLRS 322]

Owens College,
Manchester,
14 Dec 1865.

Dear Sir,

I much regret that I have not been able sooner to answer your kind letter of 23rd ult. It seems to have been detained some weeks at University College, London, and only reached me yesterday.

All the laborious thought & work, and some disappointment connected with my Coal Qu. are more than repaid when I find the result so highly approved. The subject when I had once got into it – strongly excited my interest and even my feelings, and lead me to spend great exertions upon making the argument as clear and conclusive as possible.

Your kindly expressed opinion is sufficient to convince me that I have not been mistaken in any important point. If as seems not unlikely at present, the work has no commercial success, I shall have no cause to regret my undertaking it.

I have studied almost all your works for many years back, as examples of the clearest exposition and most perfect reasoning, and when you so fully endorse one of my first works it will give me renewed confidence in future attempts. At the age of 30 I presume I may regard myself as quite a youth in Science.

You mention Liebig's criticisms on Bacon – the character of Bacon has often perplexed me. Though I cannot but regard many parts of his writings as almost perfect, his physical researches seemed to me (both

---

supported him initially and passed a Contraction Act in April 1866; however, public support for a vigorous contraction policy quickly evaporated. See Unger, *The Greenback Era* (Princeton, 1964) chapter II; Barrett, *The Greenbacks and Resumption of Specie Payments 1862–1879* (Cambridge, Mass., 1931) chapters V and VII.

before and after reading Liebig's remarks) as anything but, corresponding to the excellence, and promise, of the Organum. His reputation has
been and always will be so great, that we seem in danger of exaggeration
rather than detraction. From time to time however I hope to have
opportunity of reconsidering any opinion I may have about him.

I enclose the slip of paper you desired – and beg to remain, Dear Sir,

Yours very faithfully,

W. S. Jevons.

230.   E. LASPEYRES TO W. S. JEVONS

Basel, 22/12 1865.

Dear Sir,

I regret from all my heart that I have not yet had occasion since your
friendly visit at Basel,[1] to write you. Now the ending year drives me to
thank you for your kind visit. Your visit was very agreable to me, and
would have been [of] still greater use for me, if the difficulty of speaking
your language had not impeded my, to ask still very much more than I
did.

I begin my lettre with asking, wheater you have had occasion to
publisch the *very* prices from which you have abstracted your ratios of the
comodities since 1782 in the Journal of Statistical Society.[2] For my
purpose the very valuable but too short inquiry into the prices of the 12
groups of comodities do not suffice. I must be in possession of the ratios for
each comodity separately, and if it is possible of the very prices.

I know that you have taken the most prices from the history of prices of
Tooke and Newmarch, but there are also something what you did not
allways take from this book but which are found in the McCullochs
Dictionary the Journal of the Statistical Society, the London Gazette etc.,
which are not under my eyes.

If you have not yet published the very prices and if you are not yet
about publishing them, or if you do not intend at all to publish them, you
would very much oblige me, if you could get me in possession of the
prices. I am not quite shure wheater you understand, what I beg, because
I cannot express me very well what it is because I mean it better, to make
the comparison of raising and falling prices not only for groups of
commodities but for each commodity separately, and not only to make
the comparison the prices of 1782 taken as 100, but also the nine years
1782 taken as 100.

---

[1] Accompanied by his brother Thomas, Jevons spent a month in Switzerland in August and
September 1865; he arrived in Basel on 29 August 1865. See LJ, pp. 207–8.

[2] See above, Letter 209, n. 3, p. 61.

Mr. Soetbeer[3] at Hamburgh also has been so kind, to send me the prices of the 48 commodities treated in my essay on prices, for the years 1820–1850 each year separately. I am about publishing them and should be very glad to have the same prices of London.

The second question is, wheather you have continued to excerpt from the price current of the Economist the prices of your 118 commodities treated in your "Serious Fall" later to 1863.[4] If you have not done so I will do it, because the most necessary matter in our inquiries is the comparison of prices in various places. I ask you wheather you are about publishing the prices if you have continued to collect them. I for my person have collected my Hamburgh prices to the January 1866, and will continue to collect them the following years. I beg you to send me every thing you write on this highly interesting matter, and I promise you to send you every thing, what I do publish on the matter of prices.

Thirdly, you said me this summer that Mr. Rogers would send me his history of prices since 1259. I have not yet received any thing, and would be very glad, if I could make the Germans acquainted whith his probably *very* valuable researches, but I am not in the condition to buy this very dear book, which does not have the same interest for us, as for English people.

If you can help me, to come in the possession of this "History" I should do my best to lead the attention of German Economists on this matter by writing something on this book.

You see Dear Sir, my lettre is full of asking and begging but I did not hesitate to ask and to beg, because it is not in my interest but in the interest of Science. In the hope, I shall soon receive answer,

I am Sir Your bad writing but faithful
Dr. E. Laspeyres

---

[3] Adolf Georg Soetbeer (1814–92), an exponent and advocate of the gold standard who became concerned in statistical studies of the production of precious metals and related price movements. His best-known work was *Edelmetall-Produktion und Werthverhaltnis zwischen Gold und Silber seit der Entdeckung Amerikas* (Gotha, 1879). A native of Hamburg, Soetbeer was secretary of the Hamburg Kommerzdeputation and was elected an honorary professor of the University of Göttingen in 1872.

[4] There is no direct evidence as to whether Jevons in fact did this. In a further paper on 'The Depreciation of Gold' (originally contributed to the *Economist*, 8 May 1869, pp. 530–2, reprinted in *Investigations*, pp. 151–9) he presented an index number based on the prices of fifty commodities quoted in *The Economist* for the years 1847 to 1869. From Laspeyres's letter to Jevons of 7 July 1866 (see below, Letter 263, p. 125) it would appear that Jevons did supply some price quotations in answer to this request.

231.   W. S. JEVONS TO SIR JOHN F. W. HERSCHEL
      [HLRS 323]

Plas Eife,
Clynnog,
Carnarvon.
29 Dec 65.

Dear Sir,

I take the liberty of enclosing you a note I have received from MacMillan.[1] I cannot take upon myself to ask you to incur so much trouble – but if you should already have any inclination together with the time to write some sort of notice of the work, it would be of the utmost advantage to the work, and probably quite alter its chances of success.

I may add that I feel under some degree of obligation to Mr. MacMillan, who kindly and liberally undertook the publishing of the work at his own risk, without, I should suppose, hopes of any profit worth considering. Without his aid my labour must probably have been thrown away.

Believe me to remain Dear Sir,
            Yours very faithfully,
            W. S. Jevons.

Sir John Herschel
   &c &c

232.   SIR JOHN F. W. HERSCHEL TO W. S. JEVONS

Collingwood,
Jan 8/'66.

Dear Sir,

I reinclose Mr. MacMillan's letter about an article on "Burnt Out" in his Journal.[1] I have not in me the necessary conversance with the great subjects of statistics & manufacturing, Social Economy and general politics to put myself forward – but there are abler than I who I have no doubt will do so. The matter must be fully and fairly put before the world in all its bearings – & more than that – the enormous & outrageously wasteful consumption of every other article that the Earth produces which in 2 centuries if it go on in the present increasing ratio & populations calling themselves civilised – but in reality luxurious and selfish – spread themselves over the now sparingly inhabited continental tracts and even make the Earth a desert or at least reduce it to the state in

---

[1] Returned by Herschel to Jevons: see below, Letter 232.
[1] The letter from Macmillan is not now in the Jevons Papers.

which it was in the early periods when the vegetable products at least
(– for of the mineral there will then be no question?) sufficed for its
population, & when population itself shall be forced to shrink back to a
limit so bounded.

I remain,

Yours truly,

J. F. W. Herschel.

233.   A. MACMILLAN [1] TO W. S. JEVONS

Macmillan and Co.
Publishers to the University
of Oxford,
16, Bedford Street, Covent Garden, W.C.
London,   Mch. 3 1866. [2]

Dear Mr Jevons,

I enclose a letter from the Chancellor of the Exchequer,[3] which you
will like to see. May I ask you to return it to me. I dont know whether you
will think it well to communicate with him. I think I would in your
place.[4] I have written to say that I had sent you this note. I think the book
must attract more notice by and by.

Yours very truly

A Macmillan.

---

[1] Alexander Macmillan (1818–96), founder, with his elder brother Daniel, of the publishing
house, in Cambridge in 1843; the head office was moved to Bedford Street in 1863; publisher to
Cambridge University, 1860–80; to Oxford University, 1863–80; published *Macmillan's Magazine*
from 1859 (to 1907) and *Nature* from 1869. See C. L. Morgan, *The House of Macmillan, 1843–1943*
(1943). In 1851 Macmillan married as his first wife Caroline Brinley, by whom he had three sons and
two daughters, the elder of whom assisted Jevons with the preparation of the English version
of Cossa's *Guide to the Study of Political Economy*. See Vol. V, Letter 603.

[2] The original manuscript of this letter was pasted into the Journal by Jevons. See Vol. I, p. 202,
n. 3.

[3] Jevons made a copy of this letter in the Journal. See Vol. I, p. 203.

[4] See below, letter 238, n. 2, p. 87.

234. W. S. JEVONS TO SIR JOHN F. W. HERSCHEL
[HLRS 324]

9 Birch Grove,
Rusholme,
Manchester,
7 Mar   66.

Sir J. Herschel
&c &c

My dear Sir,
I beg your permission to use the letter you recently favoured me with concerning my 'Coal Question' as a testimonial in an application I shall shortly have to make to the Trustees of Owens College, for the prof$^{\underline{p}}$ of Logic and Political Economy.

I could not desire testimony of a more gratifying kind, as it certainly could not be more weighty.

I also desire to send a copy of your letter to the Chancellor of the Exchequer who seems to have been struck with my chapters, and has expressed a strong desire for some authoritative scientific opinion upon the work.[1]

I have the honour to remain,

my dear Sir
Yours very faithfully,
W. S. Jevons.

235. SIR JOHN F. W. HERSCHEL TO W. S. JEVONS

Collingwood,
March 8/66.

Dear Sir,
You are perfectly welcome to use my letter as a testimonial in the way you propose if you think it is likely to be of any use to you – as to sending it to the Chancellor of the Exchequer[1] as a *scientific* opinion – I do not claim this rank for it. I am hardly geologist and statistician enough to claim any attention to my opinion other than as a common sense view of a very plain case – viz: that we are using up our resources and expending our national

---

[1] Written across top of front leaf by Herschel –
'Ansd.]
Yes, only don't profess it to be a scientific opinion but a mere common sense view.'
[1] See below, Letter 238, p. 87.

life at an enormous and increasing rate and thus a very ugly day of reckoning is impending sooner or later.

> I remain
> Dear Sir
> Yours very truly
> J. F. W. Herschel

236.   WALTER BAGEHOT TO W. S. JEVONS

> 12 Upper Belgrave St.
> 10 March 1866.

My dear Sir,

I send you a public note on the Cobden Professorship, [1] which I hope is what you would like.

It is very odd but I was thinking before I received your note of asking you if you could and would sometimes wrote* for the Economist. Would it be possible for you to do so?

> I am,
> Yours very truly,
> Walter Bagehot

237.   J. T. DANSON[1] TO W. S. JEVONS

> Bellefield House
> West Derby Road
> Liverpool

W. S. Jevons Esq.   11. 3. 66.

My dear Sir,

Your published works afford to those who have read them with the care they deserve far better evidence of your fitness for the Professorship of Logic Mental and Moral Philosophy and Political Economy at Owens

---

[1] See below, Letter 256 (10), p. 114.

In 1865 the Cobden Memorial Committee gave £400 for the endowment of prizes in political economy. On 22 March 1866 the committee passed the following resolution, viz. 'That the scheme of the executive committee for the appropriation of the balance of the fund be approved, and that they may be empowered to arrange with the trustees of Owens College for the preparation of a deed embodying the spirit of the resolution now adopted.' The proposals were: 'That a sum of not less than £1,250 (it reached £1,500) be devoted to the endowment of the chair of political economy in Owens College, on condition that the professor deliver each session a course of weekly evening lectures, to which any of the public primary school teachers or pupil teachers engaged within the boroughs of Manchester or Salford should have free admission.' See Thompson, *The Owens College: Foundation and Growth*, p. 288.

[1] John Towne Danson (1817–98), lawyer, journalist, underwriter and economist. At this time Danson was Secretary of the Thames and Mersey Marine Insurance Co., and was serving as President of the Board of Directors of the Liverpool Institute Schools and Chairman of the Council of

College, than anything I could say. I have not, to my regret, and I don't doubt to my loss, been able, since you took the Professorship at Queen's College, to attend your lectures as I desired; but I may say that when, as Chairman of the Council, it became my duty to enquire somewhat closely as to your fitness for that post I was well convinced that we were fortunate in meeting with you, and finding you willing to join us. I have only to regret, for your sake, that the post is not more remunerative in every sense.

> I am Dear Sir
> Very Faithfully Yours,
> J. T. Danson.

238.   W. E. GLADSTONE[1] TO W. S. JEVONS

> 11 Carlton H. Terrace
> March 16. 66.

Dear Sir,

I return the very interesting letters from Sir J. Herschel.[2]

If in such a matter *he* disclaims scientific authority, it is scarcely needful for me to say that the impressions which were formed or strengthened in my mind by the perusal of your volume were not supposed by me to be of any weight or consequence for others.

Nor is it an absolute exhaustion of coal which appears to me near, but it is such a shifting in the conditions of supply as under economical laws will formidably change our commercial position in relation to other countries.

What perhaps most struck me in your book was that, travelling by the path you had marked out, you arrived at a practical conclusion which every year of public & financial experience serves to stamp more & more deeply on my mind. I think with you that we must accept the laws of our condition, that we should economise the use of our coal but not with the idea that we shall thereby postpone the day of difficulty – that to

---

Queen's College, Liverpool. Subsequently, in 1875, when the college had difficulty in finding a professor of political economy, Danson took over the teaching of the subject himself, his course being published as *Short Lectures on the Political Economy of Daily Life* (1876).

   [1] William Ewart Gladstone (1809–98) was at this time Chancellor of the Exchequer in the Whig-Liberal Ministry of Lord Russell. The original manuscript (BM Add. MS 44409, f. 255) is headed in another hand 'The Coal Question'. Jevons reproduced part of the letter among the testimonials in support of his application for the Chair at Owens College.

   [2] Presumably Herschel's letters to Jevons of 23 November 1865 and 8 March 1866, reproduced above (Letters 227 and 235, pp. 77 and 85). It may be inferred that Jevons had sent these to Gladstone as enclosures with a letter written in response to the prompting of Alexander Macmillan (cf. above, Letter 233, p. 84) but the manuscript of this has not survived. For a fuller account of the background to this correspondence, see Vol. I, pp. 44 and 202–5.

constrain the consumption by law would be sheer folly, and that the measure which wisdom really recommends, in view of the actual & probable state of things, is to lighten by more strenuous efforts than we have yet made the burden of that mortgage, which, under the name of the Nat. Debt, we have laid upon the property & industry of the nation.

Until the great work of the liberation of industry was in the main effected, it wd. have been premature or even wrong to give too much prominence to this view of the subject. Nor do I regard that liberation as yet having reached the point at which we might say we will now cease to make remission of taxes a principal element & aim in finance. But we are in my judgment near it. And I am most anxious that the public should begin to take a closer & more practical view of the topics which you have done so much to bring into prominence. Nothing would give me greater satisfaction than that your work was attracting as it deserves attention in a rapidly widening sphere. And I hope that the aim you are prosecuting at Manchester may have this with other good effects.

There is nothing private in my letters & you are welcome to use them as you propose. Allow me before concluding to suggest that it is most desirable to bring the attention of the followers of physical science to bear on the early portion of your work where you argue the question of substitutes in the negative. This is a very important part of the volume: it is one on which I dare not form even the shadow of an opinion.

I have the honour &c.
W. E. Gladstone.

239.   W. S. JEVONS TO HERBERT JEVONS
[LJP, 220]

9 Birch Grove
Rusholme Man^r.
24 Mar. 1866.

My dear Herbert

I am very sorry that I have been able to write so little of late –
This term however is always a heavy one and I have had and have causes of great anxiety which take up my thoughts . . .

I am myself in great uncertainty. If I can get this professorship which is now just declared vacant I shall be all right. The salary is £250 and the fees, & my private money would raise my income over £400 so that I could for some years save a good deal & have it at hand, and my prospects generally would be of a satisfactory character. Of course I have a great many things in my favour, as I am doing the full work of the Prof^{sh} & am exactly suited for it by my degree reading &c. But the Trustees will probably carry out their rule of making it an open election and we cannot be sure how that will go. And there are many things such as want of sociability which will tell much against me. Probably I exaggerate the chance against me at present.

One of the best things that has happened of late is the letter from the Chancellor of the Exchequer expressing great approval of the Coal Question & allowing that it has strengthened his desire to reduce the National Debt.

It may be a couple of months yet before the professorship is decided & until then I cannot have much peace of mind. Before I can have an answer it will have been decided for better or for worse so there is no need to say more at present . . .

Last Monday I gave an account of my *logical abacus* at the Lpool Lit & Phil Soc. for about an hour & a quarter, & those present seemed pleased & interested. Mr Higginson your old doctor first gave an account on a natural history subject.[1] He was pleased to hear of you especially that your health is better – for from the absence of any statement to the contrary I have assumed that you are quite well. I should like to know how it is.

I saw Roscoe not very long ago and will see him again in a week or two. We now have a special attendant always with him, though the man has to be changed every few months as one man cannot stand it. His condition is rather more sad even than it used to be but Henry & I cannot see that anything more can be done for him. He is quite recovered from the illness he had but is more restless, & has to be watched lest he should swallow things . . .

Thanks for papers. Hoping to hear frequently & favourably
Yours affect[ny]
W. S. Jevons

240.   J. G. GREENWOOD TO W. S. JEVONS

Chorlton View,
Fallowfield,
30th March, 1866.

My dear Jevons,

Accept my best thanks for your book.[1] It reached just in time to accompany me on a short holiday.

Can you let me have a sight of any additional testimonials that you have obtained[2] (I mean other than those I have already seen), which

[1] Alfred Higginson, M.R.C.S., 'Observed Facts in the Natural History of the Chironomus Plumosus', *Proceedings of the Literary and Philosophical Society of Liverpool*, 20 (1865–6) 173–9. The paper was presented on 19 March 1866. See Vol. I, p. 60, n. 3.

[1] Presumably *The Coal Question*.

[2] See copies of testimonials submitted by Jevons, below, Letter 256, pp. 103–20.

bear on the Mental and Moral Philosophy branch? I shall be at home again on Thursday next at the latest, and I should very much like to inspect any documents that you may have on that day – or in the evening of that day.

My address for the next few days will be

E. A. Leatham Esq.[3]
Whitley Hall,
Huddersfield.

The papers, however, – if you will kindly put them in my hands – may be forwarded to me *here* by Thursday. They will be merely for my own inspection.

Yours most truly,
J. G. Greenwood.

In replying to Gladstone's letter of 16 March 1866 (above, Letter 238, p. 87) Jevons prepared three slightly differing drafts, which follow here. It is not clear which, if any, formed the final letter sent to Gladstone, since no letter from Jevons of this date is now in the Gladstone Papers.

241.   W. S. JEVONS TO W. E. GLADSTONE

9 Birch Grove,
Manchester
April 1866.

Dear Sir,

The letter with which you honoured me concerning my book on Coal has remained unanswered solely because I had no desire to trespass needlessly on your attention.

You suggest however that the question of *substitutes for Coal* is of great importance. I would remark that this is one of the points admitting of least doubt. Not only do many men of science including Sir J. Herschel look upon a substitute as chimerical at present but the last Quarterly Review adopts this opinion.[1]

The strong point of my argument is that Coal has been a *growing* power for two centuries or more, and is now growing faster than ever, assisted by

---

[3] Edward Aldam Leatham (1828–1900), youngest son of William Leatham (d. 1842), Quaker banker at Wakefield, Pontefract and Doncaster; educated at University College London, graduating M.A. in 1851; Fellow, 1861; entered the family banking business, 1851; M.P. for Huddersfield, 1859–65 and 1868–86.

[1] 'Coal and Smoke', *Quarterly Review,* 119 (1866) 394–435.

the improvement of the engine and of furnaces which render it a more and more economical agent.

Coal is thus more and more beating all other powers, and is altogether in the ascendant.

It is quite possible that this state of things may be reversed in the course of ages by some wholly unlooked for discovery. Yet for the next century such a reversal is in the highest degree unlikely and should not be taken into account.

It is quite probable indeed that Coal is naturally the best source of power, just as iron and gold and water and air are substances of natural preeminence for certain purposes. Besides this it is in the highest degree unlikely that if such new source of power were any day found, it would be available to us in the same peculiar abundance as our coal.

The returns lately obtained concerning coal by Earl Russell[2] show our complete preeminence in the use of coal, to which we undoubtedly owe our material wealth in a main degree, and it is obvious that we cannot long maintain such entire preeminence.

I have the honour
to be Dear Sir,
Yours very obediently,
W. S. Jevons.

The R. H. W. E. Gladstone.

242. W. S. JEVONS TO W. E. GLADSTONE
[Redraft of latter part of 241]

naturally preeminent for their respective uses.

But even if some mode of turning the solar heat into power, now unthought of, were in some future age to be discovered we have no reason to suppose that this island would be endowed as happily with the conditions of this new force as with coal.

This new discovery would be in all probability a new cause tending to *undermine the peculiar material basis* of our manufacturing supremacy.

You will acquit me of confusing the *material* with the mental and moral powers of this kingdom. However we may value the latter we should not undervalue the former as that which gives efficiency to our other qualities. I should especially dislike being supposed to ignore other

---

[2] *Parl. Papers* 1866 [3580] LXXI, 427. Reports received from Her Majesty's secretaries of embassy and legation respecting coal.

On 3 May 1865 Russell had despatched a circular to British embassies and legations in various countries requesting particulars of the quantity of coal imported and exported from each country.

powers when I try to show the vast material advantage which is working on our side hitherto.

The returns lately obtained concerning coal by Earl Russell sufficiently show our present complete pre-eminence in the use of Coal.[1]

You will doubtless observe that I have entirely dismissed the notion of any interference with the coal trade and have pointed out as clearly as I could the highly obnoxious character even of an export duty on coal.

Hoping that this question may now receive the notice of men able to give weighty opinions upon subjects which I could not venture just to set forth in connection with each other. I have the honour to remain, Dear Sir,

Yours very obediently,
W. S. Jevons.

The R. H. W. E. Gladstone, M.P.

243.   W. S. JEVONS TO W. E. GLADSTONE
    [Another draft]

9 Birch Grove
Rusholme
Manchester.
April, 1866.

Dear Sir,

The letter with which you honoured me on the subject of my work of 'Coal' has remained unanswered because I had no desire to trespass on your attention needlessly.

You suggest however that the question of substitutes for Coal is of great importance. I would point out that this is one of the points admitting of least doubt. Not only do many men of science including Sir J. Herschel look upon a substitute as chimerical at present but the last Quarterly Review adopts this view.[1]

The strong point of my argument is this that Coal has been a growing power for two centuries or more and is growing now faster than ever, because the improvement of the engine and of furnaces renders it a more and more economical agent. Coal in short is more and more beating all other sources of power. All the triumphs both of Science and Art thus point to Coal as the predominating power, and though it is quite possible that this state of things may be reversed in the course of ages by some wholly unlooked-for discovery, yet for the next century such a reversal is in the highest degree unlikely, and should not be taken into account.

---

[1] See above, Letter 241, n. 2, p. 91.
[1] See above, Letter 241, n. 1, p. 90.

Besides this it is in the highest degree unlikely that if such new source of power were any day found, it would be available to us in the same peculiar abundance as our coal. Why should not Russia or Africa or Australia happen to be endowed with the peculiar conditions of this new force just as this island is endowed with coal.

The late returns concerning Coal obtained by Earl Russell[2] show our complete preeminence in the use of coal at present; to this we undoubtedly owe our *Material* wealth in a main degree, and it is obvious that we cannot long maintain such eminence. I have the honour to remain Dear Sir

Yours very obediently,
W. S. Jevons

244. E. J. BROADFIELD TO W. S. JEVONS

Accrington House.
April 20th, 1866.

My Dear Friend,

That looks a formal beginning. I think I shall plunge into 'my dear Jevons' next time although it is somewhat awful to attempt it to one who has been a lecturer and tutor to me – I hope you will excuse my delay in acknowledging and thanking you for the report of your paper and I am glad it has given me opportunity of expressing the great pleasure I have felt in reading the handsome testimony of the member for Westminster to your book and your arguments.[1] It was pleasing to read Mill on Jevons after having so often heard Jevons on Mill – and I am sure you will believe that very few would feel such personal interest in the fact that your labours and arguments were meeting with such well deserved appreciation: I suppose your name will be in leading articles in almost every newspaper in the Kingdom. I have just read an article in the 'Telegraph'[2] reminding its readers that its columns recorded the importance of the work months ago – Well I am like the 'Telegraph' I did not wait for the trumpet on the hill to convince me of the national importance of the work. Won't Macmillans be glad if Mill's advice is taken? What a noble thought that was of J.S.M's about our obligation to posterity: I told you in a brief note a week ago that I thought you had been in an amiable humour when you wrote your Logic questions. I have

---

² See above, Letter 241, n. 2, p. 91.
¹ See below, Letter 245, n. 1, p. 94.
² *Daily Telegraph*, 20 April 1866: 'More than three months since, we sounded the first note of alarm as to the startling revelations about the probable, and not remote, exhaustion of the coal measures of England, to which, in a remarkable work, Mr. Stanley Jevons has invited attention.'

since seen your 'Moral Phil' paper. I have no hesitation in calling it the *best* examination paper I ever saw in the subject. I can understand from it what must have been your plan in the lectures, but how you have managed to get through all the subjects you must have introduced in so short a time I can't even guess.

I have been continuing to act as substitute for Mr. Gaskell[3] since I saw you. The book 'Hermes'[4] the subject of the lectures in the Language class interests me much and amuses at the same time – it is an attempt to lay down principles of Universal Grammar – with metaphysics as a basis: we have just arrived at the discussion of 'tense' and next time I shall have to simplify the authors idea – that there is no such thing as present time. I heard of you being in London – but I fear you would have no time for music.

But my time is exhausted, there is indeed no such thing as present time it never ceases to be transient.

Believe me,
Yours very truly,
E. J. Broadfield.

W. S. Jevons, Esq.

245.   W. S. JEVONS TO J. S. MILL

9 Birch Grove,
Rusholme,
Manchester.
20 April, 1866.

Dear Sir,

It would be altogether out of place, if I were to thank you for your mention of my work on Tuesday night[1] as if it were a personal matter.

---

[3] William Gaskell (1805–84), Minister of Cross Street (Unitarian) Chapel, Manchester; Professor of English History and Literature at Manchester New College, 1846–53, and from 1861 lecturer in English Literature to evening classes at Owens College. He married Elizabeth Cleghorn Stevenson, who became famous as the author of *Cranford* and other novels.

[4] James Harris, *Hermes: or, a Philosophical Inquiry concerning Language and Universal Grammar* (1751), Book I, chap. VII: Concerning Time, and Tenses, pp. 100–39. The passage referred to by Broadfield occurs on page 105 . . . '*there cannot* (strictly speaking) *be any such thing as Time present*. For if all time be *transient* as well as *continuous*, it cannot like a life be present all together, but part will necessarily be gone, and part be coming. If, therefore, any portion of its *Continuity* were to be present *at once*, it would so far quit its transient nature, and be *Time* no longer. But if no Portion of its Continuity can thus be present, how can *Time* possibly be present, to which such Continuity is essential?' (italic in original).

[1] On Tuesday 17 April 1866 J. S. Mill, speaking in the House of Commons in support of an amendment favouring the reduction of the National Debt before changes in taxation, had said: 'I hope there are many Hon Members in this House who are acquainted with a small volume written by Mr. Stanley Jevons, entitled *The Coal Question*. It appears to me, so far as one not practically

Being a matter of purely public concern I have only to express my profound feeling of gratification when I can persuade myself to believe that any labour of mine can have led in any degree to a speech such as yours. I could not but feel when engaged upon the work that nearly all parts at least are impregnably strong in argument. Yet I feel that I cannot appreciate at first all that is contained in the fact that my work should so soon have received the complete approval of authorities such as yourself the Chancellor of the Exchequer, and Sir John Herschel.

Hoping that you will excuse my saying more at present.
Believe me,
Yours very faithfully,
W. S. Jevons.

J. S. Mill, Esq., M.P.

246. WILLIAM JEVONS JUNIOR TO W. S. JEVONS

21 Cannon Place, Brighton
April 23. 1866

My dear Stanley,

I have just received your kind letter, and I hasten to assure you how much I am gratified by your approbation of my article in the Theological Review.[1] I am equally gratified by the high testimony which has been borne to the merits of your book on the coal question. I read with great pleasure Mr. J. S. Mills speech, in which he recommends your book to the notice of members of parliament and takes occasion from it to inculcate upon them a very important lesson; and my pleasure was much increased when I heard from your uncle Timothy that you have received a long complimentary letter about your book from the Chancellor of the Exchequer. Your uncle justly says "we may well be proud of having so talented a nephew" and I only wish your lamented father had lived to share the pleasure which this occasion affords to us and all your relatives – Your publisher, I see, has taken advantage of Mr. Mills speech

---

conversant with the subject can presume to judge, that Mr. Jevons's treatment of the subject is almost exhaustive. He seems to have anticipated everything which can possibly be said against the conclusion at which he has arrived, and to have answered it; . . . I have myself read various attempts to answer Mr. Jevons, but I must say that every one of them, admitting the truth of everything said, has only made out that our supplies will continue a few years longer than the time which Mr. Jevons has assigned.' – *Hansard's Parliamentary Debates,* third series, Vol. 182, 1525. Cf. below, Letter 256 (21), p. 119.

[1] William Jevons, 'The Expulsion of the Traffickers from the Temple', *Theological Review,* 3 (1866) 211–27. The first page of the volume contains the statement 'the Projectors of the Theological Review . . . hold a Unitarian theology'.

to advertise your book with an appropriate extract from the speech, and if that advertisement serve, as I think it is likely to do, to promote the sale of the work, I hope that you will benefit thereby not less than *your publishers*. I am very glad to hear that you are applying for a professorship in your college. You do not say in what department; but as you call it *the* professorship, I presume it is the Headship of the college. I do not find in your letter the copy, which you intended to send, of your application. I do hope you will succeed in obtaining what you wish.

. . . We all unite in love to yourself and sister.

Yours very affectionately

W. Jevons

247.   TIMOTHY JEVONS TO W. S. JEVONS

Bridgewater, April 24. [1866]

Dear Stanley

I cannot resist the desire I feel to write to you, to congratulate you on the very gratifying notice that has been taken of your book on the Coal question by such distinguished men as Stewart Mill, as well as by the Chancellor of the Exchequer. The opinion of such men is invaluable, & will have great influence with all the most eminent literary & scientific men of the day; and in fact is as good as a fortune to you. I dare say you will have read the articles in the Pall Mall Gazette[1] which are also very important, & very gratifying. I heard from your Uncle William yesterday, expressing himself much gratified by Mr. Mill's notice of your book in his speech in the House of Commons. Mary & I intend leaving here for London on *Friday* next, & shall join Arthur & his wife[2] in lodgings at 44 Hans' Place Sloane St, S.W., where I hope we shall see you when you are in London. I dare say we can find you a bed, either in the same house, or in the neighbourhood; & you can have your *meals* with us at all

---

[1] The *Pall Mall Gazette* had originally noticed *The Coal Question* in an article 'Coal' which appeared in the issue of 4 January 1866 (43). In April 1866 the paper ran a series of three articles entitled - 'England's Prosperity - Permanent or Transient' - 20 April (1277), 21 April (1285), and 24 April (1312). The first article contained the following passage - 'The whole case is stated with admirable clearness and cogency in a very moderate-sized volume entitled "The Coal Question", by W. S. Jevons, a work which appears to have produced as strong an impression on the mind of Mr. Mill as it did upon our own . . . Mr. Jevons's figures have . . . received a few trifling corrections, and substantial confirmation in an offical report: they have been discussed and assailed, but in no important point at all shaken or impugned and we may therefore regard them as unanswered and practically established, and as a perfectly safe groundwork for any conclusions legitimately deducible from them.'

[2] See Vol. II, Letter 155, n. 4, p. 438. Arthur Jevons married Catherine Castle Dawson (1826–1906), daughter of John Dawson of Liverpool, in 1856. See Vol. II, Letter 5, n. 1, p. 10.

events. So I hope we shall meet in London in a few days. Give my best love to Henrietta, who I hope has got the full use of her leg again. Believe me

Yours affy
Tim^y Jevons

248.　W. S. JEVONS TO MRS LUCY HUTTON
　　　[LJN, 222−3]

9 Birch Grove,
26th April 1866.

. . . Your letter to me received this morning was very agreeable. I have had very pleasant congratulations from Uncle William, Uncle Timothy, Mary, and others. You will, I daresay, excuse my being a little too full of myself at present. It is hard even for me to feel the full meaning of such sudden and complete success. If I had worked ten or twenty years longer, I might have been glad to have got the result I already have got. To gain the reputation of having settled two of the most difficult questions will be no slight aid to me in future.

Does it not seem strange and incredible that what I was writing in that little cupboard in Rotten Row at Beaumaris should be altering the opinion of the whole country, and even destroying the hopes of the greatest of nations? I distinctly remember thinking in Sydney that if there were one thing I should wish to be, it would be a recognised statistical writer. How strangely my wish has been fulfilled! If I should live long and have as much success in other undertakings, what will come of it? I hardly like to anticipate anything.

I hope you will not be the least discouraged about your painting. . . . But you must remember how much time and effort is needed in all matters of this kind. What success I have comes from labouring without cessation from the earliest years I can at all remember. A woman can seldom have the inducement or opportunity to the same constant attention and effort. No one can wish that she should. Except under very peculiar circumstances, she should not sacrifice herself and others to it. I think that women are often quite sufficiently admirable in themselves and their characters without accomplishments and works . . .

249.   W. S. JEVONS TO THE EDITOR OF *THE TIMES*[1]

Sir,

Though the "Coalowner" who writes in your issue of the 26th inst.,[2] does not tell us even the acreage of his estate, I shall have great pleasure. with many others, in accepting his statement that he can supply the shipments of Cardiff for 30 years to come at the present rate. But who can suppose that the shipments will remain stationary when steam communication is spreading over all the oceans driven and to be driven by our coal? And who is to keep the blast furnaces going which are burning out the bowels of Siluria wherever the valleys enable the coal to be reached at remunerative rates?

As to the latter part of "Coalowner's" letter, it is an enigma. If the steam coal trade is a vast monopoly, and parties are clearing their tens of thousands a year by frightening consumers, why does not "Coalowner" throw his vast supplies upon the market, and either break up the monopoly or share in the tens of thousands? Is his coal too deep, or is he prudently waiting for higher prices?

I, at least, have nothing to lose or gain by the price of coal more than millions of my fellow-countrymen.

Your obedient servant,
W. Stanley Jevons.

Owens' College, Manchester, April 27.

250.   ALFRED TENNYSON[1] TO W. S. JEVONS

Farringford,
April 28th, 1866.

Sir,

I beg to thank you for your kindness in sending me your book on the Coal Question – a question which has great interest for me so that I feel

---

[1] Published in the issue of 30 April 1866.

[2] The text of the letter to which Jevons was replying, printed in *The Times* on 26 April 1866, p. 10, is as follows:

'Will you allow me to say that the idea of our coal supply running short for the next 100 years, even doubling the present rate of consumption, is simply ridiculous? There are thousands of acres in the centre of the South Wales basin as yet untouched. I myself have, on my own property which has not yet been touched, a sufficient quantity to keep the port of Cardiff going at its present rate of shipment for more than 30 years to come. The steam coal trade is at present a vast monopoly, and parties are clearing their tens of thousands per annum, even allowing them the small sum of 1ˢ per ton profit. It is the object of these parties to frighten the consumer. . . .'

[1] Alfred, first Baron Tennyson (1809–92), Poet Laureate from 1850.

sure of reading your book with pleasure.

I have the honour to be.

Sir

Your very obedient servant

A. Tennyson.

251.   E. J. BROADFIELD TO W. S. JEVONS

Accrington House.

Sunday night

April 29, 1866.

My Dear Friend,

Just a few lines tonight to acknowledge not to reply to your deeply interesting letter of yesterday. I expect a friend here tomorrow who will stay a day or two so I write tonight to ask you to excuse my waiting a day or two before writing and submitting to you a letter to the Trustees.[1]

Anything I write I shall be willing to have printed or not as you think; although I cannot see what advantage there would be in printing if you could ensure the reading of the letter by all the voting trustees. I rec[eive]d your letter last night: the printed application this morning. I was surprised to find that you had described your scheme of lecturing in almost the same words I had thought of referring to the one course of lectures I heard you deliver. If anyone at Owens can judge of your knowledge and comprehensive grasp of the general principles and various schools of Metaphysics and Ethics I think I can: to think that my testimony may even in a slight degree be of service to you gives me very much pleasure: I took your evening exam paper to Mr. Greenwood last Thursday week and called his attention to the suggested variety of your subjects. He quite agreed with my opinion of the paper. I think if you extend your list of testimonials you should print the extract from Lord Stanley's British Association speech and from Mill's speech in parliament.[2]

I have not read Beethoven's letters:[3] At present I don't desire to do: My

[1] See below, Letter 256 (20), p. 118.

[2] Edward Henry Stanley (1826–93), afterwards fifteenth Earl of Derby, was President of Section F of the British Association at its Birmingham meeting in 1865. Speaking on 'The Coal Question', he was reported as saying: 'For those who desire to go more deeply into the facts of the case, as far as they are known, than is possible within the limits of an oral address, I should recommend two books on the subject, published within the last two or three years – one by Mr. Hull, the other by Mr. Jevons. They differ somewhat widely in conclusions. The one takes what we may call "the sanguine view" of the case, the other a view comparatively despondent; but in both one and the other you will find what is, perhaps, more important than the inferences of those authors, and that is, a very ample stock of materials upon which to found your own conclusions' – *Daily News*, 11 September 1865.

For Mill's speech, see above, Letter 245, n. 1, p. 94.

[3] *Beethoven's Letters 1790–1826, from the collection of Ludwig Nohl. Also his letters to the Archduke Rudolph, Cardinal Archbishop of Olmutz* . . . translated by Lady Wallace, 2 vols (1866).

admiration and reverence for his genius strengthens. I have induced some of my young musical friends here to study and practise his pianoforte sonatas – this evening I went up to Mr. Baines[4] after the evening service – I had been more than usually occupied and rested for a while in a quiet room alone. I saw the bright moon shining through the trees and heard in the adjoining room a pianoforte arrangement of the heart warming Larghetto from the 2nd symphony, it was like the voice [of][5] a heavenly poet. I have been pausing to think it over again. Blessings in 'Representation'. I shall try to be at the dinner next Friday and hope to meet you there. You will probably hear from me before then.

Believe me,
> Yours truly,
> > E. J. Broadfield.

252.   R. B. CLIFTON TO W. S. JEVONS

> Oxford.
> May 4th, 1866.

My dear Jevons,

Pray forgive me for not replying to your letter by return of post, what with preparing for my lectures and looking after a house I was yesterday so exceedingly busy that I had no opportunity of writing. If you think it will be of any use to you to refer the Trustees to me, you are quite at liberty to do so and it will give me great pleasure, as I hope you know, to aid you. I think however the Trustees will have sufficient evidence without asking my opinion.

This place is rather a grind at first for there is nothing ready, today the electric lamp broke down in the lecture, but luckily did not altogether shut me up, still I am greatly disgusted at these accidents.

Excuse haste and with kind regards to my Owens College friends and best wishes for your success.

Believe me ever
> Most sincerely yours,
> > R. B. Clifton.

---

[4] Possibly [Sir] Edward Baines (1800–90), proprietor of the *Leeds Mercury* 1827–90, author of *A History of the Cotton Manufacture in Great Britain* (1835); M.P. for Leeds, 1859–74; knighted 1880. Baines supported the campaign for the extension of Owens College from 1865 to 1868, and was a member of the original University Court of the Victoria University of Manchester.

[5] Omitted in the original manuscript.

253. W. S. JEVONS TO MRS LUCY HUTTON
[LJN, 223–4]

9 Birch Grove,
9th May 1866.

. . . *The Coal Question* gets on apace. The papers are hammering away
about it. A Member of Parliament is going to move for a Royal
Commission to inquire into the whole subject,[1] and there will be one or
two debates upon the matter probably. The *Times* accuses me of
misleading Mr. Gladstone.[2] Of course one must be criticised and abused
a little. The more one's name is named now, the better for my
professorship appointment. I have such strong opinions in favour of the
Coal Question, and am so confident that nearly all parts of the book at all
events will bear examination, that I am not afraid. I am kept, however, in
a state of great excitement and anxiety altogether, I don't really doubt
about getting the professorship, but I can't help feeling unsettled and
nervous. There are a good many applications but few of the slightest
consequence.

I feel as if I should be able to do anything when I get £300 a year. I long
for a little rest. . . .

254. W. S. JEVONS TO THE EDITOR OF *THE TIMES*[1]

Owens College, Manchester,
12th May 1866.

Sir,

An article from a correspondent appears in The Times of the 11th inst.,
headed "the Coal Question." May I have the opportunity of stating that,
though the writer discusses certain numbers given in my volume called
the Coal Question, his remarks appear to me to have no reference to my
conclusions? So far am I from supposing that the internal temperature of
the earth will put a definite limit to our mining operations, that I
endeavour to show the contrary.[2]

---

[1] Hussey Vivian moved the motion for a Royal Commission on coal supplies in the House of
Commons on 12 June 1866–*Hansard's Parliamentary Debates*, third series, Vol. 184,241 –95. The
motion was agreed to and the Royal Commission issued on 28 June.

[2] *The Times*, 7 May 1866, p. 8 col. 4. See the passages from this leading article quoted by Jevons in
'Mr. Gladstone's New Financial Policy', *Macmillan's Magazine* (June 1866), reprinted in Vol. VII.

[1] Published in the issue of 15 May 1866.

[2] 'Now, as men can work at temperatures exceeding 100°, we are not likely to encounter the
physical limit of sinking on this account' – *Coal Question*, p. 61.

Again, so far am I from supposing that in the year 1961 the consumption of coal will reach 2,607 millions of tons,[3] that my work proceeds on the assumption that it never can reach nearly so large an amount. It is the consequences of this fact considered in connexion with the progress of foreign coal-producing countries, which seem to demand attention.

Your obedient servant,
W. Stanley Jevons.

255.   W. S. JEVONS TO HERBERT JEVONS
　　　[LJN, 224−5]

9 Birch Grove,
Rusholme,
13th May 1866.

. . . Times here are a little lively. Not to speak of an impending European war, we have a commercial panic of a most extraordinary kind, arising from unsound trading and advances by these new banks and finance companies. You will, however, read about it in the papers. It is a little annoying to me, because I have just proved to the Statistical Society that panics ought to come in the autumn.[1] However, I daresay we shall have a pressure then, this year or next, and statistics are peculiarly liable to these sorts of exceptions.

The Coal Panic, as some of the papers call it, is the most interesting event to me. It gets on very well, as Gladstone has already propounded his plan for paying off the National Debt in part, and urged its adoption on the ground of the coal exhaustion. There is also to be a motion in Parliament for a Royal Commission to investigate the subject, which will, I have no doubt, be appointed. Thus, whether people are ultimately convinced or not, I have gained my end of getting the subject investigated. It would seem that Mill, followed by Gladstone, really frightened the Opposition, composed of old landed fogies who thought their rents would go on rising for centuries to come.

[3] Starting from the actual consumption of coal in 1861, and assuming a continuing growth of its consumption at $3\frac{1}{2}$ per cent per annum, Jevons arrived at a figure of 2607.5 million tons for consumption in 1961, but stressed that 'we can never advance to the higher amounts of consumption supposed'−op. cit., pp. 272−4.

[1] Jevons's paper 'On the Frequent Autumnal Pressure in the Money Market, and the action of the Bank of England' had been read before the Statistical Society of London on 17 April 1866, and was printed in the Society's *Journal*, 29, pp. 235−53.

On the 'impending European war', see below, Letter 263, n. 2, p. 125. The 'commercial panic of a most extraordinary kind' had been set off on 10 May 1866, when Overend, Gurney & Co. Ltd. failed for over £5,000,000; the Bank Act was suspended on 11 May. See Clapham, *The Bank Of England, A History* (1944) II, 260− 70.

Thus I have had quite enough fame for the present, and I should not be altogether sorry to retire in safety. It is quite possible that I may get somewhat roasted before long, and I shall have to defend myself, or bear it as best I may. Still, a writer's purpose is to get his opinions discussed, and I suppose I could hardly have had them more prominently brought forward than in Mill's speech and Gladstone's budget.

Our trustees must, I think, be a little impressed by this time, so that I hope they will not much delay over the appointment to the professorship, but it may be some weeks yet before the matter is settled. . . .

256. W. S. JEVONS TO THE TRUSTEES OF THE LATE JOHN OWENS, ESQ.

[May 1866]

GENTLEMEN,

I beg to offer myself as a Candidate for the Professorship of Logic, Mental and Moral Philosophy, and the Cobden Professorship of Political Economy in Owens College. The following testimonials may enable you to judge of my fitness for the appointment, and I beg to add some information concerning my studies, occupations, and views with regard to teaching the subjects of the chair.

During my earlier course at University College, London, I was much devoted to Physical Science and Mathematics, which I look upon as a valuable preparation for the sound investigation of the more complex mental sciences.

In 1854 I was nominated by Professor Graham to a scientific position in the Sydney Branch of the Royal Mint. The following five years were accordingly spent in my official duties in Australia, and in scientific and philosophical inquiries.

In 1859 I returned to England for the purpose of carrying out a new and different course of study. Re-entering University College, I was elected Ricardo Scholar in Political Economy in 1860. In 1862 I completed the degree of Master of Arts in the University of London, in the Philosophical Branch, receiving the gold medal for examinations and essays in the following subjects:—

> Logic,
> Mental Philosophy,
> Moral Philosophy,
> History of Philosophy,
> Political Economy,
> Political Philosophy.

In 1864 I was elected a Fellow of my College.

Since obtaining my degree I have given constant attention to the various branches of Philosophy, and on some points I have already been enabled to publish results.

After studying the recent writings on Logic, I was led to propose, in 1863, a new general system of Formal Logic, closely analogous to the celebrated Mathematical system of the late Professor Boole, but yet contrasted to it in some important points. The opinions of logicians, as shown in the accompanying letters or testimonials, are as yet at variance concerning this system. But I have quite recently met with new evidence of its truth in the fact, practically demonstrated, that the operations of Formal Logic, when thus presented, are readily capable of mechanical performance. I have given preliminary explanations before the Philosophical Societies of Liverpool and Manchester of the Logical machine analogous to the Calculating machine, thus readily produced.

My chief publications on Economical subjects have been as follows:—

1862. Papers read at the British Association on—

1. The Mathematical Theory of Political Economy.

2. The Study of Periodic Commercial Fluctuations.

1863. Pamphlet entitled "A Serious Fall in the Value of Gold Ascertained," &c.

1865. "The Coal Question."

Also a paper "On the Variation of the Value of Gold," containing the substance of a statement to the Statistical Society of London in May.

1866. A paper "On the Frequent Autumnal Pressure in the Money Market, and the Action of the Bank of England," read to the Statistical Society in April.

In October, 1863, I became tutor in Owens College. At the same time I undertook courses of evening lectures on Logic and Political Economy. Lately I have added a course on Mental and Moral Philosophy. I temporarily held the day class of Logic in 1863, and during the present session I have the pleasure of conducting the day classes of Philosophy and Economy, at the request of the Principal and of Professor Christie. I thus perform at present the duties of the Professorship.

About a year ago, I was appointed Professor of Logic, Philosophy, and Political Economy in the Queen's College, Liverpool.

I have been led by experience to adopt the following views as to teaching the peculiar subjects of the chair which I desire to hold:—

1. In all the subjects it is indispensable to make the students acquainted with the doctrines as given in the best received text books.

2. In Mental and Moral Philosophy it is desirable to explain the doctrines of two or more of the principal schools.

3. The opinions of the lecturer, where at variance with received doctrines, should be stated only in occasional criticism, or else in lectures

professedly set apart for the purpose.

4. Logic must also be taught for the present in the received form; but I have a strong opinion that it may, by the use of frequent exercises, be made a means of training the mental powers only inferior to mathematics.

5. I have long hoped to have an opportunity of extending the teaching of Economic Science. In addition to a course on Abstract Political Economy, I should desire to give courses of lectures on Commercial History, the Social Condition of the People, &c., in which the truths of Economy would be illustrated and enforced. I would give similar abbreviated courses of evening lectures. To these I should gladly add, if required by the terms of the Cobden Professorship, a distinct free course of elementary lectures on the truths of Political Economy, adapted to school teachers.

I may say, finally, that if I am so fortunate as to receive this appointment, I shall apply the whole of my time and efforts to the work and interests of the College, or to studies, writings, or lectures appropriate to the chair.

And I may add that, in thus becoming a public teacher of the Speculative and Moral Sciences, I shall but be accomplishing the congenial work which I have long had in view.

I have the honour to remain,

Gentlemen,
Your obedient Servant,
W. STANLEY JEVONS.

P. S. My age is thirty years.

TESTIMONIALS. [1]

To the Council of Queen's College, Liverpool.

1. Alexander Bain, [2] Esq., M.A.
2. J. E. Cairnes, Esq., M.A.
3. Aug. De Morgan, Esq., M.A.
4. Henry Fawcett, Esq., M.A., M.P.
5. Rev. John Hoppus, [3] LL.D.
6. Richard H. Hutton, Esq., M.A.
7. Rev. James Martineau. [4]
8. A. J. Scott, Esq., M.A.
9. Jacob Waley, [5] Esq., M.A.

To the Trustees of Owens College.

10. Walter Bagehot, Esq., M.A.
11. William Farr, [6] Esq., M.D.
12. David Masson, [7] Esq., M.A.
13. William Newmarch, Esq., F.R.S.
14. Rev. J. E. T. Rogers, M.A.
15. Arch. Sandeman, Esq., M.A.

---

[1] Jevons obviously decided to extend this list of testimonials after it had gone to print. See above, Letter 251, p. 99.

[2] Alexander Bain (1818–1903), Professor of Logic and English in the United University of Aberdeen, 1860–80; held examinerships at University College London and in the Indian Civil Service; Rector of Aberdeen University, 1882. In 1876 he launched the philosophical journal *Mind*, for which he remained financially responsible until 1891.

[3] Rev. John Hoppus (1789–1875), an independent minister, who had been educated at Rotherham Independent College, Edinburgh University, where he studied under Dugald Stewart, and Glasgow. M.A. Glasgow, 1823; LL.D. 1839; F.R.S. 1841; Professor of Logic and the Philosophy of Mind in the University of London, 1830–66; Dean of the Faculty of Arts and Laws, 1837–8 and 1852–3.

[4] See Vol. II, Letter 147, n. 4, p. 421.

[5] Jacob Waley (1818–73), Professor of Political Economy in the University of London, 1854–66; Emeritus Professor from 1866 until his death; educated at U.C.L.; B.A. 1839; M.A. 1840; called to the Bar, Lincoln's Inn, 1842; Conveyancing Counsel for the Court of Chancery, 1871–3; member of the Royal Commission on Land Transfer, 1868–9; Joint Secretary of the Political Economy Club, 1870–3.

[6] William Farr (1808–87), medical statistician. After a medical training, entered the department of the Registrar-General in 1838 and made important contributions to the development of vital statistics; President of the London (later Royal) Statistical Society, 1871–3.

[7] See Vol. II, Letter 158, n. 1, p. 443.

LETTERS.

16. The Chancellor of the Exchequer.
17. The same.
18. Sir J. F. W. Herschel, M.A., F.R.S.
19. Herbert Spencer,[8] Esq.

1.

From ALEXANDER BAIN, Esq., M.A., *Professor of Logic, &c., in the University of Aberdeen, and Examiner in the University of Aberdeen, and Examiner in the University of London.*

University of Aberdeen,
14th Jan., 1865.

William Stanley Jevons, M.A., is known to me as having passed a distinguished examination on taking his M.A. Degree in Mental Science in the University of London. On that occasion the gold medal was awarded to him; an honour bestowed on the best candidate only when his absolute merits are of a high order, as is shown by the fact that it had not been given on any one of the three previous years.

I know Mr. Jevons further as the author of a work on "Pure Logic," which certainly displays great ingenuity and subtlety, and places the Formal Logic in a new and interesting light. As an exercise in abstract and formal thinking it does him honour.

I presume that, as a public instructor in logic, he would not confine his pupils' attention to this limited part of the subject, which he has so well mastered.

ALEXANDER BAIN.

2.

From J. E. CAIRNES, Esq., M.A., *Professor of Political Economy and Jurisprudence in Queen's College, Galway.*

74, Lower Mount-street, Dublin,
8th January, 1865.

My dear Sir, – As you think an expression of opinion from me may be of use to you in the object which you have in view, I have great pleasure in

[8] Herbert Spencer (1820–1903), philosopher. His principal works included: *Social Statics* (1855); *Principles of Psychology* (1855); *Principles of Biology* (1864–7); *The Study of Sociology* (1873); *Principles of Sociology* (1876). See David Duncan, *The Life and Letters of Herbert Spencer* (1908).

testifying to the instruction I have derived from your writings on subjects connected with Political Economy.

Every one who takes an interest in that science is aware of the attention which your work on the Gold Question universally attracted. I believe that scarcely a single essay on that subject has appeared since its publication in which it has not been referred to in laudatory terms.

Your work on "Pure Logic" would have a more immediate bearing on the chair for which you are at present a candidate, and though I do not feel myself competent to express an opinion on the merit of that publication, I may be allowed to say that I have seen it highly appreciated in periodicals of first-class position – for example in the *Spectator*.

Wishing you success in your application,

I remain, dear Sir,
Very truly yours,
J. E. CAIRNES.

––––––

3.

From AUGUSTUS DE MORGAN, M.A., *Professor of Mathematics in University College, London.*

University College, London,
January 9, 1865.

Sir, – Mr. W. S. Jevons, a former pupil of mine, is a candidate for a Professorship of Logic in your College.

Mr. Jevons was a successful student of mathematics, and, as has since appeared, he has that turn of mind which leads him to the mental applications of Mathematics.

In Logic, Mr. Jevons has published a work which will enable any one to judge him who can, and will apply himself to the recent discussions of the principles of the science.

These discussions lead to much difference of opinion, so that to give an opinion of a work would require much development of agreement and disagreement. To give an opinion of an author from his work is more easy. Mr. Jevons will be held by all who can read him to have shown great acuteness and power of systematic exposition. His views are decidedly worthy of serious attention, and actually receive it from those who follow these points of speculation.

Mr. Jevons, I am persuaded, would not, as a teacher, confine himself to his own views.

He has incidentally shown a full command of the common system; and

I can safely recommend him as a candidate whose claims merit the most attentive examination, and who will, if elected, be sure to make his subject a means of training thought, and not, as too often has happened, a literature of the thought of others, and nothing more.

I am, Sir,

Your faithful servant,

A. DE MORGAN.

———

4.

From HENRY FAWCETT, Esq., M.A., M.P., *Professor of Political Economy in the University of Cambridge.*

Having heard that Mr. W. S. Jevons is a candidate for the Professorship of Logic, Moral and Mental Philosophy at Queen's College, Liverpool, I have great pleasure in expressing my opinion that his qualifications for the office are of a very high order. I first became acquainted with Mr. Jevons through the very able pamphlet which he wrote on the Gold Question. He discussed this difficult and complicated question with great ability, and I must candidly confess that the views he propounded materially modified the opinions which I had previously held on this subject. Mr. Jevons is also the author of a very able work on "Pure Logic."

(Signed) HENRY FAWCETT,

Professor of Political Economy.

Trinity Hall, Cambridge,

January 7th, 1865.

———

5.

From the Rev. JOHN HOPPUS, LL.D., F.R.S., *Professor of the Philosophy of Mind, Logic, &c., in University College, London.*

University College, London,

13th January, 1865.

Having understood that Mr. William Stanley Jevons, M.A., of the University of London, is about to offer himself as a candidate for the Chair of Logic and Mental and Moral Philosophy, at the Queen's College, Liverpool, I have much pleasure in bearing my testimony to his merits as a student in one of my classes – that of the Philosophy of Mind and Logic – in session 1860–61. At the end of this session I awarded to

Mr. Jevons a first prize and certificate, as he was not excelled by any fellow-student, and only equalled by one, in a class in which there was rather an unusual proportion of talent and diligence. The papers of Mr. Jevons at the examination fully entitled him to the distinction which he gained.

As a proof of the great attention he has paid to Logic, in particular, I may name a work which he published last year, entitled "Pure Logic," with remarks on Professor Boole's Logical System. Of late years a strong tendency has been manifested to reduce Formal Logic to a mathematical calculus, and the name of Mr. Jevons already ranks advantageously with those writers who have ventured into this field of speculation.

I observe, also, that Mr. Jevons, at the early period of his student life at our college, was much distinguished in other branches. He obtained a silver medal for Chemistry in 1852, and the gold medal for the same in 1853, also the first prize in Experimental Natural Philosophy in 1852. He also gained the prize in Botany at the Matriculation Honours, in the University of London, 1852.

I may add that Mr. Jevons has shown the extent of his knowledge in quite another direction – that of Political Economy in the branch of Finance. I allude to his work on the "Fall in the Value of Gold," published in 1863.

Upon the whole, I cannot but think that Mr. Jevons may be fairly regarded as one of the most distinguished of our students, having the recommendation of that varied knowledge which is likely to react favourably on a man's teaching of a particular branch.

It is also much to his advantage as a candidate for the chair he is seeking that he has gained experience as a teacher, by instructing and lecturing on the subjects of that department.

From all I know of the studious habits of Mr. Jevons, I should entertain no doubt of his doing justice to the important range of study which the professorship embraces.

JOHN HOPPUS, LLD., F.R.S.,
Professor of the Philosophy of Mind, Logic, &c., in University
College, London.

———

6.

From RICHARD HOLT HUTTON, Esq., M.A.

University of London,
7th January, 1865.

I examined Mr. Stanley Jevons in the M.A. Examination of the University of London in 1862, and, though my department was only Political Economy, his answers showed the exact and precise thought requisite for excellence in all departments of philosophy, and no small amount of original power.

I have since read a very able and original treatise of his on "Formal Logic," which places him among the first logicians of the day, and I feel sure that no man of greater attainments and ability will be found for the post for which he is a candidate. I have had no experience of his powers as a teacher, but have often been told by those who have that they are very great.

RICHARD H. HUTTON, M.A., London,
Examiner in Political Economy in the
University of London.

———

7.

From the REV. JAMES MARTINEAU.

Mr. W. Stanley Jevons having for several years pursued his studies in London, and partly in my own class-room, I have been led by opportunity and friendship to be a careful observer of his career. The distinctions which he has won speak for themselves; but they inadequately attest his remarkable faculty of exact and profound thought upon abstract subjects, and his acquaintance with the history of doctrine in Logic, Metaphysics, and Political Economy.

His treatise on the "Logic of Quality" exhibits, in its relation to Professor Boole's larger work, his power of clear and compressed exposition. Nor can I omit to say that his natural gifts and acquired knowledge are rendered doubly effective by the highest moral qualities of a teacher, – a pure and unpretending love of truth, and a conscientious devotion to the work of imparting it.

JAMES MARTINEAU,
Professor of Intellectual and Moral Philosophy in Manchester
New College, London.

10, Gordon-street, London,
7th January, 1865.

———

8.

From the late A. J. SCOTT, Esq., M.A., *Professor of Logic and Mental Philosophy at Owens College.*

Owens College, Manchester, was founded with the intention that the direct instruction there should be conveyed in the method adopted at the German and Scotch Universities, that is by the continuous discourse of the professors, by whom in general the auxiliary examinations or exercises should be conducted. Experience confirmed the belief warranted by the trial previously made at University College, London, and elsewhere, that this plan of teaching might be rendered efficient in all the principal branches of study in a degree at least equal to any other.

But, from the foundation of the College, the trustees and the professors were agreed that its system could hardly fail to gain much in precision and thoroughness if the tutorial method were at least made accessible to the student as supplemental to the lectures of the professors. This has been added during the last two years. The governors of the College have not yet been encouraged to introduce this additional means to a greater extent than by the appointment of one college tutor; but they have been peculiarly happy in being able to fill that office with a gentleman whose reputation as a writer, and a thinker, are already considerable; and who gives promise, by the extent, variety, and originality of his researches, of yet more valuable contributions to science and philosophy. A severe illness rendered me incapable of resuming the duties of the Professorship of Logic at the commencement of last session. For about three months they were discharged by Mr. Jevons. I had personally some opportunity of ascertaining, by examinations, that they were efficiently discharged, and the report of the University examinations confirmed my impressions. The state of my health has greatly limited my intercourse with society since that period. From all I hear, I have reason to regret the very slight opportunity I have consequently had of cultivating Mr. Jevons' acquaintance. Should he succeed in obtaining a situation of more extended usefulness as a public instructor, the sense of our loss at Owens College will be proportionate to the feeling of its professors of the improbability that he can be replaced by a scholar of attainments equally extensive, and various, and of powers of thought so sound and original.

Thus far I have spoken necessarily on the testimony of others – of my colleagues. Mr. Jevons, is, however, an author in my own special department; and I have thus the pleasure of bearing witness of my own knowledge to his possessing some of the highest qualifications as a Professor of Logic. I have studied his "Pure Logic" or "Logic of Quality." It is a work truly original, founded on principles at once simple, and sound, and comprehensive. Much has been accomplished in this science in our day. Aristotle is no longer either idolised or slighted. By Hamilton, Thomson, De Morgan, and Boole especially, correction and fruitful development have been given to the ancient doctrines.

I know not that any contribution by any of these eminent men has, in proportion to its extent, excelled in worth the modest and compendious work of Mr. Jevons.

A. J. SCOTT.

9.

From JACOB WALEY, Esq., M.A., *Professor of Political Economy in University College, London, and Examiner in the University of London.*

20, Wimpole-street, London,
9th January, 1865.

Dear Mr. Jevons, – I have great pleasure in the opportunity of offering my testimony to your very high qualifications in the branch of knowledge in which I have been one of your examiners at University College, and the University of London (Political Economy), and of stating my belief, on sufficient grounds, in your capacity to fill with advantage a professorship in the cognate sciences of Logic, Mental Philosophy, etc.

In your examination for the scholarship in Political Economy at University College, for which you were the successful competitor, I remember well that both Mr. R.H. Hutton (my co-examiner) and I were struck with your bold and skilful treatment of some of the problem-questions set by Mr. Hutton.

We considered that you showed a singular aptitude for original economic inquiries, and our views in this respect have been verified by your very able pamphlet on the Gold Question, which has been widely circulated, and the value of which is generally admitted.

At the University of London you were again the successful competitor for the highest honours, obtaining the gold medal for the best examination for the M.A. degree in Moral Sciences Branch. Though personally I had only to peruse your papers in Political Economy, the result authorises me to say that in the other branches of the moral sciences you had attained a high degree of proficiency.

With good wishes for your success in this and other undertakings, I remain,

My dear Sir,
Very truly yours,
JACOB WALEY.

10.

From WALTER BAGEHOT, Esq., M.A., *Editor of the "Economist."*

12, Upper Belgrave-street,
10th March, 1866.

My dear Sir, – I have great pleasure in saying how exactly your abilities and studies seem to me to fit you for the first Cobden Professor. I do not think I know any recent books which show (as far as I can judge) an equal knowledge of the abstract theory of Political Economy, and an equally accurate acquaintance with the statistics of present facts. Scarcely any one has paid the same attention both to abstract argument and to complex figures, and it is in consequence of that combination that your book on the Gold Discoveries *moved* the subject to which it is devoted.

Since that tract was published there has been a sensible change of public opinion upon its principal topic, and, in consequence, I have not been able yet to read your book on "Coal" as carefully as I ought, but it is undoubtedly very able.

I am,
Yours very truly,

WALTER BAGEHOT.

Possibly it may be worth naming that I have heard the Chancellor of the Exchequer and two Governors of the Bank of England speak of your work on the Gold Discoveries with very great respect and praise.

———

11.

Registrar-General's Office, Somerset House,
March 16, 1866.

My dear Sir, – I entertain a very high opinion of your labours in the field of Political Economy.

Your researches into the effect of the Gold Discoveries on prices are conclusive.

It will give me great satisfaction to learn that you get the Professorship at Owen's College – which already enjoys a high reputation that I believe your labours would augment.

I am, my dear Sir,
Yours very faithfully,

WILLIAM FARR.

Professor Jevons.

———

12.

From DAVID MASSON, Esq., M.A., *Professor of Rhetoric in the University of Edinburgh.*

University of Edinburgh,
March 9, 1866.

Although my personal acquaintance with Mr. W. Stanley Jevons is slight, I have had good opportunities of forming an opinion of his powers through various writings of his.

Some time ago, I had the pleasure of awarding to him a prize offered by the council of University College, London, for the best English Essay "On the Effect of Climate on Nations," and since then my knowledge of him has been increased by the perusal of at least portions of his published writings. For some time he has seemed to me to be one of those in this country who have a decided, and even signal vocation for the work of speculative research, both in pure philosophy, and in questions of social and economical science. My belief is that, were he appointed to such a post as that of Professor of Logic, Mental and Moral Philosophy, and Political Economy in Owens College, he would be found not only a successful practical teacher of these subjects (his written expositions being remarkable for their lucidity and accuracy of style), but also one whose original contributions in these departments would be of such public note as to reflect credit on the post.

DAVID MASSON.

13.

From WILLIAM NEWMARCH, Esq., F.R.S.

67, Lombard-street, London,
9th March, 1866.

I understand that Mr. W. S. Jevons is a candidate for the appointment of Cobden Professor of Political Economy in Owens College, Manchester.

I consider Mr. Jevons to have high qualifications for such a post. He is remarkable for the combination of practice and theory in his investigations of economic phenomena; and, while giving full weight to the abstract view, he has sagacity, patience, and industry sufficient to lead him to elaborate verification founded on statistical evidence.

His works already published afford evidence of his good merits, and also afford evidence that, while an independent inquirer, he is not under the influence of exaggerated or eccentric opinions.

I shall be glad if Mr. Jevons obtains the appointment, and I say this on purely public grounds.

W. NEWMARCH, F.R.S.,
Vice-President of the Statistical Society
of London.

_____

14.

From the Rev. J. E. T. ROGERS, M.A., *Professor of Political Economy in the University of Oxford, and Tooke Professor of Economic Science and Statistics in King's College, Oxford.*

London, March 12, 1866.

My dear Sir, – I do not know of any person who would fill the office of Professor of Political Economy at Owens College better than yourself, and I hope that the application which you make will be successful. I am well acquainted with the laborious and patient research which you have given to some of the most obscure and difficult problems in the science.

Yours faithfully,

JAMES E. T. ROGERS.

_____

15.

From ARCHIBALD SANDEMAN, Esq., M.A., *late Professor of Mathematics in Owens College.*

Queen's [*sic*] College, Cambridge,
9th March, 1866.

My dear Jevons, – I am happy to state, as you wish, what I know of you, and shall be still happier if aught I can say be of any use to you.

Your diligent and studious habits, large acquaintance with books, way of seeing things for yourself, and character as a writer – all with more or less leaning to the Sciences of the Mind – are well known, and need no word from me. But from the many talks we have had, I can specially bear witness to the great heed you have given to Logic. And although we are far from at one on many points, yet, as to the late Professor Boole's very remarkable system, you and I have been led, each in his own way, to view some things nearly if not quite alike. You have also contrived a simple piece of mechanism to show how, when classes of objects are related to one another in a given way, any one of these classes is related to the rest.

The wideness of your knowledge in many branches of learning can hardly but bring about that soberness, and that looking at things from many sides, which philosophy most of all needs.

Believe me,

Very truly yours,

ARCHIBALD SANDEMAN.

Testimonials 16–18 were copies of letters relating to *The Coal Question* from Gladstone and Herschel. See Vol. I, p. 203; and above, Letters 238 and 227. pp. 87 and 77.

———

19.

From HERBERT SPENCER, Esq., *Author of "Social Statics," "Principles of Psychology," "First Principles," &c.*

88, Kensington Gardens Square,

January 9, 1866.

Sir, – I acknowledge with much pleasure the copy of your work on "Pure Logic," received yesterday, with much more pleasure indeed than I usually acknowledge the receipt of books; for I perceive from the glance I have already taken over the earlier pages of your work, that it has a special interest for me, since it asserts and works out in its logical aspect a distinction between the two orders of reasoning which I have myself worked out in its psychological aspect, and which also I found myself obliged to make when seeking a rational classification of the sciences. I send by this post a copy of the short essay in which this distinction is drawn. The psychological aspect is dealt with in the second part of the "Principles of Psychology." But for the establishment of this doctrine it needed working out from a logical point of view, and I am delighted to find by your little work that it is practicable to formulate the processes of pure qualitative reasoning in as exact a manner as those of quantitative reasoning – all the more so as I have been attacked by Professor De Morgan, I believe, for asserting that pure logic is non-quantitative.

I am, faithfully yours,

HERBERT SPENCER.

———

20.

From E. J. BROADFIELD, Esq., B.A., *Associate and Lecturer in Owens College.*

Accrington House,
Accrington,
May 2nd, 1866.

To the Trustees of Owens College, Manchester.

Gentlemen, – Having heard that Mr. William Stanley Jevons, M.A., is a Candidate for the Chair of Logic and Mental and Moral Philosophy at Owens College, I feel desirous of offering my testimony to his high qualifications for the duties of the position, especially as it is founded on considerable practical acquaintance with his opinions, attainments, and method of teaching.

In October, 1863, I entered the Logic Class at Owens College, with the understanding that the late Prof. Scott would deliver a course on Metaphysics; during his temporary absence of three months, Mr. Jevons delivered a course on Logic. I venture to speak in decided terms of these lectures, because at the time I had considerable familiarity with the subject of Logic. I cannot well imagine a course better designed to give general views, and concise notions of the particulars of Logic. The common principles, the general rules, and the technicalities of Logic recognised in every system were clearly stated and systematically taught: the distinctive features of the different doctrines held by the leading Logicians of modern times were most fairly sketched. The definitions of writers like Hamilton, De Morgan, and Thomson, on the one hand, of Whately and Mill on the other, were often texts for comprehensive and candid discussions, but peculiar views were never unduly prominent.

Mr. Jevons's style of lecturing I considered very appropriate to the discussion of a subject like Logic. It was calm and argumentative, his explanations were clear and void of technicalities, and his illustrations remarkably apt and effective. The questions submitted as exercises to the class were drawn up and selected with great care – they gave the student ample opportunity for judging his own progress and grasp of the subject. The opinion here expressed was shared by several distinguished students who heard the same course. And I remember remarking that in the Logic paper of the B.A. Pass Examination of the University of London, about that time, no question was asked which might not readily have been answered by a diligent student of Mr. Jevons's class.

About this time I began to read privately with Mr. Jevons, and had the benefit of his assistance in the study of Mental and Moral Philosophy; to his great extent of knowledge, and clear views, I acknowledge myself greatly indebted. His extensive reading and remarkable powers of classification I could not but notice, both in Metaphysics and Ethics. He led me to a general knowledge of the varied opinions in the chief systems from the days of the Greek Philosophers to our own times. His candour and justice to the views he could not accept were very noticeable here also. Of the extent of his knowledge of these subjects I have had frequent opportunities of judging. His system of teaching can only be judged by results, but from no slight knowledge of his views gained by the freest discussions of the subjects in the intercourse of private friendship, as well as in the classroom, from hearing his sketches and plans for his various courses of College Lectures, I have no hesitation in saying that for a Professor of Mental and Moral Philosophy Mr. Jevons must have eminent qualifications, and that under his guidance and instruction the students of Owens College (whether as candidates for degrees, or simply as students of Philosophy) would enjoy inestimable advantages in their study and pursuit of subjects so intricate in character and so vast in range.

Believe me, Gentlemen,
Yours truly,
E. J. BROADFIELD.

———

21.

Extract from the speech of Mr. JOHN STUART MILL, *in the House of Commons, 17th April, 1866.*

"He commended to the notice of hon. members a small work entitled *The Coal Question*, by Mr. Stanley Jevons. It was, as far as he, not practically conversant with the subject, could judge, exhaustive in its treatment of the question; Mr. Jevons seemed to have anticipated and answered all ordinary objections to his conclusions, which briefly amounted to a statement that at the present rate of consumption of coal three generations at the most would see an end of all workable British coal nearer the surface than 4,000 feet, and that the expense of working coal at a depth beyond this would prevent competition in manufactures with countries richer in fuel. If Mr. Jevons's conclusions could be shown to be fallacious in any way by any hon. member it would be most desirable that it should be done; but up to the present time no answer had been given to him which led to more than a comparatively short extension of the time during which a supply of coal may be expected."

———

22.

From JOHN STUART MILL, Esq., M.P.

Blackheath Park, Kent,
May 4, 1866.

Such of Mr. Jevons's writings as I am acquainted with give evidence of decided originality, much knowledge and mental vigour, and an unusual degree of precision of thought and investigation.

His Essay on the Gold Question was the first starting point of the important series of discussions which has changed, and, it may now almost be said, settled the opinions of instructed men on the subject.

The merit of his investigation of the "Coal Question" can hardly be rated too highly.

His "Logic of Quality" showed extraordinary familiarity with and power over Formal Logic, and if I had a fault to find, it would be that the expenditure of power was greater than any result to be obtained by that mode of employing it would sufficiently remunerate.

Of Mr. Jevons's teaching powers I can say nothing; of these, however, the authorities of Owens College can judge from their own experience. But as regards his knowledge both of Logic and of Political Economy, so far as the whole can be judged from a part, I should form a very high estimate of it.

J. STUART MILL.

257.   W. S. JEVONS TO MRS LUCY HUTTON
[LJN, 225–6]

9 Birch Grove,
Rusholme,
21st May 1866.

. . . I write now to say that there is no doubt about the professorship. The committee of trustees had a first meeting last week, and seem to have found that none of the candidates could at all oppose me; and Mr. Greenwood even said in a letter to me in London that there was no need of further trouble. One cannot realise at first how satisfactory this is.

My visit to London was very gratifying. The visit to Gladstone was especially so, as he was pleasant and communicative – in fact talked so that I could get little in. It is something to make the acquaintance of the leading minister, and who is likely to be even more powerful than he is now. [1]

[1] See also the entry in Jevons's Journal for 23 May 1866, and notes thereto: Vol. I, pp. 206–7.

When I called on Macmillan, he at once proposed a second edition of the *Coal Question,* as the last copy was going, and there seemed to be orders on hand. I shall have to work hard to get it ready quickly. . . .

258.   R. C. CHRISTIE[1] TO W. S. JEVONS

> 7, St. James Square,
> Manchester.
> Wednesday, May 31. [1866]

My dear Jevons,

Pray accept my thanks for the valuable present of your new book which I received yesterday and of which I read a considerable portion last night with gratification. I am not quite prepared to say how far I agree or disagree with your conclusions but I can have no doubt as to the value and interest of the facts and details which you have brought together nor as to the great ability displayed in dealing with them.

I trust I may before long have the pleasure of resigning my office of Prof. of Pol. Econ. in favour of a "Cobden Professor" who will be able to carry out the Economical studies in the College far more efficiently than I have ever been able to do.

> Believe me to be
> Very faithfully yours,
> R. C. Christie.

W. S. Jevons, Esq.

259.   WILLIAM JEVONS JUNIOR TO W. S. JEVONS

> 21 Cannon Place,
> Brighton.
> June 4. 1866.

My dear Stanley,

I have this morning received your letter of the 2[d] inst. informing me of your appointment to the Professorship which you applied for, and the information has given us also great pleasure. Most heartily do I congratulate you on the attainment of this object of your honourable ambition, and I trust in your ability to fulfil your new duties to the satisfaction of those who have appointed you, and to the benefit of your

---

[1] Richard Copley Christie (1830–1901), Professor of History at Owens College, Manchester, 1854–66; Professor of Political Economy, 1855–66; Barrister of Lincoln's Inn, 1857; Chancellor of the Diocese of Manchester, 1872–93; Governor of Owens College, Manchester, and Royal Holloway College. See also Vol. I, p. 42.

future pupils. I am also very glad to know that you are preparing a second edition of your book on the coal question. When that task is finished, you will be able to devote yourself more entirely to those studies which appertain more immediately to your professorship, and I can hardly think that such vast subjects as Logic, Mental & Moral Philosophy, and Political Economy will leave you much time for the study of other subjects, more especially if you retain the professorship in Liverpool as well as that at Manchester. . . .[1]

. . . We all unite in love to yourself and Henny, and I remain

Affectionately yours
W. Jevons.

260.   W. S. JEVONS TO SIR JOHN F. W. HERSCHEL
        [HLRS, 3257]

9 Birch Grove
Rusholme
Manchester
23 June 1866.

My dear Sir,

The message which you were so good as to send me through Mrs. Herschel was highly flattering to me. I had hoped with many others to have had the pleasure of both seeing and hearing you at our prize meeting and universal regret has been expressed that you were unfortunately prevented from coming on this occasion.

I hope that your illness has proved a very slight affair and that you are now recovered.

The wish has been widely and strongly expressed that you will consider your visit to be only deferred to the next convenient opportunity.

As you have taken interest in the utilization of the tides it has occurred to me that you would like to see the enclosed extract from the new Journal "Engineering".[1] It has the marks of being written by an engineer of ability, but I have not gone over the calculations as I am inclined to agree with the writer that the works required would probably be quite impracticable upon the shifting sands of the River Dee. I apprehend that a tidal reservoir would almost always silt up as a matter of course.

I take the liberty of sending also a copy of the preface to my new

---

[1] Jevons in fact resigned his appointment at Liverpool on 7 June 1866. See Vol. I, p. 198.

[1] 'The Power of the Tides', *Engineering*, 1 (1866) 195–6. The author examined the possibilities of obtaining tidal power from the Dee Estuary and concluded that while it might be technically feasible it would be 'commercially impracticable'.

Edition.[2] You will see that I have ventured to quote a single sentence from one of the letters with which you have favoured me. I could not give more because your expressions were too flattering and I thought I might give as much as Mr. Gladstone had already mentioned the views you hold on the subject.

Now that a Royal Commission is to be appointed the subject must be left very much to them. Whatever[3] becomes of any particular views – it is not to be doubted I think that good must come out of an inquiry into the use of such an article as[4] Coal. The French seem to know the value of Coal better than do we who are careless of it and I am glad to find that the Prevost Paradol concludes an article in the Journal des Débats as follows:—

"Ce n'est pas seulement au profit de l'Angleterre, mais au profit du monde entier que va commencer cette sérieuse enquête sur cette réserve houillière qui est devenue la source principale de la force et du mouvement dans le monde."[5]

I have the honour to remain

My dear Sir,
Yours very faithfully,
W. S. Jevons.

261.   SIR JOHN F. W. HERSCHEL TO W. S. JEVONS

Collingwood
June 30/1866.

Dear Sir,

Many thanks to you for the Preface of your 2nd edition and for the extract you have been so good as to send me from the Engineer.[1]

I am far from denying (indeed in my general rejection of the notion of utilising tidal power on the grand scale I always kept a reservation in favour of such local cases) that in certain localities as in the Estuary of the Severn or in the Bay of Fundy[2] where the rise and fall of the tides is enormously increased by local circumstances (acting in effect something

---

[2] In this Jevons wrote that 'Sir John Herschel has most kindly expressed a general concurrence in my views', quoting a passage from Herschel's letter of 23 November 1865. *The Coal Question*, Preface to the second edition – page xxxix in third revised edition, 1906.

[3] 'Whether' was deleted here in the original manuscript.

[4] 'of' was deleted here in the original manuscript.

[5] Lucien Anatol Prevost-Paradol, *Journal des Débats Politiques et Littéraires*, 20 June 1866, p. 1. The author gave a brief account of the debates in Parliament on the coal question and emphasised the importance of considering future supplies.

[1] This reference to the *Engineer* was a mistake on Herschel's part; for the correct reference see above, Letter 260, n. 1, p. 122.

[2] Nova Scotia, 45°N, 65° 40′ W.

like the Hydraulic Ram) tidal force might perhaps be availably utilised – even now – much more so when coal becomes dearer.[3] Yet I still hold that as a *substitute for* our coal mines the whole tidal power which it is conceivable that human engineering could ever avail to utilise would be utterly insignificant. In the calculation which I sent you which was made hastily and carelessly – I must have neglected some points – as on going over it again I find the total answer for 1170 miles of coast laid under contribution by a tide basin 1000 feet broad and allowing 100000000 foot pounds for the work of 84 lbs of Coal would give an equivalent in Coal of 6818 tons per diem or $2\frac{1}{2}$ million tons per annum – i.e. half the consumption of London or about 23 Great Easterns kept constantly under full steam which after all is a fleabite compared to our actual annual expenditure of 96,000,000 tons.

Then too – for our iron works – we want not only *power* and *heat* which we shall have to find out of our tide power – at an immense expense of the original staple commodity. Who knows however whether before our coal is burnt out we shall not have devised the means to grind nitric acid out of atmospheric air or sulphuric out of Gypsum etc. (and so make the tides supply us with our great bases of Chemical power) as we now grind ice out of water and light and magnetism out of horsepower.

Thanks for your kind enquiries as to my health. I have had a *very severe* pull but am now able to get down stairs for some hours in the day, you will easily understand how very much I was disappointed by this untoward interruption of my visit to Manchester. I read the account of the proceedings with great interest. May I beg you to present my best regards to your Principal with thanks for his obliging letter, and believe me to remain

    Dear Sir,
        Yours very truly,
        J. F. W. Herschel.

262. W. S. JEVONS TO A. MACMILLAN
     [MA]

                                   Oban
                            4 July '66.

A. Macmillan, Esq.,

My dear Sir,

Having been out for the last week or more on a tour making myself acquainted with your delightful country I am not aware whether you

---

[3] Tidal power in the form here envisaged by Herschel has in fact been utilised since 1966 to produce electricity at the generating station on the estuary of the River Rance, between Dinard and St Malo.

have yet got the 2nd Ed. of the Coal Q. out. I suppose it must be ready by this time.

I omitted to mention before perhaps that I should be particularly glad if you would send a copy for review to the Editor – (Zerah Colburn) of the Journal "Engineering" your nearly opposite neighbour at 37 Bedford Street, C. Garden.[1]

The Review in the Times was on the whole very gratifying being fair and moderate.[2]

In case you should have anything to write to me my address may be on or before next Monday, Post Office, Inverness and till the Monday following, Post Office, Edinburgh.

I beg to remain,
My dear Sir,
Yours faithfully,
W. S. Jevons.

263.   E. LASPEYRES TO W. S. JEVONS

Basel.
7/7/1866.

My dear Sir!

It is very long that I received your kind letter which contained the valuable appendix of some prices not contained in Tooke's history of prices. I must beg pardon that I did not yet say you my utmost thanks, but I were in such a hurry of business, that it was wholy impossible. The one of those business was that I am about going from here to Riga in September. I have been named there Professor of political economy at the Baltican Polytechnikum.[1] The last time I were also occupied by the war in Germany[2] in such degree that I were not able to write.

The last time bevore your letter I were also very much occupied by the same subject you are about writing the variations of discount and its causes, but since I heard your intention to take upon yourselves this

---

[1] No doubt for the reasons stated in the opening paragraph of this letter, Jevons was apparently unaware that the *Coal Question* had been reviewed in *Engineering* for 15 June 1866 (I, 400–1). It was perhaps the only notice of the book which was both unfavourable and perceptive, ending with the words 'It is quite as likely that with the constant discoveries in science we shall yet require a gradually decreasing rather than an increasing supply of coal.'

[2] *The Times*, 26 June 1866, p. 12.

[1] The Riga Polytechnical School was established in 1861, but full courses only began to be taught there in 1863–4. Laspeyres was appointed Professor of Political Economy from 1 September 1866, and remained in Riga until 1869. In 1919 the Polytechnical School became the basis for the Latvian State University.

[2] The Seven Weeks War of June –July 1866, which arose out of the dispute between Austria and Prussia over Schleswig–Holstein.

difficult and interesting inquiry I desisted from my intention. I am very curious to compare the results of your researches and I say you already now my thank, that you promised to send me a copy. I am myself occupied with an essay on the wages in France and particularly in Paris founded on the two enquetes sur l'industrie de Paris 1847 and 1860 edited by the chambre of commerce, which contain a very rich material on all the conditions of the french labouring classes. I fear only that I shall not find much time in Riga. As soon as the work will be published, probably in French, I send you a copy.[3] My researches on prices have been interrupted for some time, for I must wait till the work of Mr. Rogers has been published, I regret that you wrote in your last letter, that you did not know, how soon it might appear and possibly I remind you also now too soon your kind promise to procure me from the author or the editor a copy for criticising it in one of our reviews. It should be heavy, if the work should not appear.[4] Your kind answer on this letter written in a hurry (what I beg to pardon) of bellicose accidences, I beg till the end of August to Basel, from September to Riga under the address of Professor *Nauck*.[5]

I am Sir your most obedient

Dr. E. Laspeyres.

264.   W. S. JEVONS TO MRS LUCY HUTTON
        [LJN, 229–30]

Durham.
Wednesday, 18th July, 1866.

. . . I hardly remember when I last wrote to you; it seems a long time ago. I have been to a great many places since. . . .

I was charmed with Edinburgh, the most beautiful city existing, I should think. It looks like a crowd of castles and monuments, or rather like two groups of castles and monuments on two hills, with all manner of fine buildings and gardens disposed between. I found the Manchester Theatre Company playing the *Midsummer Night's Dream* at Edinburgh just as at Manchester. . . . I enjoyed the play amazingly, having just read it over a few days before. It seemed to me perfectly suitable for acting, and wonderfully entertaining.

This morning I went from Newcastle to Monkwearmouth, and called

---

[3] The work was in fact published in German in 1869, as *Der Einfluss der Wohnung auf der Sittlichkeit. Eine moralstatistische Studie uber die arbeitenden Klassen der Stadt Paris.*

[4] The first two volumes of Thorold Rogers's *History of Agriculture & Prices* did appear in 1866.

[5] Ernst Nauck (1819–75), first Director and Professor of Chemistry, Physics and Mineralogy, Riga Polytechnical School, 1862–75.

on the manager and viewer of the large and celebrated colliery there.[1] They were very civil, seeming much interested in the *Coal Question,* which one of them had partly read, while the other was just beginning some experiments for the Royal Commission. They gave me every convenience for looking over the mine to its deepest parts. It was dreadfully hot and oppressive in some places, and the men worked naked. After two or three hours below I came up all grimy, and in a suit of mining clothes, in which you would not have known me.

The *Coal Question* seems to sell well in Newcastle. In one shop the man told me they had sold a *good few*, and had only two copies left. At the railway station I took up a copy there, and was much amused by the man saying, "Fine work that, sir. The first edition sold off very quick". There is a palpable want of truth about the latter part at least which takes away from the first.

I am pleased with Durham, and the cathedral and castle look grand. I shall stay most of to-morrow here to hear the service, which is said to be very finely performed. Then I go on to York, where I want to see the Minster. On Friday or Saturday I hope to get home to Manchester, after a tour of a most varied character.

Some time in the following week I hope to be with you at Clynnog; and I shall be glad to rest among friends, after so long coasting about among strangers. . . .

265.   TIMOTHY JEVONS TO W. S. JEVONS

St. Michael's Hamlet
Sept 30 [1866]

Dear Stanley

I expect that by this time you will have got back to Birch Grove, to be ready for the Feast you will doubtless enjoy next week at the Social Science meetings.[1] I hope you have enjoyed your wanderings the last few months, and all the various *occupations* you have been engaged at, *some* of which we have heard from *Lucy*. I am only sorry you have not favoured us with your company for a few days at the Hamlet, during your vacation; though I fear we have no *work* for you here to put your hands to. However, enough of that sort of chaff, and I will come to the object of my writing to you now. I want you to take up the subject of the *Labour*

---

[1] Jevons made several references to the Monkwearmouth colliery in *The Coal Question*. One of the deepest pits in Britian at the time, it had been commenced in 1826, and in 1845 had reached a depth of 1,794 feet. *The Coal Question*, third edition, pp. xxxvii, 57 and 89.

[1] The National Association for the Promotion of Social Science met in Manchester from 3 to 10 October 1866.

question, in all its bearings on the Country. It is really becoming the great question of the day, and its importance on the future welfare and prosperity of the Country, cannot be over estimated. I do not at all mean in a *Political* sense; but *solely* in an *Economical* point of view; for the working classes are now fast becoming the controllers of our most important manufactures, (by means of their combinations and unions,) and, with or without *votes*, are gaining enormous influence on the commercial interests of the Country. In our business as Iron Merchants, we are continually hearing of the despotic tyranny they display in their conduct towards the Iron Masters, who are now positively afraid of them, and hardly dare speak to them. There is a strike now pending in the Cleveland Iron district, against a reduction of wages, the issue of which is very uncertain, though it has continued for several months. The manufacture of Iron has become a losing business with the Masters, owing to the long continued depression of business, and the competition with Foreign Manufacturers; and yet the men will not submit to any reduction of wages from the highest point. We know it for a fact, from our own experience, that the French and Belgians have been supplying the Continental demand for Iron for the last 2 or 3 years; and have supplanted English Iron almost entirely by their lower prices. Our business with the Continent has dwindled away to nothing, owing to that cause; and we have no end of letters telling us, in reply to our quotations and solicitations for orders, that the writers can buy what they want cheaper in France and Belgium. What then is to be done? Until lately England was the cheapest market in the world for Iron, and now we are undersold by our nearest neighbours. The wages now demanded by our workmen are double what their Fathers and predecessors were paid for the same kind of work; and yet they will not submit to any reduction. Is England then to lose its prestige[2]

The following exchange of letters (266–70) in the *Manchester Examiner and Times* and the *Manchester City News*, arose out of the delivery, on 12 October 1866, of Jevons's *Introductory Lecture on the importance of diffusing a Knowledge of Political Economy*. Since Jevons's two letters, of 19 October and 1 November, were prompted by the criticisms of other correspondents, the letters of these correspondents are reproduced here also.

Jevons's reaction to the controversy is given in the Journal (see the entry for 1 November 1866, Vol. I, pp. 207–8) and the lecture itself is reprinted in Vol. VII. See also W. H. Chaloner, 'Jevons in Manchester: 1863–76', *The Manchester School*, 40 (1972) 73–82 (pp. 77–8).

[2] The remainder of the original letter is missing. The concern expressed by Timothy Jevons about foreign competition and the growth of trade unionism was typical of the views of ironmasters at this time. See D. L. Burn, *The Economic History of Steel-Making* (Cambridge, 1940) chapter 1.

266. 'A BRITISH WORKMAN' TO THE EDITOR OF THE *MANCHESTER EXAMINER AND TIMES*[1]

TRADES' UNIONS.

Sir,

Many persons will have read with interest and pleasure Professor Jevons' lecture on political economy, reported in your issue of last Saturday; and some will have noted with regret the following sentence in it: "These organisations (trades' unions), as the *Times* stated the other day, were pitiless as they were powerful, and such atrocities as that reported from Sheffield were but extreme instances of the tyranny which at this moment is paralysing the trade of a large part of the country." Now, sir, I put it to common fairness whether it is just or honest to speak of a diabolical attempt to blow up a workman's house as if it were the deliberate action of a trades' union, unanimously resolved upon and executed by a special deputation! In the trades' union to which I belong each member is expressly told, upon entering, that he is not to use any intimidation to induce men to join the union or comply with its rules, yet violence has, I grieve to say, occasionally been used by some of our members during trade disputes; but no man ever inferred from this that the trade union ordered an oppositionist to be thrashed. Teachers of political economy may find real faults enough in our trades' unions without noticing the base and irrational insinuations of the *Times*.—

If you kindly print this you will oblige

A BRITISH WORKMAN.

163, Higher Cambridge-street,
Chorlton-upon-Medlock, October 15, 1866.

267. 'A COBDENITE' TO THE EDITOR OF THE *MANCHESTER EXAMINER AND TIMES*[1]

THE COBDEN LECTURESHIP, OWENS COLLEGE.

Sir,

I was glad to observe in your issue of this morning a letter from a working man complaining of the partizan view expressed by Professor Jevons on the subject of strikes. As one who voted at the meeting of

[1] Published in the issue of 17 October 1866.
[1] Published in the issue of 19 October 1866.

subscribers to the Cobden memorial fund that a portion of that fund should be devoted to the endowment of a lectureship on political economy at Owens College, I venture to express my disappointment that the introductory discourse of the "Cobden lecturer" was by no means consonant with that enlarged and genial sympathy for the masses which pre-eminently distinguished the illustrious reformer whose name and services this lectureship was to commemorate. I felt, on reading your report, that the address of Professor Jevons was calculated to aggravate that distrust of economical science amongst working men which it was the main object of this lectureship to remove. It was essentially a plea for the employer, to the detriment of the employed. This opinion has been expressed to me by several intelligent artisans. These men alleged that, while strikes were most unsparingly, not to say unfairly, handled, "lockouts" were not mentioned. Now, "lockouts" interfere as seriously with the labourer selling his labour in the dearest market as strikes may interfere with the master buying his labour in the cheapest. If, therefore, strikes are opposed to the principles of political economy, so are "lockouts". Why, then, did not the professor protest against the "ignorance" of many capitalists? Far better would it have been if the Cobden lecturer had shown by what means strikes and lock-outs could have been superseded to the advantage both of employer and employed. Assuredly such a course would have been more in harmony with the spirit of Richard Cobden, and more conducive to the true interests of this commercial community.

But the least satisfactory feature of this preliminary lecture was the political animus which evidently inspired the lecturer. Though avowing that the professors at Owens College had nothing to do with politics, he discussed at length the political objections to strikes, and even to the enfranchisement of the working classes. This, I respectfully submit, was injudicious in the extreme, especially for a "Cobden lecturer", whose task should have been – as it would have been with Richard Cobden – to propitiate, rather than to estrange the working classes.

If ignorance of the fundamental principles of political economy be a political disqualification, does not the objection apply to the upper as well as to the lower classes; for who exhibited such gross ignorance of economical laws during the anti - corn - law agitation as the very class who now wish to withhold the franchise from the people – the aristocracy? Despite their ignorance, they are allowed to monopolise one whole House to themselves, as well as two - thirds of the other.

The assumption of the professor that "most of the upper classes in this country" desired"to introduce a large part of the working classes to the franchise" is opposed to facts, since they recently rejected the most moderate Reform Bill ever submitted to parliament by a Liberal ministry. I have no wish, however, to enlarge upon the political question on this occasion; I am merely anxious to observe that the "Cobden lecturer" should be the last public teacher to disparage the claims of those whose welfare was so dear to the immortal "Manchester Manufacturer."

A COBDENITE.

Moss Side,   October 17, 1866.

268.   W. S. JEVONS TO THE EDITOR OF THE *MANCHESTER EXAMINER AND TIMES*[1]

Sir,

The letter of a "British Workman", in your issue of the 17th instant has only come to my notice this morning. May I be allowed to explain that, in quoting a certain sentence from the *Times,* in my introductory lecture at Owens College, I had no intention whatever of implying that the trades' unions were chargeable with the late outrage at Sheffield. As to the letter of a "Cobdenite", in this morning's *Examiner,* I beg altogether, and most emphatically, to deny that I advocated the employers' interests, or took a partisan view of the question of strikes. I advocated what I believe to be the workman's true interest as well as that of the whole country – that strikes should cease. There are such abundant openings for the employment of capital here and abroad that we may be sure the capitalists will in the long run take care of themselves. The men are injuring themselves more than anyone else. In this opinion I have been confirmed by the writings of Dr. John Watts, the secretary of the Cobden Memorial Committee, than whom it would be hard to find a more sincere, enlightened, and, as far as I can presume to judge, a more sound friend of the working classes. Dr. Watts seems to me to have conclusively proved, by actual computation, that strikes are a dead loss to the workmen, even more than to any class in the community. And he has admirably pointed out that the energy, endurance, and skill, in combination, which the men display during a strike has only to be properly applied to make the men their own masters, acquainted with the sweet as well as the bitter side of capital. I do not know what "Cobdenite" means by "propitiating the working class". Does he mean that the Cobden lecturer ought to disguise or distort what he conceives to be the truth, because it is not at present accepted by certain of the working classes? This ill accords with the character of a Cobdenite, nor is it what I conceive to be the duty of a teacher, in searching after and disseminating the truth. I think, indeed,

[1] Published in the issue of 22 October 1866.

that in a college class room it is best for a lecturer to keep to his subject, and I abstain there from political questions. But in a public lecture on the importance of a knowledge of economy it seemed impossible to avoid alluding to the political side of the question. For my part I wish to see cherished and developed in England such liberalism as Mr. Mill has deliberately described in his brief but great essay on liberty. I referred to the mistaken actions of workmen in strikes, because they tend to retard the advent of reforms political and commercial. "Cobdenite" says that it would have been far better if the Cobden lecturer had shown by what means strikes and lock-outs could have been superseded to the advantage of both employer and employed. This I did attempt to do briefly in a portion of my lecture which was omitted in the abridged newspaper report. Co-operation and the saving of capital form the panacea. Every workman should, in my humble opinion, be more or less of a capitalist, and in every trade a considerable portion of the mills, factories, and works should in time be owned by workmen and managed by their deputies. The workmen will thus have in their own hands the means of breaking up combinations or lock-outs of the masters, and of becoming informed precisely concerning the employers' side of the question as well as their own. It avails not to say that the men cannot save the money. The large sums raised by unions to support strikes, and the loss of comforts endured by those engaged in them, show what vast funds could be raised if the men had half the perseverance and abstinence in making their own fortunes that they have in marring alike the fortunes of themselves and their employers I think I am doing far better in pointing out these plain truths than in trying "to propitiate the working class".

W. Stanley Jevons.

9, Birch Grove, Rusholme, 19th October.

269.   W. MACDONALD[1] TO THE EDITOR OF THE *MANCHESTER CITY NEWS*[2]

TRADE OUTRAGES. – PROFESSOR JEVONS ON THE MORAL CHARACTER OF ASSOCIATED LABOUR.

Sir,

It seems almost a profanity to offer up that petition, "Give us this day our daily bread," while our bakers are starving. The same Manchester

---

[1] William Macdonald, housepainter and early trades union pioneer in Manchester; at this time secretary of the Manchester Alliance, the strongest of a number of housepainters' unions in the area, founded in 1852; one of the thirty-three delegates who attended the first Trades Union

that may be said to have fed the people of Britain, is permitting a large portion of her own industrious citizens to be ground to death by overwork, or to find homes in our infirmary and workhouses. It is miserable policy to reduce men to the condition of patients and paupers, and then grant them in charity what was due to them in wages. The trades' societies and their council seem the only good Samaritans to lend a helping hand to the bakers in their struggle. But every bread eater who has had his share in consuming the half of the bakers' wages is bound in justice to make some return. And if our economists were imbued with a fine sense of public interest, they would calculate what is due to the baker for his loss in low wages and long hours; for until he is restored or elevated to a true position in civil society, we can hardly, without offending the ear of heaven, lift up our voices and say, "Give us this day our daily bread."

The master baker is like other men, he is the victim himself of a vicious system and false opinions, propagated to maintain class interest, and not the welfare of society. The employer is told that his men are "ignorant, tyrannical, and rebellious;" that every combination is a league against him and his capital, or that the honour of his order is at stake in opposing the claims of the workmen; that the prosperity of commerce and national interests all depend on his keeping his workmen in due subjection; and if one claim is yielded it only makes way for another. How often has this selfish sophistry been employed to resist a fair claim and block up the path of progress. The moral and social maxims that ought to promote truth and equity between the strong and weak members of the same community are perverted to pamper greatness, rank, and wealth; but why should not science be quoted to uphold white slavery, when black slavery can be preached from Scripture?

Sir, I have been so busy with my fellow operatives, the bakers, that no time has been left me to notice the opening address of the Cobden Lectures at Owens College. Professor W. S. Jevons will excuse me when I say that this is the first time I have seen the name of the immortal Cobden associated with such sentiments. I am far from questioning the lecturer's high attainments. He may have fathomed the depths of the coal question, be a profound geologist, and an infallible mathematician, and able to discern the flow and ebb of national wealth in its great ocean and minor channels. But the character, wants, and aspirations of that class from whose brain and muscle all that wealth springs he does not so well

Congress in Manchester in June 1868; author of *The True Story of Trades Unions contrasted with the caricatures and fallacies of the pretended economists being a reply to Dr. John Watts, Professor Jevons . . . and others* (Manchester, 1867). This was a pamphlet consisting of eight letters from Macdonald, originally published in the *Manchester City News* between August and December 1866, on the subject of trade disputes in Manchester involving joiners, bakers and housepainters.

² Published in the issue of 27 October 1866.

understand. I am proud to acknowledge myself as one of that class – never having been able to reach the halls of Oxford University. I am a graduate of that college which had George Combe for its professor of moral philosophy, and Richard Cobden for its political economist. He was the apostle of free-trade – Professor Jevons is only the bishop. The working classes of England were free-traders long, long before the learned and ruling classes embraced the doctrine. To show that I have not forgotten my first lesson, let it be given as I had it from the teacher's lips 25 years ago: "Buy in the cheapest market and sell in the dearest." Buying in the cheapest market is simply purchasing where the necessaries of life are most abundant, and selling in the dearest, carrying them to where they are most wanted; thereby using the blessings of Providence to the best advantage. The selfishness, the benevolence, and conscientiousness of men have full scope in obeying this maxim; and hence this new gospel has spread and worked gigantic miracles in regenerating and uniting mankind in a common brotherhood. It is, however, affirmed that trades' societies are monopolies. I reply that they are monopolies only in the same sense that capital is a monopoly. The small capitalist must often sell to a disadvantage, and suffer great loss thereby; the same as an individual workman, whose necessities are ever pressing on him, would be often obliged to sell his labour in the cheapest market. By combination he is able to wait for weeks until his terms are accepted. To ask the workmen to lay aside their unions is equivalent to telling the largest capitalist to forego the advantages of his wealth, or a joint-stock company to break themselves up into individual traders. The editor of our Liberal Manchester paper once observed on the loss of the South Lancashire Election, that landlordism was in itself an organisation which must be met by counter organisation. The same might be said of capital.

The employer who can set to work a thousand men has in his hands a power equal to that thousand united, and it is only when they are united that they can be called free workmen – free to accept or reject the terms offered them by one employer. To argue that labour will always get full justice without resorting to combination is a fallacy contradicted by all experience. Why could the corn laws not be repealed without a league? For what purpose do the Reform and the Conservative Clubs exist, the Union and Emancipation Association, and all the leagues and Reform Societies at the present day; the innumerable societies of lawyers, doctors, &c.? The leading distinction between masters' associations and workmen's is this, that while employers have very often used their organisation to suppress the workmen's union – the engineers are a case in point – no single instance can be adduced where workmen, however powerful, have made a like tyrannical attempt. The oppression of the workmen is not to be proved by learned declamation, but by facts and instances. Professor Jevons, however, knows little about trades unions, and takes up with such second-hand descriptions as he can fall in with, and places himself at the mercy of the London *Times* for his information. In his lecture above referred to, delivered on Friday, October 12th, at Owens College, and reported in the *Examiner and Times,* he says: "These organisations, as the *Times* stated the other day, were pitiless as they were powerful, and such atrocities as that reported from Sheffield were but extreme instances of the tyranny which at this moment is paralysing the trade of a large part of the country." On Monday last, after a remonstrance from "A British Workman", he observes: "May I be allowed to explain that in quoting a certain sentence from the *Times,* I had no intention whatever of implying that the trades' unions were chargeable with the late outrage at Sheffield." The charge of conniving at assassination is withdrawn, but he need not have been so particular; its circulation has served the purpose of the *Times,* and it is as well supported as the other portion of the Professor's indictment against trades societies. He still maintains that they are pitiless as they are powerful, tyrannical, ignorant, at the mercy of the prevailing opinion of a few workmen and often a few leaders of the union. The saw-grinders of Sheffield are so far from shielding the intended assassin, that they offer a reward and every assistance for his discovery, and there are grave doubts whether the whole thing be not a plot to strike horror into the public mind, and raise a false prejudice against extending the franchise to working men. The enemies of liberty are in desperate circumstances, and spare no means to stem the tide of democracy. There is, a real murderer, proved but not convicted – ex-Governor Eyre – a man whom our governors are screening from justice and the laws of England, because he was a governor, and belongs to their union. The *Times* is the greatest slanderer in the press. On one occasion it imputed the pleasant contemplation with which John Bright would divide the land of the country. Cobden's masterly exposure of the venomous calumny was a fine example of that incisive logic for which he was so distinguished, and the great editor, after eating his filthy words, shrunk back into his assassin darkness, with the pity and contempt of every honest man.

Professor Jevons's mission in Manchester is to "disseminate among the working class a comprehension of the principles of political economy." "It was desirable that this instruction should be given at a very early age, to prepare them for a proper use of the franchise, 'the present unions causing great uneasiness to those who were entrusted with the government of the country.'" The uneasiness is mutual, for the people generally are much troubled with the members sent to Parliament by the upper classes. Robert Lowe is one of this class, and his follower in the cave of Adullam. Mr. Robert Lowe is very high in "economic knowledge," but in principle remarkably low. He does not admit any morality into his aristocracy and the governing party for the time being. We ignorant unionists have been able to find this out, and we have very queer suspicions that he intends further to confine the electoral monopoly to the hands of its present possessors. Professor Jevons should demand free trade in legislation, in land, and education, as well as in labour, for these monopolies are a real tyranny, and a bar to the progress of England. It is to be feared that Oxford itself, the great university, has some elements of monopoly about it. Let that be looked to. Suppose we test the ancient institution by its political creed and its present representative in Parliament; I must be forgiven, but I have forgot his name. But it lately had a gentleman, a scholar, an orator, a statesman to represent it, in the person of Mr. Gladstone. He possessed all the qualifications, and only lost his seat because he was a free-trader. "A little learning is a dangerous thing," but a great deal seems more dangerous still to true liberty; and the great man came to Lancashire and stood a contest for a seat for that county. He won in spite of all the influence of monopoly. The enthusiastic shout in Market-street, Manchester, at the close of the poll told that he had the suffrages of every workman in his favour. After such an example as this our Cobden lecturer need not fear that the people will err in choosing a proper person to send to Parliament. It is equally true that our chancellor is at present on strike, with all the best workmen at his back. The Government shops are filled with knobsticks, who never did a piece of good work in their lives; their only claim to a job is that they have been long idle and have large families to support and expenses running on. It is supposed that they have got hold of some moulds and patterns belonging to the late workmen, and intend to try them in the market as their own. Whenever the imposture is found out the nation itself will strike, and demand their dismissal, to make room for the honest, skilled workmen, with the great foreman at their head.

Yours truly,

W. Macdonald.

57, Coupland-street, October 25.

270.   W. S. JEVONS TO THE EDITOR OF THE *MANCHESTER
CITY NEWS* [1]

TRADE OUTRAGES.

Sir,

In answer to Mr. Macdonald, will you allow me to say, I never desired that workmen should lay aside their unions. The following are the words I used in the introductory lecture of the Cobden course, at Owens College, criticised in your columns:—"Let it be distinctly understood that it is not against the existence of combinations the political economist protests. We cannot have too much co-operation and combination among men for purposes in accordance with the laws of nature and the laws of the country. All classes of people, all districts, and villages should have their unions, institutions, societies, and meetings of various kinds. And it is highly desirable, at the same time, that every class of tradesmen and workmen should meet in their societies and unions to exchange information and assistance, and to concert every means of really and permanently benefiting their own body and the community. Any matter concerning the convenience and health of the workmen, such as the length and arrangement of the hours of labour, and the time for meals, the allowance of holidays, the mode and time of paying wages, the wholesomeness and safety of factories, should be discussed by workmen among themselves in their own unions. But this is where the want of a knowledge of economy and the laws of the working of society is so indispensable. When they pass from these matters, in which an employer should consult the welfare of his men collectively, to regulate or raise the rate of wages, or to enforce equality of earnings, they bring their own and others' welfare into peril."

In any manufacture there are some arrangements which are at the will of the employer or his men, and in these I think the employer ought to defer to the comfort of his men. But the rate of wages, and the demand and supply of labour, are things which cannot be regulated at the will of anyone. They depend upon the natural advantages of the country or the locality, the abundance of capital attracted to the trade, the course of foreign commerce, the state of the money market, and many other causes. Trades unions cannot alter or govern these things; they cannot, therefore, raise wages at all in the long run. They may seem now and then to gain an advantage of five or ten per cent., but they cannot tell how much capital they drive away from a branch of trade by each strike or forced concession. There is no such thing among employers as a rule to prevent

---

[1] Published in the issue of 3 November 1866. Further letters from W. Macdonald, to which Jevons did not reply, appeared in this same issue and those of 10 November and 15 December 1866.

or force the bringing of new capital into a trade. The movement and investment of capital is perfectly free. It is only by attracting new capital to a trade that wages can be permanently and truly raised in it. And yet workmen will not trust in their own case to the operation of free trade and free industry.

Mr. Macdonald need not tell me I "should demand free trade in legislation, in land and education, as well as in labour." I do demand and expect these things – if not from the present, then from a reformed Parliament. I hope to see land bought and sold as freely and easily as the funds. I hope to see every child educated, and every exception to the equality of all classes before the laws of justice removed. But after devoting myself to the study of those principles of free industry on which our prosperity mainly depends, I must say that my heart somewhat sinks when I observe most of the intelligent artisans of England act dead against those principles and their own true interests. I do not know whether it is by good or ill fortune that my labours are, even in the slightest degree, connected with the high name of Cobden. But I am certain that I should be wholly unworthy of any connection with that name if I failed to uphold unflinchingly the truth of those principles of freedom which he upheld.

I hope to see the time when workmen will be to a great extent their own capitalists. If trades' unions, with all the skill in organisation which they possess, and all the funds at their command, would only devote their energy to the erection of co-operative mills and works, they might readily attain all they desire, to the best of my judgment. When they find it necessary to contend with a group of illiberal employers, they should do it by planting mills or works in their midst, owned and managed by workmen and their deputies. This is the way in which wages may be permanently raised and the exclusive interests of capital effectually destroyed. I believe that a movement of workmen towards co-operation in the raising of capital would be anticipated by employers admitting their men to a considerable share of their profits. This has already been done by a few employers with excellent results to their men and themselves. I beg to join my small voice to that of men like Mr. Mill, Prof. Fawcett, Dr. Watts, and Mr. Hughes, who say that a new era will open to the workmen of England when they take measures for sharing in the possession, management, and profits of capital. They cannot do without capital, and therefore they ought themselves to hold and enjoy a large portion of it.

Yours truly,
W. Stanley Jevons.

Owens College, 1st November, 1866.

271. W. S. JEVONS TO A. MACMILLAN
[MA]

9 Birch Grove
Rusholme.
7th Nov. 66.

My dear Sir,

I shall be happy to undertake to prepare a logic of the size of Roscoe's Chemistry.¹ I will certainly not exceed 400 pages and I will try to make it less in quantity than Roscoe's, as I should like the type to be leaded somewhat to make the page lighter.

The arrangement I should prefer is certainly that of half profits.

I am glad to hear that Fawcett is writing a small Pol. Econ. as I hope it will suit my evening students.²

Is it indispensable to call the divisions of the book Lessons? I should rather prefer *Chapters* but of course I will make it as you think best.

I have not heard how the Coal Question is selling since the first week or two after the appearance of the 2nd Ed. I should be happy if you could let me [know]³ at your perfect convenience.*

Yours very faithfully,
W. S. Jevons

* have a *general notion* how it is going.

272. W. S. JEVONS TO THE EDITOR OF *THE TIMES*¹

Sir,

In the report of a lecture reprinted in The Times of the 16th inst., I am reported to have said concerning the working of deep coal, that "no one was so absurd as to suppose that they should ever get to that depth" (4,000 ft.). What I said, however, was that no one could suppose we should work out the coal to that depth in 100 years, or any such period. I

---

¹ H. E. Roscoe, *Lessons in Elementary Chemistry* (1866), part of 'Macmillan's School Class Books' series.

² It was not Fawcett but his wife, Millicent Garrett Fawcett, who wrote *Political Economy for Beginners,* first published by Macmillan in 1870. In the Preface she explained how 'when I was helping my husband to prepare a third edition of his *Manual of Political Economy*, it occurred to us both that a small book, explaining as briefly as possible the most important principles of the science, would be useful to beginners and would perhaps be an assistance to those who are desirous of introducing the study of Political Economy into schools'.

³ In the original manuscript Jevons stroked out the word 'know' and substituted the phrase which follows his signature, indicating the continuation by an asterisk.

¹ Published in the issue of 20 November 1866.

believe that fine seams of coal may easily be followed to a greater depth than 4,000 ft., the question being entirely one of cost.

Yours obediently,
W. S. Jevons.

Owens' College, Manchester, Nov., 16.

273.   W. S. JEVONS TO J. MILLS[1]
    [TLJM, 336–7]

9 Birch Grove, Rusholme.
November 23, 1866.

My dear Sir,

I have been wishing not only to thank you for the copy of your pamphlet[2] which you kindly sent me, but to tell you how thoroughly I concur in all the opinions you have expressed. So much nonsense was talked at the Social Science Association, and so much is constantly talked about currency and the bank, that I was delighted when I saw from the brief report of your paper how thoroughly you supported the principle of the Bank Act. You seem to me to bring out in the most convincing manner that instead of the Bank Act being the cause of the disaster, it really saved us from we know not how worse a disaster.

At the same time you do not deny, if I read your paper rightly, that the banking system somewhere wants a little correction. This is strongly shown in the pamphlets of Mr. J. B. Smith[3] and Mr. David Baxter.[4] The conduct of the great J-S [sic] banks is obviously reckless, and their dependence on the Bank of England altogether unsound. It is the position of the banking department, not the issue department, which is anomalous and dangerous, and that of course is in no way regulated by law, but by custom.

The fact is, the panic in the spring was caused by bad banking, not by bad currency; and it is proposed to remedy things by giving over the issue of currency to those who have brought us to the verge of national bankruptcy.

---

[1] John Mills (1821–96) began his career as a clerk in the Manchester and Liverpool District Bank, 1838; became manager of the Nantwich Branch, 1852, and of the Bowdon Branch, 1864; drew up plans for the Lancashire and Yorkshire Bank which opened in Manchester, 1872, and was its general manager until 1889. Succeeded Jevons as President of the Manchester Statistical Society, 1871–3.

[2] John Mills, 'The Bank Charter Act and the late Panic', read to the National Association for the Promotion of Social Science at Manchester on 5 October 1866, and subsequently reprinted as a pamphlet (24 pp., Manchester, 1866).

[3] John Benjamin Smith, *An Inquiry into the causes of money panics, and of the frequent fluctuations in the rate of discount* (Manchester, 1866).

[4] Presumably a reference to Robert Dudley Baxter, *The Panic of 1866 with its Lessons on the Currency Act* (1866).

The *Publishers' Circular*[5] of November 15 carelessly describes you as an opponent of the Bank Act.

    Believe, my dear Sir,

         Yours very faithfully,
         W. S. Jevons.

274. W. S. JEVONS TO THE EDITOR OF *THE TIMES*[1]

IRONMASTERS AND IRONWORKERS.

Sir,

Without in the least attempting to anticipate the important information which we may expect from your correspondents at Brussels, Messrs. Creed and Williams,[2] may I be allowed to point out a great peculiarity of the iron trade, which partially explains the present position of that trade? It is that while the means for the production of iron remain constant or nearly so, the home demand for iron undergoes great fluctuations according to the amount of capital which is being invested in railways, bridges, factories, and other large permanent erections, which absorb much solid material. If the prices and qualities of timber, bricks, and the metals consumed were examined for many years back there would be found a remarkable excess of demand for these materials at times of great prosperity, when a large fixation of capital is in progress. Iron is, of all articles, the most affected by this varying demand. The following account of the average price of British bar iron in each year since 1845, drawn from monthly quotations in the *Economist* newspaper, will be sufficient to show this:—

Year.	£	s.	Year.	£	s.
1845	9	5	1856	9	1
1846	9	11	1857	8	8
1847	9	15	1858	7	4
1848	7	4	1859	7	0
1849	6	5	1860	6	11
1850	5	18	1861	6	5
1851	5	11	1862	6	5
1852	6	4	1863	7	0
1853	9	5	1864	8	7
1854	9	18	1865	7	17
1855	8	11	1866	7	11

[5] *Publisher's Circular*, 15 November 1866, p. 716, lists Mills's pamphlet with the comment 'The writer is an opponent of the Bank Act of 1844'.

[1] Published in the issue of 17 December 1866.

[2] H. Herries Creed and Walter Williams, Junior, published a series of letters in *The Times* under the heading 'Foreign Competition with British Manufactures', comparing the economic position of

It is apparent that the price of bar iron was very high during the periods of years 1845, 1847, and 1853–7, when much capital was in course of investment in railway and other fixed works. The revulsions both of 1847 and 1857 were followed by considerable depressions of price.

Since 1862 another variation of the same kind has taken place, and if we look to the present sudden cessation of railway schemes, produced by the late pressure in the money-market, to the temporary suspension of the iron ship building trade, and to the general absence of all speculative or large undertakings, it is apparent that the home demand will be reduced for several years to come.

The effect of these variations upon our foreign trade is at once apparent; a large home demand so raises the price that foreigners are enabled to compete with us. This is partly the reason why during the last two or three years we have been quite cut out of the continental market, and have been partially undersold in other markets, or almost in our own. It is now, when the home demand is falling, that we shall be enabled to compete on something like our old terms with continental producers. I am informed by merchants engaged in the trade that the continental demand is already showing signs of revival from the moderate fall of prices accomplished. I am far from denying, at the same time, that Continental iron and steel makers are advancing upon us in a manner which should make us look round very carefully.

But what I should wish now to point out is the suicidal character of any attempt, either on the side of the masters or the men, to maintain, during a period of depressed home demand, a high range of prices and wages only warranted in a period of brisk demand. The result, if accomplished, would infallibly be the destruction of one of the most important branches of our foreign trade. The fact, however, is that an endeavour of the kind must break down, and can only lead to an increased loss of employment in the iron and many other trades, to a withdrawal of capital, and to a generally contracted and possibly bankrupt state of the trade.

It is said that one firm in South Wales lost a Russian order for 40,000 tons by hesitating to make a reduction of price. It is especially to be hoped that the ironworkers of South Wales will not be induced to resist the notice for a reduction of wages lately given. A strike now must inflict great loss and suffering upon them, and cannot possibly succeed. We have seen how disastrous to the men, at least, has been the strike in the Middlesborough district. A similar reduction cannot long be avoided in South Staffordshire. If I am rightly informed the iron trade there is in an

---

Belgium and England. The first letter, written from Brussels on 4 December 1866, was published on 11 December; the second appeared on 24 December. The letters were subsequently reprinted as a pamphlet, entitled *Handicraftsmen and Capitalists*. Cf. below, Letter 278, p. 151.

unsound condition; the masters cannot profitably carry on their business at present prices and wages, nor can they stop their works; nor do they venture to propose a reduction of wages. Such a state of things can only redound to the injury of all concerned. If the men demand higher wages than the condition of the trade warrants they will run the risk of losing their employment altogether, and deferring and lessening their own future prosperity from a returning period of activity. A seasonable reduction will result in benefit to all, especially to the operatives. It alone can enable us to recover our position in the foreign trade, and to lay the basis of renewed prosperity a few years hence in home and foreign undertakings.

But I must say, Sir, I am often inclined to think that the masters are to blame for the difficulties they encounter with their men. It is because the masters are always thought to be making secret, but vast profits that their men display profound distrust in all negotiations. I believe that this secret system of trade is beginning to be broken down by the prevalence of joint-stock concerns, of which the profits are known to many, the accounts being submitted to an auditor, and the balance-sheet made more or less public. The sooner publicity is substituted for secrecy the better for the interests of all. It will then be practicable to combine the interest of masters and men by the division of all profits exceeding a certain fixed amount – say 10 per cent. This arrangement, which has worked so well in the case of the Messrs. Briggs's collieries, seems to me the only panacea for the unreasonable contest between capital and labour. So long as the masters surround their accounts with mystery they may make large profits one year, but may expect at another time to be driven into losses and difficulties by the distrust and resistance of their men. Few can doubt that the present relations of capital and labour are becoming very threatening to the prosperity of trade, and everything seems to point to the advantage that would be derived from the union of interests long advocated by Mr. Mill and Professor Fawcett.

Yours obediently,
W. STANLEY JEVONS.

Owen's College, Manchester, Dec. 13.

275.   *W. S. JEVONS TO THE EDITOR OF THE TIMES*[1]

Sir,

The dreadful colliery explosions which happened on the 12th and 13th inst. are not improbably connected with a rapid fall of the barometer which was proceeding at the time. If so, they are undoubtedly preventable, and lie upon the national conscience. Considering the dire importance of the subject, you will perhaps allow me to explain the nature of the connexion as far as I can. I impute blame to no particular persons, and regard the explosions merely as natural events, which may have natural causes under the average degree of caution observed in coal-pits.

We should remember, in the first place, that two distinct causes are needed to produce an explosion:—

1. The cause which leads to the fouling of the air.
2. The cause which ignites the explosive mixture of gas and air.

These are quite independent. The air may be foul for days without an accident, but the first lamp that is then opened occasions the death of hundreds.

The fall of the barometer is evidently a cause which will lead to the fouling of the air in a pit. For the diminution of atmospheric pressure which it indicates is felt in the pit just as on the surface, and the consequence is that all inflammable gas accumulated in crevices of the coal, in grooves in vacant spaces left by the partial fall of the roof, or that possibly which lies by its low specific gravity in cavities of the roof in tranquil, remote parts of the pit, expands slightly. Thus, if the barometer fall one inch, all accumulations of gas give off one-thirtieth part of their bulk, so that a vast addition may suddenly be made to the ordinary evolution of the gas. Now, ventilating arrangements which may be quite adequate to carry off the gas in ordinary circumstances, and keep it fully below the exploding point, may be quite inadequate when a sudden addition is made to the inflammable gas involved.

From the table of the variations of the barometer below it will be seen that between 9 a.m. on Tuesday, the 11th, and 3 p.m. on Thursday, the 13th, the barometer fell one inch. On Wednesday, at 1 p.m., the great explosion at the Oaks occurred; on Thursday, at 11 a.m., the second explosion at Tunstall occurred. These two coincidences alone would prove nothing; but similar coincidences between explosions and falls of the barometer are well known to persons engaged in coalmining to have happened before. When it is added that the physical connexion or reason of the coincidence is evident, a serious probability arises that we have here the cause of these terrible events.

[1] Published in the issue of 22 December 1866.

The subject, however, is not free from some difficulties. I give below a table of the variations of the barometer since the beginning of the month, which has been kindly furnished to me by Mr. Bryan, optician, of Manchester:—

1866 December		9 a.m. Inches.		3 p.m. Inches..	9 p.m. Inches.
Saturday,	1st	29.86		29.78	29.74
Sunday,	2d	29.73		29.70	29.60
Monday,	3d	29.59		29.53	29.52
Tuesday,	4th	29.48		29.44	29.57
Wednesday,	5th	29.70		29.74	29.81
Thursday,	6th	29.84		29.51	29.36
Friday,	7th	29.29		29.32	29.70
Saturday,	8th	30.24		30.37	30.45
Sunday,	9th	30.18		29.89	29.84
Monday,	10th	30.03		30.14*	30.22
Tuesday,	11th	30.34		30.31	29.13
Wednesday,	12th	29.76	**	29.70	29.73
Thursday,	13th	29.36	**	29.35	29.34
Friday,	14th	29.34		29.36	29.43
Saturday,	15th	29.44		29.35	29.40
Sunday,	16th	29.59		29.70	29.94

** This mark indicates the occurrence of an explosion.

It appears that throughout this period the atmosphere has been in a remarkably perturbed condition. There have been four considerable falls of the barometer since the beginning of the month, as follows:—

1st, 9 a.m., to 4th, 3 p.m.	Fall,	.42 inch.
6th, 9 a.m., to 7th, 9 a.m.	"	.55 inch.
8th, 9 p.m., to 9th, 9 p.m.	"	.61 inch.
11th, 9 a.m. to 13th, 9 p.m.	"	1.00 inch.

The first of these falls of the barometer was comparatively slow and limited. The other three were all rapid, and dangerous to coalminers. My difficulty is not that explosions occurred on the last occasion, but that none occurred in the two previous falls. This is perhaps explained in the case of the third by the fact that it reached its climax on Sunday, the 9th, when there could be but slight chance of the gas becoming exploded. The exact moment of the occurrence of explosions is of course determined by

* An explosion occurred at Bolton at 2 p.m. on Monday afternoon, but it was caused by an accidental discharge of gas, and had no connexion with the barometer, which was rising.

the moment at which the top of a lamp is taken off, or when a blast or some other accidental cause ignites the gas. It is quite possible, therefore, that the air may become seriously fouled by a fall of the barometer without any explosion occurring, or that explosions originating in the same fall of the barometer may not happen the same day.

It may be asked, will not one fall of the barometer so clear the reservoirs of gas that there will be less chance of a second fall having a dangerous result? The barometer fell lower on the 8th than on the 13th, when an explosion occurred. Ought not the first fall to have prevented a calamity on the second occasion? The fact, however, is not so. All depends on the rapidity with which the barometer falls. If the barometer falls very slowly, the inflammable air in all the crevices swells very slowly, and the ventilation is sufficient to carry the gas off without any great danger. However low the barometer falls, provided it falls slowly, no evil results. But if it rise again and then fall suddenly there is danger. By the rise of pressure a little air is driven back into the crevices, supposing they are not filled up with new gas evolved from the coal. The next fall of the barometer causes as great an outpour of gas as the former, and if sudden the ordinary ventilation of the mine may for the time be quite inadequate.

Two kinds of precautions are taken in coalpits against explosions:—
1. The guarding of lights, to prevent ignition.
2. Ventilation, to prevent the gas reaching the inflammable point.

It is a maxim among coalminers, or, if it is not, it ought to be, that the second kind of precaution can alone be relied upon. The first kind of precaution is subject to all sorts of accidents beyond human foresight, as well as to all the carelessness of individuals. It is the very fact that ventilation generally renders a pit secure that makes colliers too confident and reckless in the use of lights. The dangerous conjuncture, then, is when some incident like the fall of the barometer interferes to render the ventilation insufficient. Then an act of carelessness (repeated, perhaps, hundreds of times before with impunity) brings sudden death to hundreds.

Those who employ machine ventilators, like the powerful new one of M. Lemielle, which seems likely to come into use, should observe that, if they too suddenly increase the draught of air from the pit when the barometer is falling, they will only increase the evil they wish to avoid by still further lowering the pressure of air in the mine.

Now I ask, Sir, are precautions generally taken in coalmines against this obvious tendency of the air to foul during a rapid fall of the barometer? I know that the barometer is carefully observed in many deep mines; it ought to be constantly observed in all mines of any extent and of fiery character. Any viewer who has omitted it hitherto would do well to begin tomorrow, and no more intermit his observations for the future than a cautious sea captain would intermit his observations of the weather when he was in the region of the typhoons.

Any barometer will do, provided it is not one of the old wheel barometers. An aneroid barometer would be very convenient, and not liable to breakage. The instrument, however, which I should most recommend would be the sympiesometer, invented by Adie of Edinburgh, and to be had from all instrument-makers. It acts by measuring the volume of air enclosed in a tube, and thus exactly represents the expansions and contractions of the gas in the crevices. The instrument would thus serve to indicate and explain to the under-viewers and others the necessity of caution. A good sympiesometer placed in the mine and a barometer in the office at the bank would be sufficient. Observations should be made the first thing in the morning on entering the pit, and at noon, and, perhaps, 6 p.m. The observer need only watch for a sudden fall of the barometer, and when that is occurring he should cause a very careful examination of the mine to be made, and the men should at once be withdrawn from any part of the mine where unusual symptoms of firedamp are observed. It does not matter whether the barometer be high or low, provided it be stationary, or rising, or only slowly falling.

I should like to know in how many collieries the new instrument of Mr. Ansdell, founded on the discoveries of Mr. Graham, the Master of the Mint, is used for detecting the presence of fire-damp. 15L. or 20L. would furnish the largest colliery with abundance of barometers, sympiesometers, and fire-damp indicators, and their observation would be a pleasure rather than a trouble or expense to any intelligent viewer or under-viewer. And yet a little niggardliness and a great deal of stupidity inherent in the English character may cause the neglect of all such precautions, and may lead to catastrophes which weigh upon the conscience of the nation.

Coalowners are fond of assuring us that we need be under no apprehensions of a want of coal, for they can easily sink to any depth, and work any number of square miles of country from a single shaft. Have they all of them clear consciences? Have they all of them adopted the latest and most efficient means for ventilating their mines and detecting danger? If not, I wonder that they can sleep in their beds at night for thinking of the heaps of blackened corpses in the burning pit, and the villages full of orphaned children and widows.

Yours obediently, W. S. J.

276.   WILLIAM JEVONS JUNIOR TO W. S. JEVONS

21 Cannon Place, Brighton
Dec 24.   [1866]

My dear Stanley

It is a long time since we had any correspondence with one another. But now that Christmas is come again to make us think of absent friends, I cannot resist an inclination to write to you, though I have little to say. I have been reminded of you more than usual by your letters in the Times which I have read with much interest; more particularly your last letter which treats of colliery explosions. I have no doubt you are right in thinking that variations of atmospheric pressure have a good deal to do with the escape of foul air in mines, and I hope your letter will be the means of directing the attention of colliery proprietors to this important subject. I think also you are right in the main in what you say (in the Times of last Monday) about the causes of variations in the price of iron and the necessity of greater friendship and natural confidence between masters and men; though the strictures of "An Employer" in the Times of Friday last are not unworthy of consideration. I am very glad to see you coming forward as you do in the Times, and I do not at all grumble at the favour you enjoy with the editor of that paper, though he lately rejected a letter of mine on the Athanasian creed.

I want to know how you are getting on with your professorship. I also want to know how it fares with dear Henny, and what news you have of your brother in America, and your brother in a more distant part of the world. Your aunt and cousin would be equally interested in such intelligence and I am sure they unite with me in offering the usual good wishes of the season to yourself and sister. Believe me
my dear Stanley

Very affectionately yours
W. Jevons

277.   W. S. JEVONS TO HERBERT JEVONS
[LJP, 231–2]

Beaumaris
28 Dec 66.

Dear Herbert

I was glad to get your letter not long since although it was not a full one. You have not recently written as much as you used. Many people ask how you are going on & how you like New Zealand, and I tell them you are pretty well satisfied with it & that the climate agrees with you as I infer from the fact that you never speak about your health now.

Sometimes I think I have some tendency to the kind of health you used to suffer under viz, low pulse, weak digestion and general depression, but I take great care of my health now having for some years now given up working at nights. I make a point like old Lord Palmerston used, always to take a full nights rest if I can however late I get up in the morning, & I find 8 or 9 hours & sometimes more necessary to me. The three years that I first spent at Owens College tutoring, lecturing, & writing at the same time were undoubtedly too hard & would have done me up if continued but my work is now so much more easy, familiar & congenial & I have had such plenty of holydays* that I shall be all right for the future I hope.

Henny & I are spending the Christmas holydays* here with John & Lucy who found Clynnog too dreary & solitary for the winter, & who were also disturbed by the prevalance of measles & other sickness in the country round and cholera in Carnarvon.

About 400 people have had cholera or diarrhoea in Carnarvon & 60 have died. I think it is therefore well for the children as well as J & Lucy to have a little change. We were at Emily Roscoe's[1] house till yesterday & had a merry time of it. She then went with all her family to Derby & John has just got into new lodgings just overlooking the sea, at the extreme corner towards Bangor of the little square over looked by his old house. It will be cheerful enough for them for the month they will spend here.

Lucy seems well now but she appears to have been rather frightened & depressed by the dark stormy months we have lately had, & by the sickness or perhaps exaggerated reports of sickness she heard. John suffers much from *tic* & other sickness but gets on some way or other. The quarry seems now to be in a safe & even sound condition. There are plenty of orders, enough money I suppose to carry them over the winter, a balance sheet showing 10 p. c. profits to enable them to offer fair prospects to new partners. I hope that the easy state of the money market which now exists & will continue for some time will enable them to fill up the capital and carry out some improvements in the harbour. The new incline to carry the *Setts* down to the harbour with considerable reduction of cost is in progress.

Eddie is here now having returned from India some weeks. He is thin rather pale, & somewhat weak having had an attack of liver complaint there but his quick return has saved his life & he is rapidly recovering I think. He is to return to school at Oxford under his old head master D[r] Hill who wishes to have him again. He is full of accounts of his travels to Singapore, Simla, and other places & is exceedingly pleasant and a very

---

[1] Emily, wife of Jevons's cousin William Caldwell Roscoe. See Vol. II, Letter 55, n. 12, p. 123.

good fellow in every way. The other children are growing and improving without exception, though Grindal looks a little thin.

I have not seen the sodium amalgam but I think there was no difficulty in using it & certainly no danger. I shall be glad to hear how it answers & what the success of your companies is. My speculation of £300 in Alfred Booth & Co^s Brazil Steam Ships has not been fortunate as yet, the voyages this year having left no profit as I understand. I hope they will pay better in a little time but I fear the steam trade has been somewhat overdone.

I have posted you a *Times* containing some remarks on a letter of mine.[2] I find it easy now to get attention to anything I like to write and sometimes get a little abuse but I am already somewhat seasoned to criticism. I feel it to be very necessary to be careful what I write so as not to fall into any scrape or get shown up in a mistake. One man in the Manchester City News[3] has taken to abusing me systematically every week to the amusement of the College people and other friends. It is very difficult to know what view to take of this Reform agitation. I am not a democrat as perhaps you know and dont much care to adopt popular views to please the mob. However I dont think any reform bill that is likely to pass will really upset our system here, while it may lead to many real improvements.

I find myself a good deal taken up at present with my College work, with some additional public lectures or papers which I have undertaken but if nothing else turns up I shall have the Summer pretty clear to go on with more important work.

The professors have been a good deal engaged of late in elaborating a scheme for rebuilding Owens College which at present is in a small dingy building in one of the worst parts of the town. We want to raise a great Scientific University College in Manchester with all sorts of engineering, mining, & Scientific Schools. Harry Roscoe is perhaps the moving spirit in it but most of the other professors especially the new ones are ardent about it.

£6000 have already been promised for the engineering School which is very popular & will doubtless succeed but we want altogether some £100,000 which it will not be easy to raise even in Manchester. The beginning however is not altogether unpromising & our present trustees are quite willing to promote the scheme & place it on a more public & important footing.

[2] Probably *The Times* of 21 December 1866, which contained a long letter signed 'An Employer' discussing the letter from Jevons published in the issue of 17 December 1866 (see above, Letter 274, p. 141), under the heading 'Iron Masters and Iron Workers'.

[3] W. Macdonald. See above. Letter 270, n. 1, p. 137. In his letter of 15 December 1866 Macdonald declared himself 'very curious to know why Professor Jevons is hiding his light under a bushel'.

Manchester is a fine place for public spirit. It is a kind of metropolis of the manufacturing districts and I do not know whether there is any place out of London I should prefer to it. Indeed there is some use & satisfaction in being out of London & having a somewhat distinct position, not involved in the great crowd of competitors of London.

It is a great satisfaction at last to find myself really living under my income with a prospect of saving £100 or £200 a year, which I shall take care to invest beyond chance of loss.

I hope you got the copy of my account with you sent last month & find it correct.

Lucy & Henny send their best love.

Your affect. Brother
W. S. Jevons.

278. W. S. JEVONS TO THE EDITOR OF *THE TIMES*[1]

PARTNERSHIPS OF MASTERS AND MEN.

Sir,

I am sorry to find that Messrs. Creed and Williams, in the last of their important letters, oppose as unsound a scheme which seems to me most promising for the future prosperity of English industry.[2] I mean the scheme of a partnership in results between masters and men. In a former letter, which you did me the favour to publish, I briefly alluded to this scheme, and the result was an almost pathetic protest from an "Employer" against any such unsound notions. But, in spite of all weight of opinion to the contrary, I feel so strongly that theoretical soundness and ultimate practicability are on the side of this scheme that I must beg a little space for explanation.

This kind of partnership was put into successful operation by the Messrs. Briggs in their collieries, as is pretty well known. It has been introduced into the iron trade by Messrs. Fox, Head, and Co., of the Newport Rolling Mills, Middlesbrough, whose works are now actually conducted on a plan elaborated by them after an inquiry into the arrangements of the Messrs. Briggs. By the kindness of the Messrs. Fox I have been freely furnished with a copy of the constitution of their

---

[1] Published in the issue of 19 January 1867.

[2] In a letter published on 15 January 1867 H. Herries Creed and Walter Williams compared the labour markets of Belgium and England, contrasting the freedom of capital and labour in Belgium with the restrictions imposed on them by trade unions in England. Considering possible reforms in industrial relations they rejected profit sharing as 'simply a device for bribing the men to abjure Unionism'.

partnership, which I forward with this letter for publication, if you think desirable.[3]

The Messrs. Creed and Williams misunderstand the conditions, thinking that the masters are to content themselves with 10 per cent. profit on their capital; whereas they will receive in addition half of the excess of profits above 10 per cent. The other half of the excess is to be divided among all the workmen, clerks, or other *employés*, in proportion to the amount of wages or salary received during the year. It will be further seen that the proprietors secure to themselves 5 per cent. interest on their capital in any case which if not realized one year is to be paid out of future years' profit. The depreciation or renewal of capital, again, is provided for by a reserve fund of $12\frac{1}{2}$ per cent. of the total capital, to be gradually raised and maintained by yearly contributions of $2\frac{1}{2}$ per cent. out of profits. A good auditor or accountant would probably insist on laying by such a reserve fund before declaring the profits.

The working of the plan is, then, as follows:— The men have advanced to them by the capitalist such ordinary wages as are sufficient to meet current expenditure. The masters receive current interest on their capital as is done in ordinary partnership arrangements. The capital is kept intact by a sinking fund. Efficient management and labour on the part of the masters is then compensated by an additional 5 per cent. if realized; and, lastly, the zeal and care of all concerned in the works are rewarded by a fair division of all profits exceeding 10 per cent.

We have here the division of the proceeds of industry as it has always been recognized by political economists – the wages of labour, the interest of capital, the wages of superintendence, the compensation for risk in the sinking fund, and the extra profits of successful years.

Messrs. Creed and Williams say that this scheme "does not contain within itself any economical principle capable of vivifying it and making it march." To the very best of my judgment it contains the great vivifying principle of political economy – that reward should be in proportion to desert. This is the great principle which underlies all the laws of property, and is their only sufficient warrant.

It has, indeed, always been strange to me that workmen labour so hard as they do, seeing that they are not better paid for working harder. Yet a gang of navvies or a shop full of mechanics may often be seen working as if their life depended on the result, even without the master's eye upon them. The highest qualities of fidelity, energy, and love of good labour, must animate those who thus voluntarily give a fair day's labour, and it is only fair that they should be rewarded by at least a portion of the extra

---

[3] Published in full in *The Times*, following Jevons's letter. Details of this scheme were given by Jevons in a lecture 'On Industrial Partnerships', delivered to the National Association for the Promotion of Social Science on 5 April 1870 and reprinted in *Methods*, pp. 122–55.

proceeds due to their diligence. There are many, of course, who are not so upright, or active, and these must be bribed, if you like to call it so, by hope of a bonus. Neither in principle nor in practice is this scheme really new. Mr. J. S. Mill, in advocating it many years ago (*Principles of Political Economy,* book iv., cap. 7, sec. 5), pointed out many instances where labourers share results.[4] It is not at all uncommon for firms to give bonuses to their clerks during good years, and it is evidently a most salutary principle to make the remuneration of managers, secretaries, agents, and others at least partially dependent on the success of the business they manage.

As to the subordinate advantages of the scheme they are more than I can possibly specify here. The discontent of the working classes would be removed by learning that on an average of years the masters' profits are not so excessive as may be thought, or that, if great, they are shared by themselves. A well-managed concern, too, by declaring good bonuses, would attract the best workmen, desirous of working under the best masters. Many men who now spend every penny of their weekly wages might be induced to lay by the half-yearly bonuses, thus laying the basis for an increase of providence which is essential to a real advancement of the people. Again, a free variation of remuneration between firm and firm, and between one year and another, would not only tend to prevent strikes, but would counteract the hurtful notions held by some men that all earnings should be equal.

I am far from being blind to difficulties which must prevent this plan from coming into operation, except by slow degrees. As to "Employer's" chief objection to my previous remarks that secrecy is indispensable to the success of business, I cannot see any difficulty. No one proposes that a firm should take a thousand workmen into counsel before concluding a bargain. Just as a managing director or a board of directors manages the affairs of a joint-stock company with perfect independence and secrecy, only publishing half-yearly or yearly results, so the firm will retain the independent conduct of transactions. There may be some kinds of business to which the co-operative plan is inapplicable; but so there are some which joint-stock companies should not undertake in spite of the great development of such companies which is taking place.

It seems to me, Sir, that the great difficulties which must impede the establishment of these partnerships arise from the prejudices and customs of both masters and men. The principle, on the contrary, is that vivifying principle which lies at the base of industry. Many must share the opinion expressed by Mr. Waley in his recent communication to the Statistical

[4] The reference is to the section headed 'Examples of the association of labourers with capitalists' in the well-known chapter 'On the Probable Futurity of the Labouring Classes'.

Society[5] – that strikes are almost inevitable in the present state of things. And I do earnestly recommend this scheme to masters and men as one which, however difficult in practice, is, to the best of my judgment, thoroughly sound in principle, and calculated to effect that union of interests by which alone our trade can prosper.

Yours obediently,

W. STANLEY JEVONS.

Owens College, Manchester.

279.   R. I. MURCHISON[1] TO W. S. JEVONS

16 February, 1867.

My dear Sir,

In replying to your letter of yesterday, I beg to send you 4 copies of the Questions prepared by the Committee of which I am the Chairman in the Royal Commission on Coal.[2]

If these are not sufficient and that you think you can obtain useful knowledge by the circulation of any larger number other copies will be sent.

These questions are only those prepared by Geologists. I will request the Secretary to send you copies of the sets of questions prepared by the other Committees of the Commission, as I am well aware that you who have written so ably on the subject, may be able to aid our enquiry materially.

I remain

Dear Sir,

Yours faithfully,

Rod. I. Murchison.

[5] Jacob Waley, 'On Strikes and Combinations, with reference to Wages and the Condition of Labour', *JRSS*, 30 (1867) 1–20.

[1] Sir Roderick Impey Murchison (1792–1871), one of the leading geologists of his time, who won fame for his establishment of the Silurian system; President of the Geological Society, 1831, and Director-General of the Geological Survey, 1855–71.

[2] Murchison was Chairman of two committees of the Royal Commission on Coal: Committee D, Geological Committee, on the probability of finding coal under Permian, New Red Sandstone and other superincumbent strata, and Committee E, on Mineral Statistics. Although Jevons's work was clearly most related to that of Committee E, paragraph three of this letter suggests that the questions enclosed with it were those prepared by Committee D. See *Report of the Royal Commission on the Coal Trade*, vol. 1 *Parl. Papers*, 1871 [C. 435] xviii.

279A.   W. S. JEVONS TO SIR BENJAMIN BRODIE[1]

9 Birch Grove
Rusholme
Manchester
25 May 1867.[2]

Dear Sir

I beg to thank you for your kindness in forwarding me a copy of your Paper on the Chemical Calculus.[3] I had however had the pleasure of reading it in another copy, and felt much interest in the subject. I am truly sorry that I cannot feel convinced of the truth of all your views. So strongly indeed do I feel the insecurity of your fundamental equation that I have been led to write out a few remarks on this point.

I have written them in the form of a communication to the Philosophical Magazine,[4] but I much prefer in the first place to submit them directly to your consideration. I have therefore posted you the M.S. hoping that you will excuse the liberty of criticism of which I have availed myself.

I beg that you will deal with my remarks just as you think fit. But you will doubtless desire that the truth of your system should be freely tested and if as is most probable, you consider your position unshaken by my objections, I presume that you would rather desire their publication than not.

I beg to remain Dear Sir
Yours very faithfully
W. S. Jevons.

Sir B. C. Brodie Bart.

279B.   SIR BENJAMIN BRODIE TO W. S. JEVONS

Cowley House,
Oxford.
May 27 1867.[1]

Dear Sir,

I thank you for your consideration in forwarding to me the copy of your criticism before publication.

---

[1] See Vol. I, p. 81, n. 2.

[2] The original manuscript of this letter is now in the University Library, Leicester.

[3] Sir Benjamin Collins Brodie, 'The Calculus of Chemical Operations; being a Method for the Investigation, by means of Symbols, of the Laws of the Distribution of Weight in Chemical Change. Part I. – On the Construction of Chemical Symbols', *Proceedings of the Royal Society*, 15 (1867) 136–9; the paper was presented on 3 May 1866.

[4] No such communication was published in that journal.

[1] The original manuscript of this letter is now in the University Library, Leicester.

You do not of course expect me to admit the validity of your objections, which, I must candidly say, appear to me to rest on an imperfect comprehension of my statement[2] but still more on an inadequate appreciation (at least according to my ideas) of the general principles of algebraic reasoning and expression.

As I have already given my opinion very fully upon the points which you raise I really do not think that anything would be gained by a further discussion of the subject on my part, and must leave your remarks to the consideration of those who are competent to form a judgment upon them.

As you have been good enough to apprise me of your intention it is only due to you to inform you that I hope before long to publish a short abstract of the way in which I propose to proceed to the treatment of the equation; which perhaps might[3] modify your ideas (and certainly ought to modify some of your statements) in regard to the calculus considered as an analytical method.[4]

Faithfully yours,
B C Brodie.

Prof. W. Jevons.

279C.   W. S. JEVONS TO SIR BENJAMIN BRODIE

9 Birch Grove
Rusholme
29 May 1867[1]

Dear Sir

I am very much obliged to you for replying to my letter. You may rely upon it that I shall carefully consider the subject many times over before venturing to print anything upon it, & if I discover any reason at all to suppose my criticism unfounded, I should at once apologise for having troubled you at all on the subject.

My objections you will have noticed do not bear against the employment of systems of equations in chemistry, which I should perfectly agree with you must form the basis of chemistry as of every other exact science, but against the special condition

$$xy = x + y$$

---

[2] Brodie first wrote 'the statement which I make . . .' but altered it.

[3] Altered from 'and which is calculated to . . .'.

[4] Altered from 'a mathematical system'.

[1] The original manuscript of this letter is now in the University Library, Leicester.

But I have no desire whatever to enter into a personal discussion of the subject, & I will take time to consider before saying more about it.

> Believe me
> > Dear Sir
> > > Yours very faithfully
> > > > W. S. Jevons.

Sir B. C. Brodie Bart
  &c &c &c

280. W. S. JEVONS TO HERBERT JEVONS
  [LJP, 236]

> 9 Birch Grove
> 25 Sept 1867

Dear Herbert

Your last letter was a considerable relief to us as you had left six months or more without writing & those who are nervous began to think something must have happened to you.

As I was uncertain too as to your exact address I wrote a note to the Manager of the Dunedin Bank to ask for it. I hope you will not let so many months nor anything like it pass again without writing; even once a month would not be too much. I do not know whether the letters I have lately written will reach you as they were addressed to *Greymouth*: if not I cannot help it as the best maps here do not enable one to find out what Greymouth or Hokatika is or what is their relative position.

I am now glad to feel settled at home after a long holyday*. Someway or other I am sick of travelling about and wish for nothing so much as to be settled at home. It is yet however some 10 or 12 days before the Session begins. There is already some signs* that the classes will be well filled this year.

I am now much engaged upon the construction of my logical machine. I have found a young clockmaker in Salford who has begun this week to work for me at 35^s a week. It will be necessary for me to go there almost every day to see that he is getting on right. I find it necessary to have each step of the work done separately in order that I may see whether I have planned every thing rightly. I think it will certainly be done before Christmas, & I intend to send it to the Royal Society with a complete paper on the Subject.

Henny has just got home this afternoon from Lpool where she has been for a few days besides a previous visit. I also spent Saturday & Sunday there. Poor Will[1] does not get on at all with his schemes for setting up a business. In fact I am afraid he is no nearer one than he was nine months ago.

Henny seems decidedly well & cheerful after her holydays*.

We expect Lucy's confinement[2] within a month from the present time. I think she will probably go to Beaumaris on the occasion but I have not heard precisely.

I am not sure whether I have written to you since my continental travels to Paris & through Belgium & Holland, but I can hardly undertake to tell you of what I saw. The Paris Exhibition[3] was very interesting though rather hard work, & in fact before I got home I managed to do myself up pretty completely & find myself now immensely better for a little quiet work at home.

I have now made it a habit to walk about 3 hours a day & as much as 8 or even 10 miles & I take work in very moderate quantities so that I can hardly fail to be well.

I am glad to say that Tom will shortly be on his way home for a visit & for the purpose of deciding on his future business. He is just at present at the head of the N York business during Busk's absence, with full powers, & seems rather pleased at his position. I do not know precisely the terms of Rathbone's & Jevons offer but they both refer to N York, & though Rathbones promise no permanency at present the terms are so favourable that I think Tom is likely to take them & he is evidently much more inclined to their alliance than that of the old business.

Would you like us to send you out any new things? I have been thinking of getting up a box but it would perhaps be well to wait till you have let us know of any things that you may specially want. What is [the][4] port to which the box should be sent by sea & how could it reach you at Hokatika wherever that may be. I wish you would go back to Dunedin as then we knew where you were, but now we have a very vague idea that you are somewhere on the west coast among mountains & lakes & swift rivers. You must take care & not get drowned. I must say I should like to see the New Zealand scenery of which I got a rather terrible notion from the narrative of poor Howitt's unfortunate journey.[5]

---

[1] i.e. William Edgar Jevons. See above, Letter 199, n. 2, p. 49.

[2] Mary Josephine Hutton (1867–1910), daughter of John and Lucy Hutton, was born early in October.

[3] The Paris Universal Exposition of 1867 was intended to demonstrate the rapid progress of French industrial development. Over forty thousand exhibits were housed in an elliptical building designed by Alexander Eiffel, constructed on a forty-one-acre site on the Champs de Mars. Jevons was among almost seven million visitors to the Exhibition, at which English manufacturers, particularly in the iron and steel industry, were for the first time outclassed by foreign competitors. Cf. above, Letter 265, n. 2, p. 128.

[4] This word is omitted in the original letter.

[5] Herbert Charlton Howitt, a surveyor who had attempted to cut a track over the great dividing

You will have heard of the rather alarming act of the Fenians in seizing the police van and releasing their leaders. It was rather startling news to find so bold an act of war carried out with firearms within a mile of us. The excitement it created was immense. I hope they will make such an example of the many men concerned whom they have already caught that the repetition of such a thing will be impossible. [6]

Henny is also writing to you. Hoping to hear further from you

Ever your affect Brother

W. S. Jevons.

281.   SIR JOHN LUBBOCK [1] TO W. S. JEVONS

15, Lombard Street, E. C.

5, Dec. 67

My dear Sir,

I have now the pleasure of sending you the dates of 1000 sovereigns and 500 half sovereigns which have been taken down by one of our cashiers. [2]

None of these were illegible. Indeed few illegible sovereigns come I think into the hands of London Bankers, excepting indeed from the Brewers.

Your idea seems a good one and I should much like to hear the result you arrive at if you would kindly drop me a line when you have worked it out.

Believe me, dear Sir,

Very sincerely yours,

John Lubbock.

W. Stanley Jevons, Esq.

---

range from Canterbury down the Taramakau to the west coast of New Zealand. In June 1863 he was drowned in Lake Brunner with two of his party. See *Cambridge History of the British Empire*, Vol. VII, pt II, pp. 40–1.

[6] On 18 September 1867 two Fenian prisoners, Thomas Kelly and Timothy Deasy, were being transferred to Bellevue Gaol, Manchester, on remand; an attack was made on the prison van by other Fenians, during which a police sergeant was fatally wounded. The three men who were hanged for his murder, Allen, Larkin and O'Brien, became known as the 'Manchester Martyrs'. See *The Times*, 19 September 1867; Rose, *The Manchester Martyrs: the story of a Fenian Tragedy* (1970).

[1] Sir John Lubbock (1834–1913), created first Baron Avebury, 1900. Head of the banking house of Robarts, Lubbock & Co., first President of the Institute of Bankers, 1879, and chairman of the committee of London clearing banks, 1898–1913.

[2] This letter is the first of a number which Jevons received as a result of enquiries made in the course of preparing his paper 'On the Condition of the Metallic Currency of the United Kingdom with reference to the question of International Coinage', read before the Statistical Society of London, 17 November 1868; *JRSS*, 31 (1868) 426–64. The paper was reprinted in *Investigations*, pp. 244–96, with a slightly altered title – 'On the Condition of the Gold Coinage . . . with reference to the question of International Currency'.

282.   W. S. JEVONS TO A. MACMILLAN
        [MA]

9 Birch Grove,
Rusholme,
7 Dec. 67.

My dear Sir,

I forward herewith by post an essay on an Economical or Political subject by my brother Mr. Thos. E. Jevons which seems to me so clear and so applicable in some respect to the present time that I think it just possible it might be admitted into your Magazine.[1] I shall be glad if you will be so kind as to submit it to the consideration of your Editor. If it should appear his name might be added or not as you liked.

The success of Roscoe's work is very gratifying, and I hear now that it is to be translated into Russian.[2]

Yours very faithfully,
W. Stanley Jevons.

A. Macmillan, Esq.

283.   SIR JOHN LUBBOCK TO W. S. JEVONS

15, Lombard Street, E.C.
12 Dec. 67.

My dear Sir,

The return I send you was just as they come to us over the counter, and I cannot account for the increased proportion of new sovereigns in the Manchester returns unless it arises from the Bank in question weighing all sovereigns and rejecting those which may be at all light.

We take them from the Public just as they come.

Believe me,
Yours very sincerely,
John Lubbock.

W. S. Jevons, Esq.

[1] There is no record of any contribution by Thomas E. Jevons, signed or unsigned, having appeared in *Macmillan's Magazine*, according to the lists in the *Wellesley Index to Victorian Periodicals*, vol. i.

[2] H. E. Roscoe, *Lessons in Elementary Chemistry* (1866). On its various editions and translations, see his *Life and Experiences* (1906) pp. 149–50. Cf. Letter 271, above, p. 139.

284. J. BRIGHT[1] TO W. S. JEVONS

Rochdale.
January 20. 68.

Dear Sir,

I believe my lamented friend Mr. Cobden has not left any expression of his opinions on Trades' Unions[2] in any of his speeches or letters. From his views on freedom of trade and of industry, I think there cannot be much difficulty in determing what were his views on Trades' Unions – I speak of Combinations to raise wages by strikes, and by creating a monopoly of employment within the limits of a particular trade.

I have however no authority to state what his views were, and do not wish to be quoted in any way in connexion with them.

I am very faithfully yours
John Bright.

W. Stanley Jevons, Esq.,
Owen's College,
Manchester.

285. J. LAING[1] TO W. S. JEVONS

Bank of England,
London,
24 Jan. 1868.

Dear Sir,

Since posting a note to you yesterday it has occurred to me to suggest the fitness of your communicating with the Bank *authorities* with a view to securing their assistance in the matter of public interest which you have taken in hand.

Mr. Alfred Latham[2] I believe takes, or did take, an interest in the late Mr. Miller's[3] (chief cashier) "quantity of gold coin in use" investigations and would be, I think, a good person to apply to.

---

[1] John Bright (1811–89), M.P. for Durham, 1843–7; for Manchester, 1847–57; and for Birmingham, 1857–85; President of the Board of Trade in Gladstone's first administration, 1868–70. Met Richard Cobden in 1835 and after 1841 devoted himself mainly to helping him promote the Anti-Corn Law League.

[2] Jevons at this time was probably preparing for the lecture on 'Trades Societies' which he gave to the Trades Unionists Political Association, Hulme, Manchester, on 31 March 1868. See below, Letter 298, n. 1, p. 183.

[1] John Laing (1832–72), entered the service of the Bank of England on 10 July 1856, and in 1868 was a clerk in the Accountant's Bank Note Office.

[2] Alfred Latham (1801–85), of the firm of Arbuthnot Latham & Co., merchants and East India agents, director of the Bank of England for various terms from 1838 to 1878; Deputy Governor, 1859–61; Governor, 1861–3.

[3] William Miller (1809–66), Chief Cashier of the Bank of England, 1864–6; author of the tables used at the Bank for reducing the gross weight of gold and silver to standard.

If I am correctly informed Mr. Miller's investigations proceeded on the plan of *assuming* an amount of coin as in use; then statedly *adding* the new coin received from the mint, *subtracting* light pieces returned for coinage and coin exported. Any reflux of sovereigns from Portugal, Brazil or other foreign countries was I understand allowed to go as a set-off against the multifarious inroads on the coinage unsusceptible of estimation, such as withdrawals for melting for trade purposes, or by travellers going abroad etc.

Were the Bank to take up the enquiry the sovereigns returned daily by the bankers and the public, either before or after they had passed the weighing machines, would provide a very extensive field of observation.

Possibly you are already in communication with the Bank in which case I must ask you to excuse my troubling you unnecessarily and to believe me,

Yours faithfully,
John Laing.

Professor Jevons.

Should you, acting on the suggestion now made, address Mr. Latham I think that introducing my name would *not* prove advantageous to you.

J.L.

286.   A. LATHAM TO W. S. JEVONS

23 Norfolk St. Park Lane.
January 31st 1868.

Dear Sir,

As I am on the point of taking my departure, to be absent for a few days from London, you will excuse me if I answer too briefly to your note of yesterday's date.

The Governors, who are the executives of the Bank (it is not a matter for the Directors) will I am sure afford you every facility in their power for examining and classifying the Gold Coins that may be conveniently within their reach – indeed would feel it their duty provided it can be done under the inspection of one of their own officers – They will not, or rather they cannot, undertake that the returns should be issued under Bank responsibility – unless in their own way, which might easily happen not to be yours, of arriving at the desired results.

When I was myself the Deputy Governor or Governor, 1859 to 1863 I took some pains to determine the rate of wear and tear of coined money whether of Gold or Silver under different conditions of circulation, therefore your subject is not new to me and I remember examining

William Millers tables and calculations of the number of Gold coins in the U. Kingdom. He certainly convinced me that the amount, at that time, more nearly approximated to 100 millions than to 70. His own words were to the effect that he would defy any body to reduce his estimate to 90. We have no man, now, for an object of this kind, that we can call a successor to poor Miller; who in whatever he undertook was almost painfully laborious and exact as well as methodical and ingenious.

In these enquiries so much depends on the meaning of such terms as the metallic *circulation*, the *currency* and *money* market, that I will not venture to concur in your last para:[1] without mutual explanation, which in writing would be very tedious, to enable us to understand each other.

I will send your note and paper to the Governor who will thus be prepared to see or hear from you and a reference to these will save you the trouble of repeating to him the same matter.

I am,

Dear Sir

Yours very truly,

Alfred Latham.

W. S. Jevons, Esq.

287.   A. LATHAM TO W. S. JEVONS

Brighton, 1 Feby 1868

Dear Sir,

I have been considering the subject of your note since I wrote to you yesterday and I am a little apprehensive that in your proposed basis of calculation you will find yourself check-mated by some disturbing cause peculiarly affecting the year 1863. – You are aware, no doubt, that some foreign countries have adopted the British Sovereign as their legal tender – for example the U. States, Portugal, Brazil and I suppose also Egypt as they are constantly going there. – In the United States they are affected by an under-rating i. e. that is that a given weight of pure gold in foreign Coin pays less debt than in U. States coin, but in Portugal and in Brazil it is the other way – at least I imagine so as I was myself at Rio de Janiero in the autumn of 1863 and every steamer was bringing out from one to two hundred thousand sovereigns at a cost of nearly two % to the Imperial Bank which by an extreme of folly (as I ventured to point out to one of their directors) was lending simultaneously at 8% p ann$^{m.}$ on 3 mos

---

[1] The content of this can only be surmised since there is no trace of Jevons's letter in the archives of the Bank of England: those of Messrs Arbuthnot Latham & Co. were destroyed by enemy action during the Second World War.

engagements.[1] It is contrary to the practice of the Bank here to issue new coin for the purpose of exportation, they issue coins, not as they receive them from the Bankers or over the counter, but after being passed thro' their own weighing machines – about 60,000 coins are weighed daily, of which on the average about 3% are ejected as light and cut. The Bank takes in its gold coin by three channels –

(1) from the mint (2) from the Bankers in bags of 1000 each and (3) from depositors over the counter. – Since 1844 the Bank has always been able to supply the exporters on a large scale with gold in bar (i.e. the pound stg. or 123¼ grains) whereas in a current sovereign he might receive only 122½ and were he to melt the sovereign he would suffer in the difference of assay as well as of weight. The Bank cannot refuse either to give coin or, practically to receive it but might, and hereafter probably will be, unable to supply bar, since from the recent establishment of branch colonial mints the Bank has lost its control or power of limiting the number of coins. The stock of Coin in the Bank at any given time is somewhere, I think, between 3 and 5 millions. When it runs down towards 3 the mint is set to work and when it runs up to 7 it is stopped. The *new* sovereigns are passed out to the public, chiefly at the period of paying the quarterly dividends – each dividend carries out, I think, about 2 millions, and an equal number of light or current coins is gradually returned during the quarter.

These thoughts, written from memory, may perhaps serve suggestively for the pursuit of your investigation.

Faithfully yours,
Alfred Latham.

W. S. Jevons, Esq.

288.   T. GRAHAM[1] TO W. S. JEVONS

R. Mint
3 Feby. 1868

My dear Stanley Jevons,

I am much pleased to hear that you are settled and congratulate you on the prospects before you of a happy and useful life. The Australian episode occurring so early in your career will form I can easily conceive a pleasant souvenir.

---

[1] A financial crisis occurred in Rio de Janeiro in the following year, leading to a suspension of specie payments on 15 September 1864. See 'The Financial Crisis in Brazil', *Bankers' Magazine*, 24 (1864) 1004–8; Joslin, *A Century of Banking in Latin America* (1963) pp. 68–9.

[1] For biographical details, see Vol. I, p. 65; and pp. 13–14 for Graham's influence on Jevons as one of his teachers.

Till the last four years when my brother² introduced a more regular system, our practice as to using dies was not such as to justify the inference with any degree of certainty that a coin has been issued in the year corresponding to its date. The cause of this irregularity was the necessity of holding a stock of dies, particularly of sovereigns, to be ready for any sudden demand for coin on the part of the Bank of England. We have generally closed the year with a stock of 50 or 100 dated dies, which were used up in the early part of the following year. Indeed the case has occurred of the surplus dies of one year serving for the whole of the following year where the coinage was small.

Perhaps a comparison might be instituted between periods of 3 or 4 years, but for single years it would be decidedly unsafe.

My brother, who succeeded Mr. Brande³ as superintendent of the Die and Coining departments introduced the practice of numbering each individual die and commencing rigidly with No. 1 at the beginning of each year. But this holds only for 1864, 5, 6 and 7.

With the best wishes for your continued happiness and prosperity I remain

Sincerely Yours
Tho. Graham

Professor W. S. Jevons

289.   W. S. JEVONS TO G. J. HOLYOAKE¹

Owens College,
Man^r.
5 Feb 68.²

Dear Sir

I shall be very glad to send you a contribution or two soon, when I can find a little time. In case you have not noticed it I send an extract giving the result of the first years working of Fox Head & Co^s works.³

² John Graham (d. 1869), Superintendent of the Coining Department of the Royal Mint from 1866 until his death.

³ See Vol. II, Letter 27, n. 11, p. 50.

¹ George Jacob Holyoake (1817–1906), son of a Birmingham engineer; became a Chartist at the age of fifteen and in later life devoted himself to the co-operative movement and social reform. In 1875 he published a *History of Co-Operation in England*. See his autobiography, *Sixty Years of an Agitator's Life* (1892).

² The original manuscript of this letter is now in the Holyoake Papers in the Library of the Co-operative Union, Manchester.

³ This extract is no longer with the manuscript: cf. above, Letter 278, n. 3, p. 152. Jevons was presumably referring to the *Reasoner*, a co-operative newspaper of which Holyoake was the proprietor and which he edited from 1846 to 1866. There is no evidence that Jevons ever did contribute to it.

I enclose subscription for a year for myself to be addressed
 Parsonage Road
  Withington
I also enclose 2/6 for a copy which I shall be glad if you will send to

  Mr. George Whitehead[4]
  Holybush Mount
  Parkgate
   Rotherham.

He is an operative who is much disposed to push co-operative principles among the Parkgate men. He seems a very intelligent man.
      Yours faithfully
      W. S. Jevons.

Some of the background to the ensuing three letters is explained in an undated fragment in Jevons's handwriting, found along with other miscellaneous notes in the Jevons Papers, which reads as follows:

In regard to this and certain other essays of Professor Fleeming Jenkin, it seems desirable that I should make the following explanation, to prevent misapprehension. My theory was originally read at the British Assoc. in 1862 & printed in the Stat. Journal in 1867. In March 1868 Prof. Jenkin wrote an article for the Br. Quarterly Review[1] in wh. he stated(?)[2] at pp 13–14 the law of supply and demand in math. language. He courteously sent a copy to me & requested my opinion thereon; in replying I sent a copy of the paper mentioned above, & a correspondence ensued concerning the correctness of the theory in the course of wh. curves were used in illustration by both parties.

In 1870 appeared Prof. Jenkins "Graphic Illustration......[3] in wh no reference is made to my previous

Partly in consequence of this I was led to write and publish the Theory in 1871.

In 1872 Prof Fleeming Jenkin published in the Proceedings of the Roy Soc Edin (?)[2,4]

---

[4] See below, Letter 324, n. 1, p. 225.

[1] This was a mistake on Jevons's part. Jenkin's paper 'Trade Unions. How far legitimate?' appeared in the *North British Review* for March 1868, vol. 48, 1–62.

[2] Part of the manuscript is obscured at this point.

[3] 'The Graphic Representation of the Laws of Supply and Demand, and their application to Labour', first published in *Recess Studies*, edited by Alexander Grant (Edinburgh, 1870).

[4] 'On the Principles which regulate the incidence of Taxes', *Proceedings of the Edinburgh Royal Society* (1871–2) 618–31. All these papers were reprinted in *The Graphic Representation of the Laws of Supply and Demand and other Essays on Political Economy* (L.S.E. Series of Reprints of Scarce Tracts in Economic and Political Science, No. 9, 1931).

290.   H. C. F. JENKIN[1] TO W. S. JEVONS

March 4, 1868.
6 Duke St. Adelphi.

Dear Sir,

I think I now thoroughly understand your "fluxion" theory of exchanges; but I do not think you have stated it quite correctly in your letter to me. I will state my view of the theory first and then show how far it differs from that in your letter.[2]

Let the Area of curve A represent the desire Jones has for a certain quantity of silk corresponding to & measured by the horizontal ordinate

---

This note of Jevons is quoted by Keynes in *Essays in Biography, Collected Writings of John Maynard Keynes* (1972) x, 130. Cf. also Vol. IV, Letter 353, in which Jevons also commented on his priority *vis-à-vis* Jenkin.

[1] Henry Charles Fleeming Jenkin (1833–85), an engineer with wide interests, who also produced a number of highly original papers on economic subjects, most notably 'The graphic representation of the laws of supply and demand and their application to labour' (1870). Professor of Engineering of University College London, 1866, and at Edinburgh University, 1868. See A. D. Brownlie and M. F. Lloyd Prichard, 'Professor Fleeming Jenkin, 1833–1885, Pioneer in Engineering and Political Economy', *Oxford Economic Papers*, 15 (1963) 204–16.

[2] It has unfortunately proved impossible to trace the letter which Jevons wrote to Fleeming Jenkin, but it is apparent both from the assumptions and the notation used here by Jenkin that the explanation provided by Jevons must have been closely similar to that which he later gave in *T.P.E.*, first edition, pp. 95–102. In the first part of the section on 'The Theory of Exchange' Jevons used the technique here employed by Jenkin of reversing and superimposing one utility curve on another – and also the assumption which it entails of a one-for-one ratio of exchange between the two commodities involved (loc. cit., pp. 97–8).

The argument put forward by Jenkin in Letter 290 that this would not necessarily be an equilibrium ratio of exchange acceptable to both 'trading bodies' is essentially correct; and it is notable that in *T.P.E.* Jevons presented the superimposed utility curves for one party only. The following section, 'Symbolic Statement of the Theory', which contains the well-known 'equation of exchange'

$$\frac{\phi_1(a-x)}{\psi_1 y} = \frac{y}{x} = \frac{\phi_2 x}{\psi_2(b-y)}$$

ab. The vertical ordinates represent the corresponding intensity of desire (utility) for each increment of quantity.

Let the Area of curve B represent the total desire which Brown[3] feels for a quantity of Cotton

measured by the horizontal ordinate – cd, and let us further suppose the units in which the quantities of silk & cotton are measured, to be so chosen that one unit of cotton exchanges for one unit of silk (I will return to this point by and by).

---

does not involve the assumption of a ratio of exchange fixed at one for one, or any other level, and is therefore not open to the objections put forward by Jenkin.

There was presumably another letter from Jevons to Jenkin between 4 March and 11 March; the manner in which Jevons endeavoured to meet Jenkin's point can only be inferred now from the text of *T.P.E.*, but it is notable that in Letter 291 Jenkin introduces and concentrates on the idea of a variation in the rate of exchange between the two commodities. He seems here to be approaching the concept of a varying rate of substitution between the two commodities in the mind of each trader, but using cardinal utility he is led to express his idea in terms of three-dimensional diagrams where Edgeworth and later writers used the indifference map.

Although recognising that there will be one rate at which 'both Jones and Brown would desire to exchange exactly equal quantities' (and which therefore satisfies the Jevonian equation) Jenkin remained convinced that there was 'no motive operating on their minds to induce them to agree on this rate'. Jevons, in his 'Symbolic Statement of the Theory', appears to take what is still essentially the accepted view of this problem, that each trader would adopt a consumption pattern which makes the ratio of the marginal utilities of the two commodities to him equal to the ratio of their prices *as given in the market* – and his whole discussion is subject to his Law of Indifference 'that in the same open market, at any one moment, there cannot be two prices for the same kind of article'. In other words, although Jevons referred to only two 'trading bodies' he conceived them as price takers and quantity adjusters in a situation where both price and quantity could vary freely [and in infinitely small amounts]. On the other hand Jenkin took the more natural interpretation of the trading bodies as simply two persons in a bargaining situation and his argument is essentially that which in more recent terminology could be expressed by saying that in that situation exchange may or may not take place at a point on the contract curve. Cf. Scitovsky, *Welfare and Competition* (1952) chaps IV and XIX; R. D. Collison Black, Introduction to the Pelican Classics edition of *T.P.E.* (1970) p. 22.

[3] In the original manuscript 'Jones' has here been crossed out in the text and 'Brown' written in above, but 'Jones' has been left unaltered in the diagram. The notation of all the diagrams is reproduced here exactly as in the original letter: but it is clear from the text that Jenkin intended figures A & C to relate to Jones's *preferences* and B & D to Brown's.

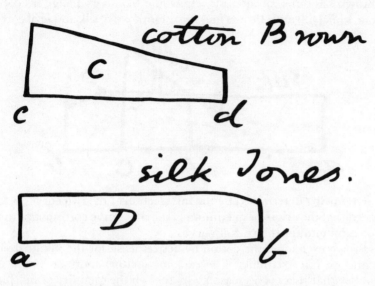

Let curve C represent Jones total desire for Browns cotton let curve D represent Browns total desire for Jones silk.

Now, Jones would like to exchange his silk for Browns cotton until

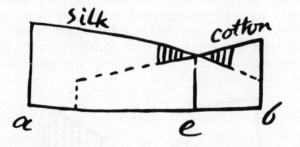

Jones has the quantity eb of cotton and only ae of silk the point e being determined by the intersection of the two curves A & C placed together so that the origin of the cotton[4] curve corresponds with the end of the silk.[5] The total area enclosed by the full lines will represent the total desire Jones has for his possession in silk & cotton after the exchange or what you call the total utilities of these commodities to Jones. If he has either more or less cotton the total area of the curve will be diminished by one of the two triangular shaded portions of the diagram (not necessarily equal even when infinitely small).

[4] replaces 'shortest', crossed out in the original manuscript.
[5] replaces 'longest', crossed out in the original manuscript.

But Brown has different interests. He would like to exchange his cotton for Jone's [*Sic*] silk until Brown had the quantity af of silk and fc of cotton;

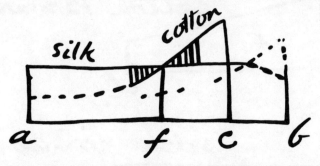

the point f being determined by the intersection of the two curves B & D so placed that the origin or maximum of the silk[6] curve corresponds to the end or minimum of the cotton curve.

Thus Brown exchanges the cotton he desires least, for the silk he desires most and his interests suffer if he exchanges either more or less.

But we see that there is no reason why the[7] eb the quantity of silk Jones wishes to give away should be equal to af the quantity of silk Brown wishes to receive or should bear any one ratio to it. Jones would like to exchange to the extent eb. Brown would like to exchange much more, viz. af.; but it is Brown's interest to exchange any smaller quantity than af whereas Jones will flatly refuse to exchange more than eb and this will therefore be the actual quantity exchanged. We may then represent the utility of the exchange to the two parties by increase of area shaded in the diagram annexed which clearly shows how much Brown would like to go on exchanging, only Jones won't.

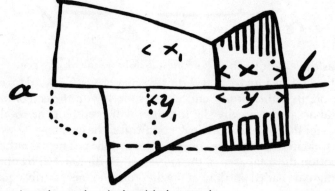

---

[6] replaces 'cotton', crossed out in the original manuscript.

[7] Here Jenkin had originally written the 'ratio of $\dfrac{ac}{eb}$ should be the same as $\dfrac{fc'}{a}$' but crossed this out.

There is of course a point at which the increase of utility or happiness to the two collectively would be a maximum, but Jones & Brown do not exchange with that object; each wants to be as happy as he can and either of them will stop exchanging as soon as his utilities begin to decrease even though the other's increase at a faster rate.

Now I think it is pretty clear that knowing the four curves A B C D we could determine exactly how much of the goods would change hands. But to plot these curves, the unit of desire or utility must be the same and the unit of quantity as above said must be such for each commodity that "one" of silk will exchange for "one" of cotton.

In the language of your letter we require to know the ratio $\frac{y}{x}$. When I know this, I plot my curves with such units of quantity that $y = x$ and $\frac{y}{x} = 1$ so that then $\frac{\phi(a-x)}{\psi y} = 1$

where ϕ is the coefficient of utility expressing the last increment of silk to Jones

& ψ is the coefficient of utility expressing the last increment of cotton to

Jones. (of course the device of making $\frac{x}{y} = 1$ was only required to facilitate the graphical expression)

But now I think you must perceive that $\dfrac{\phi' x}{\psi'(b-y)}$ is not equal to $\dfrac{y}{x}$ or to 1 or to $\dfrac{\phi(a-x)}{\psi y}$

That would only be the case if the quantities given in exchange had been $\dfrac{x_1}{y_1}$ equal no doubt to $\dfrac{x}{y}$ but ϕ' would be applicable to x_1 not to x & ψ' to $(b-y_1)$ not to $(b-y)$.

So that I should say you had three equations, but four unknown quantities

$$\frac{\phi(a-x)}{\psi y} = \frac{y}{x}$$

$$\frac{\phi' x_1}{\psi'(b-y_1)} = \frac{y_1}{x_1}$$

and as $\dfrac{y}{x} = \dfrac{y_1}{x_1}$ we have $\dfrac{\phi(a-x)}{\psi y} = \dfrac{\phi\ x_1}{\psi\ (b-y_1)}$

If the ratio $\dfrac{y}{x}$ be known then these equations allow us to determine x y &

x_1 $y_1$and the *exchange will take place which corresponds to the smallest pair of values* of x & y but I see in this theory no means of determining the ratio $\frac{y}{x}$. If you assume that Jones & Brown [are] both perfectly satisfied & would exchange neither more nor less then you can find x & y but in practice the one point is to find what determines $\frac{y}{x}$. This being given your theory is necessary to determine the amount of business that will be done.

One point is brought out very prettily viz. the increased utility to both parties resulting from any bona fide sale. The increased wealth produced by the simple change of hands. This cuts all the knots about the gain by imports exports etc. I shall be very glad to learn if you agree with my view of your theory. I will send you a copy of my complete article in a day or two. The same number of the North British contains an article of mine on Lucretius. [8]

Yours very truly,
Fleeming Jenkin.

Prof. Stanley Jevons

291.   H. C. F. JENKIN TO W. S. JEVONS

March 11, 1868.
6 Duke St. Adelphi.

Dear Sir,
    The difference between us is I think this. I demur to one of your two equations. I agree that two are wanted. I acknowledge the truth of one of

yours $\dfrac{\phi(a-x)}{\psi\, y} = \dfrac{y}{x}$ but   I   deny   the   truth   of   the   other

$$\frac{\phi'\, x}{\psi'(b-y)} = \frac{y}{x}$$

I will try to make my difficulty plain and then you may be able to explain it away.

---

[8] 'The atomic theory of Lucretius', *North British Review*, 48 (1868) 211–42.

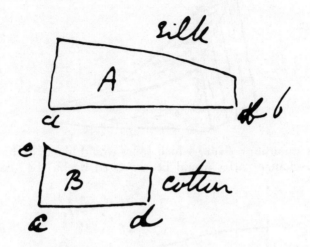

If curves A & B represent the desires of Jones for fixed quantities of silk & cotton at a given rate of exchange. Then if the rate of exchange vary so that more cotton is given for the same quantity of silk (sticking to the device of $\frac{y}{x} = 1$), then the curve A being left constant, the horizontal ordinate cd of B will shorten and the vertical ordinates of B must be increased if the utilities of cotton per pound to Jones remain constant; thus supposing the curve A to remain constant variations in the rate of

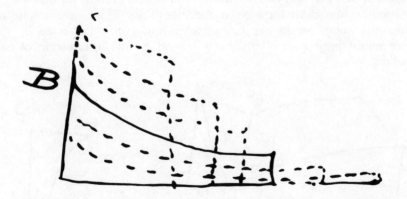

exchange would modify B successively into the form of each dotted line — (a solid might be used to express this)

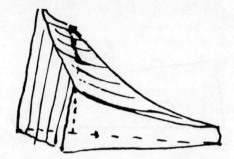

Then the quantities of silk[1] which Jones would like to exchange as the rate of exchange varies would be expressed by ba_1 ba_2 ba_3 ba_4 the

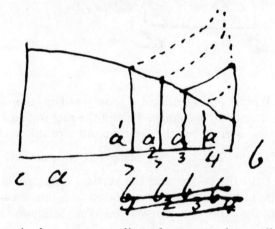

smallest quantity ba_4 corresponding of course to the smaller quantity of cotton exchangeable for a given quantity of silk. (This variation in the quantity Jones would like to exchange might be represented by the horizontal projection of the curve caused by the intersection of two solids).

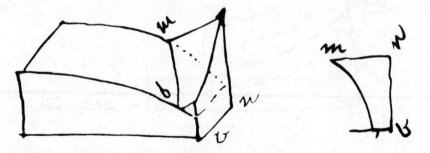

[1] 'and cotton' has been crossed out here in the original manuscript.

This expresses the fluxional theory of the manner in which a variation in the rate of exchange affects Jones' mind. at first he is willing to exchange very little and gradually his willingness increases according [to] a law determined by the intersection of the two fluctuating curves the fluctuation in which can however be easily deduced on the assumption that the utilities to Jones are not altered by an alteration in the quantities exchangeable. Quite similarly Brown's mind is affected by the rate of exchange, but he is willing to give less and less of his cotton when Jones is willing to take more and more of it. Calling mb Jones exchange curve

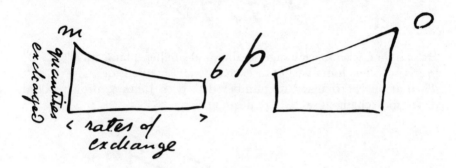

determined as above, & op Browns exchange curve, putting these two curves together as sketched we shall find the rate fixed by your equations.

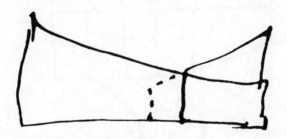

Let us now consider the effect on Brown. Supposing as before the silk curve to remain constant the effect of varying the rate of exchange so that more cotton is given for the same quantity of silk may be of two kinds. The variation may be due to causes wholly external to Brown so that the utility of a given quantity of cotton is constant to him – then his cotton curve will vary after the same fashion as Jones cotton curve. The vertical ordinates will rise as the horizontal ordinates contract.

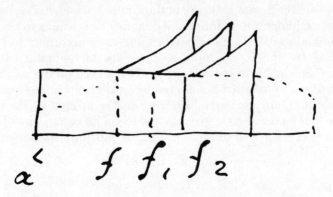

$$a \qquad f \quad f_1 \quad f_2$$

He will then wish to exchange smaller and smaller quantities af_2 af_1 af_0 precisely when Jones wishes to exchange larger quantities.

Then at one particular rate numbered 2, both Jones & Brown would desire to exchange exactly equal quantities.[2]

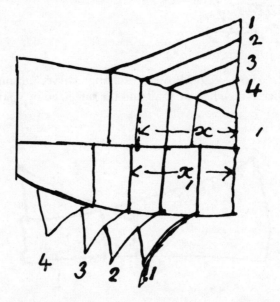

At the rate Numbered 1 Jones would like a larger exchange but Brown would like a smaller exchange; at the rate 3 Jones would like the smaller exchange & Brown the larger. Is there any reason why one rate should prevail more than another? I think on the above hypothesis absolutely none. A fall in the value of cotton as compared with Silk will please

[2] As Jenkin has drawn the diagram, this rate is numbered '2' for Brown but '3' for Jones.

Jones – a rise will please Brown. The quantities exchanged will vary at every variation of the rate of exchange but I see absolutely nothing in the above considerations to induce Jones and Brown to agree on a particular

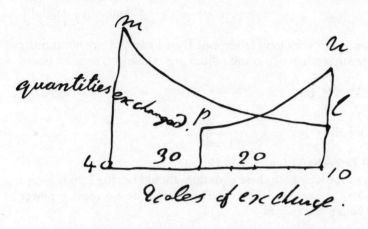

rate of exchange. If ml be Jones exchange curve & np Browns exchange curve their intersection determines the rate of exchange at which each would be satisfied to exchange exactly the same quantity, but there is no motive operating on their minds to induce them to agree on this rate. Jones would like more cotton for his silk, Brown would like more silk for his cotton and I do not see how any of the considerations as to the rate at which their desires fluctuate with the quantity can determine their desire for any one quantity. This must it seems to me be determined by wholly different considerations. You appear to me to assume that the ratio of exchange would be that fixed by the intersection of the curves ml and np but in order that this should be true it would be necessary that the aggregate utilities to *each* party should increase up to that point which is not true. As the quantity of cotton given increases Jones aggregate utilities increase as the quantity exchanged increases; but Brown's aggregate utilities *decrease*.[3]

---

[3] The letter is unfinished, but attached to it on a separate sheet is the following passage in Jenkin's handwriting – also crossed out: –

'. . . exchange, determined by their intersection at which the *maximum* amount of goods will be exchanged and the maximum amount of utilities obtained for the two exchangers. This is the rate of exchange fixed by your equations, but I say that it is not the true rate which will obtain in any market except accidentally.'

292.   H. C. F. JENKIN TO W. S. JEVONS

March 11, 1868.
6 Duke St., Adelphi.

Dear Sir,

I have written you a very long letter; but I see I can put my point quite shortly. I agree that when two commodities are exchanged then for one of

them $\dfrac{\phi(a-x)}{\psi\, y} = \dfrac{dy}{dx}$ but

I deny that for the other $\dfrac{\phi'\, x}{\psi'(b-y)} = \dfrac{dy}{dx}$

I cannot tell beforehand which will be true.

If you can show me why both these equations should be true I shall accept all your theory, at present I only accept part. I see no motive power tending to change the curves

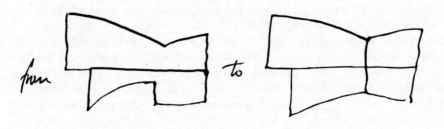

| where one equation
is true | where both
are true |

At a certain rate of exchange the second curves are true but I see no reason why this special rate should obtain.

Yours very truly,
Fleeming Jenkin.

293. A. LATHAM TO W. S. JEVONS

23 Norfolk St
Park Lane
20 March '68.[1]

My dear Sir,
  The Sovereigns now in the London vaults are of the
  Coinage 1864 – 600,000
           1865 – 500,000
           1866 – 2,300,000
           old   – 2,600,000
  Australian   100,000
I have a return of poor Wm Millers which may be useful in your investigation; it is dated the 3 Augt 1866
  Since 1816
Sovereigns coined   171,813,377
Half Sovereigns   20,289,532
                     —————————
                      192,102,909

Obviously he intended to express not the number of the "Halves" but the amount in pound Stg.

Faithfully yrs
Alfred Latham.

W. Jevons Esqr.

294. W. S. WALLIKER[1] TO W. S. JEVONS

Post Office, Hull.
24th March, 1868.

Dear Sir,
  The return I sent you includes the greater part of the gold coin received at the Money Order Counter of this Office during the day and also that received for Money Orders issued at the Town Receiving houses and sub-Offices in my District – for instance Flamboro' Hornsea Barton-on-Humber, Aldbrough – Medon etc., etc.
  I was anxious to include the money received from these outlying offices as gold coin is often hoarded for a considerable time in such places—.

---

[1] The original manuscript of this letter is now in the possession of the Royal Statistical Society, London.
[1] William Samuel Walliker (1821–92), Postmaster of Hull, 1864, and Birmingham, 1861–91; Surveyor of Birmingham district, 1886–91; member of special committee to enquire into the money order system, 1876.

By the way – the coin was in part received for Savings Bank deposits —.
If you wish anything more precise on the subject I shall be happy to
furnish it.

I am much pressed for time or would have written you more fully now.

Yours very truly,

S. Walliker.

W. Stanley Jevons Esqr.

P.S.   I shall look for the result of your labours with great interest – I
hope you will be able to send Bridlington a paper as he (the Sub-
Postmaster) took much pains with his report.

295.   WILLIAM JEVONS JUNIOR TO W. S. JEVONS

21 Cannon Place,
Brighton
March 24, 1868

My dear Stanley,

On looking to the date of your last letter, I am surprised to find that full
two months have passed since I received it. It called for no immediate
reply, and nothing has since occurred to make it worth while to interrupt
you in your busy and happy life. I have not been forgetful of the paper
you sent me relating to your statistical inquiries about our gold coinage.
But all I could do to aid you was to put the paper into the hands of Annie,
requesting her to enter on it the dates of the sovereigns which pass
through her hands. She promised to do so: but under present circumstances it is hardly possible for her to pay attention to the matter, though
she is very desirous of doing what she can to aid you. Almost her every
thought is occupied about her Mother, and I am sure you will excuse her
if she has forgotten to do what she intended.

We have all been much pleased to hear of your lecturing at the Royal
Institution.[1] Kate[2] sent us an account of your lecture, and I have since
read a brief notice of it in the Illustrated London News.

.... [3]

Very affectionately yours,
W. Jevons.

---

[1] On 13 March 1868 Jevons had lectured at the Royal Institution 'On the Probable Exhaustion of
our Coal Mines'.

[2] Probably Susan Katherine Hutton (1850–1915), known generally as 'Kate' among members of
the Jevons family. See Vol. I, p. 46.

[3] The remainder of the letter is concerned only with family matters.

296. C. RIVERS WILSON[1] TO W. S. JEVONS

6 Old Palace Yard,
30 March, 68.

Sir,

In reply to your letter of yesterday I beg to inform you that the International Coinage Commissioners[2] will only sit once after tomorrow before Easter, viz on Friday next – I shall have the honor of laying your letter before the Commissioners tomorrow, and will at once inform you whether it would be desirable that you should give evidence on Friday next or at the first meeting after Easter.[3]

Any evidence that you could tender respecting the present amount and condition of the Gold Currency would be very acceptable. Upon the first question no reliable information has been produced – indeed all estimates that I have ever seen amount to little more than guesses – and no two estimates even approach each other. Upon the other point viz the state of the gold coin it is generally understood that the average shows a considerable depreciation by wear, and upon this head we could doubtless obtain tolerably accurate data thro' the Bankers – Mr. Hendricks[4] estimates the depreciation I think at circa 1/- in the sovereign.

I am Sir,
Your faithful servant,
C. Rivers Wilson.

Professor Jevons.

297. R. VALPY[1] TO W. S. JEVONS

Board of Trade
April 11th, 1868.

Sir,

In reply to your letter to Mr. Fonblanque[2] of the 6th instant, I have the pleasure to enclose a Statement of the Imports and Exports of British

[1] Sir Charles Rivers Wilson (1831–1916), civil servant and financier; entered the Treasury in 1856 and was appointed private secretary to James Wilson and later to Robert Lowe; Comptroller-General of the National Debt Office, 1874–94; Vice-President of Anglo-French Commission on revenue and expenditure of the Egyptian Khedive, Ismail, 1878, and Finance Minister of Egypt, 1878–9.

[2] The Royal Commission on International Coinage, which had been set up in February 1868, under the Chairmanship of Lord Halifax, to examine the recommendations of a conference held in Paris in June 1867 on 'the best means for securing a common basis for a general international coinage', and their adaptability to the circumstances of the United Kingdom.

[3] Jevons in fact gave evidence on Friday, 24 April. See Minutes of Evidence of the Royal Commission on International Coinage, *Parl. Papers*, 1867–68 [4073] XXVII, pp. 95–103.

[4] Frederick Hendricks (1827–1909), actuary; for further details see below, Letter 329, p. 232.

[1] Richard Valpy (d. 1889), of the Statistical Department of the Board of Trade; author of a series of papers, mostly on trade and currency, read to the Statistical Society of London between 1846 and 1874; F.S.S. 1842; a member of the Council of the Statistical Society, 1859–64.

[2] Albany William Fonblanque (1793–1872), manager and editor of the *Examiner*, 1830–47, sole

Gold Coin, as Registered at the Custom House, the only information it is in our power to give you upon the subject of your inquiry.

I am sorry that we cannot help you with any estimate of the amount of coin that leaves the country by private channels, or of the amount of the gold coin melted down for the excess of weight above the current standard. Unless gold coin is privately sent abroad upon mercantile account the quantity otherwise taken is perhaps not so very considerable, now that circular notes are so largely used by travellers.

I am,
Sir,
Yours very faithfully,
R. Valpy.

W. Stanley Jevons, Esq.

P.S.

The accountant I had when you last wrote me has since been removed, but I wrote him to know whether he knew that the sovereigns then fixed upon were to his knowledge exceptionally light. This would not be unless they were then thrown aside as being so light that the public even declined them, and that he in error may have selected from that lot. I don't think it probable, but as it is possible, and would readily explain the point at issue I shall write him by this post.

298.   W. S. JEVONS TO HERBERT JEVONS
[LJN, 240-1]

Parsonage Road, Withington,
Manchester 18th April 1868.

. . . We are now pretty well settled in our new house, and are enjoying a quiet Easter Holiday at home, than which nothing can be more pleasant. We get breakfast about 9 a.m., then I work till 1.30 p.m., dinner; then a little more work till 4 p.m. Then we have a little gardening or a walk out till 6.30, and about 8 p.m., we have a little more work. Harriet does a great quantity of work for me, especially copying and arithmetical work, which relieves and helps me much. Our house satisfies us in nearly every way. It is very convenient and cheerful, and quite large enough. We have

---

proprietor thereof, 1847–60. Head of the Statistical Department of the Board of Trade from 1847 until his death.

also a nice-sized garden, which I have begun to cultivate with considerable vigour. It furnishes me with a kind of excercise I have long wanted.

I find a great deal to do between the engagements of married life and those of college, in addition to my own work. On the 13th March I gave a lecture to the Royal Institution, London, on the Coal Question, which went off tolerably well, as I am told. I have also given a lecture[1] to some Trades' Unionists' in Manchester, although very few came. I will, in a little time, send you copies of them.

Next week I have to go to London to give evidence before the Commission on International Currency, and I am busy getting up a variety of things about coins.[2] . . .

299.   W. S. JEVONS TO J. B. SMITH[1]

Parsonage Road
Withington
Manchester
21 April 68.

Dear Sir

Mr Browning of the Chamber of Commerce here mentioned to me that you would like to speak with me previously to my being examined by the International Coinage Commission.

I will in consequence try to call at your house on Thursday afternoon but as I have a very narrow margin of time & might be prevented or might unfortunately find you out I may as well mention briefly the kind of evidence I am prepared to give.

I am much in favour of our joining the Monetary Convention to the extent of assimilating the sov^n & the 25 franc piece because I think the sov^n would then become the principal coin & medium of exchange all over the world. It seems to me that gold must be adopted as the future money everywhere & this is now recognised by the International Convention. The question arises, what coin is to replace the old Spanish dollar which was the predominant silver coin, & the goodness & general

---

[1] 'Trades Societies their Objects and Policy', delivered by request of the Trades Unionists' Political Association in the Co-Operative Hall, Upper Medlock Street, Hulme, Manchester, 31 March 1868. Reprinted in *Methods*, pp. 101–21.

[2] See above, Letter 296, n. 3, p. 181.

[1] John Benjamin Smith (1794–1879), Manchester cotton merchant, President of the Manchester Chamber of Commerce, 1840, and first Chairman of the Anti-Corn-Law League. M.P. for Stirling, 1847–52, and for Stockport, 1852–74.

The original manuscript of this letter is now in the J. B. Smith Papers, Central Reference Library, Manchester.

currency of which must have facilitated commerce in a very high degree. Now it seems to me that if we join the Convention the 25 franc piece will be the most general coin & being issued mainly from our own mints in London, Australia & before long perhaps in India, as well as at the United States & some of the other principal mints on which we can rely, it will become an invaluable medium of exchange & standard of value all the world over. If we do not enter the convention, the napoleon may become the more common coin of circulation & we shall be shut out.

I think the change of the sov^n can be effected with great ease & that if a seignorage be imposed to a moderate amount (say $\frac{3}{4}$ per cent) there will be absolutely no disturbance of contracts &c. I believe moreover that a considerable part of the currency which I can give some estimate of is already light enough to pass as a 25 franc coin, *if not too light*.

I have of late been making a somewhat new kind of inquiry into the amt of the gold circ which lies I think [at]^2 about 85 million & certainly does not exceed 93 or 95, and I have evidence to show that nearly $\frac{1}{3}$ of this coin is now too light to be legal tender at present & would pass as the new coin. I enclose a paper which will give you a notion of the nature of my little inquiry.

I believe that a seignorage of 1 per cent will not do any real harm especially when it is uniformly exacted by all mints but I think $\frac{1}{2}$ or $\frac{3}{4}$ per cent would be enough.

The introduction of the 10 & 20 franc piece here are matters of smaller importance. I think it would be a great mistake to try to decimalise our coin at present & there is no fear of its being attempted, but if we join this convention & it be extended very widely there will at some future time be a chance of the question settling itself, & a real sound decimal system being chosen. But with this we have very little to do as I think there are immediate advantages attaching to the alteration of the sov^n quite sufficient to induce us to make it.

Believe me   Dear Sir
Yours faithfully
W. S. Jevons.

P. S. I take the liberty of sending a paper or two of mine.

---

^{2} Omitted in the original manuscript.

300.   W. S. JEVONS TO HERBERT JEVONS
       [LJP, 241]

Parsonage Road,
Withington
Man^r
23 June 68.

My dear Herbert

I enclose a bill of lading for a box which is now on its way to you. There is nothing very beautiful or valuable in it but there are a few things which will prove useful I think . . .

I have not heard much of you just lately but hope that you are getting on all right. We are now at the end of the session, the distribution taking place on Friday next. Harriet & I are going first of all to stay a few days in Wales with John & Lucy – For the main part of our holidays we have various plans but are most inclined to stop 6 weeks or more at Heidelberg as we both of us want to see a little of Germany & to learn a little German.

We are pretty well settled in our house now though we have not done all the furnishing yet. We have had several visitors lately. Uncle Timothy stayed from Easter day till Monday & seemed pleased with our house.

Fred & his wife are coming next Saturday to stay over Sunday.

I have been very busily engaged the last two or three weeks on my logical machine, having begun a new one altogether. I have now got it to work fairly & there can be no doubt of my finishing it now with success although many little troubles arise in a new form of mechanism. I am thinking of exhibiting it with a paper to the Royal Society next session. The machine works in a few moments any logical problems involving no more than four distinct terms or things. It will be in appearance like a large accordion or a very small piano, & has 21 keys exactly like white piano keys.

. . . I have not heard from Tom for some time myself but I believe he is getting on well, being in command of the business now Mr Busk is away in England.

. . . I should very much like to hear how you are getting on now, & what sort of work you have. I have never been able to find your position on any map & should like to have an account of the position of the places you refer to with a sort of map of the district.

Hoping you will approve of the box & get it safely as it has been a matter of some anxiety to me to send it off rightly,

Believe me
Your affectionate Brother
W. S. Jevons.

301.   G. B. AIRY[1] TO W. S. JEVONS
Royal Observatory, Greenwich,
London, S.E.

1868 July 1

Sir,

I am much obliged by your transmission to me of your paper "On the International Monetary Convention etc."[2]

I carefully abstain at present from expressing an opinion on the recommendations; but I ask leave to point out to you an error of fact which, in reference to the purpose for which you use it, is important.

In page 84, line 3 from the bottom, you state "the French currency is nicely adjusted in connexion with the metrical system of weight."

This is not now correct.

The original value of the franc was 5 grammes of silver: and, if it had remained so, your remark would have been strictly correct. But, in consequence of the use of a double standard, the silver disappeared from circulation (the opposite change had occurred 30 years before) and it was found necessary to debase the silver coin very greatly to the fineness $\frac{835}{1000}$; and so it remains.

Practically; silver is now only a token: gold is the standard; and the 20-franc piece contains 5.8064 grammes of pure gold, or 6.4526 grammes of alloyed gold.

I am, Sir,
Your obedient servant,
G. B. Airy.

302.   THOMAS GRAHAM TO W. S. JEVONS

R. Mint.
1 Oct. 1868

Dear Stanley Jevons,

I scarcely know what to say on the subject of the destruction of gold coin by the practice of picking out and melting down the heavier pieces and turning the lighter into the circulation. One result of the enquiry is very unexpected, namely that the practice is justified by the parties

[1] Sir George Biddell Airy (1801–92), Plumian Professor of Astronomy and Director of the Cambridge Observatory, 1828–35; Astronomer Royal, 1835–81; Chairman of the Commission to superintend the construction of new parliamentary standards of length and weight, which reported in 1854; advocate of the 'pound and mil' system of decimal coinage. See Vol. II, Letter 154, p. 435.
[2] 'On the International Monetary Convention, and the Introduction of an International Currency into this Kingdom', *Transactions of the Manchester Statistical Society*, 1867–8, pp. 79–92. Reprinted in Vol. VII, Part I.

engaging in it, which include the *highest* foreign capitalists, and we are told that it is our business to protect ourselves against it in the best way we can. None of the information we could get was sufficiently precise to be made the basis of an estimate. All allusion to the subject has been suppressed in the Report, out of a feeling of delicacy I believe to certain individuals, although this will not be publicly stated.

I send a copy of my evidence before the Decimal Com[n]. of 1857,[1] for the sake of some information which may assist you in your enquiries respecting the statistics of the silver coinage. The results could be brought down to the present both as to pieces issued and withdrawn, by reference to the Mint Annual Return of the coinage for late years. The *Coinage Report* will I fear be found disappointing.

I am faithfully yours,
Tho. Graham

W. Stanley Jevons, Esq.

303. B. W. FAREY[1] TO W. S. JEVONS
   [WM]

B. DONKIN & CO.	Engineers Works,
Engineers & Iron	Bermondsey,
Founders, Etc.	London, S.E.,

Oct. 2nd, 1868.

Nr. Bermondsey Station.
From Charing + or Cannon Street.

Professor Jevons,
The College,
Manchester.

Dear Sir,

Mr. B. Donkin Jun[r. 2] who is at present abroad, writes me that he gave you a paper written by me relative to economical steam Engines, and

---

[1] Minutes of Evidence taken before the Decimal Coinage Commission, *Parl. Papers*, 1860 [2591] xxx, 439–53, Evidence of Thomas Graham, Esq., 30 July 1857.

[1] Barnard William Farey (1827–88), Member of the Institution of Civil Engineers, 1865; nephew of John Farey (1791–1851), an authority on steam-engine practice. Farey, who had begun his engineering career in France under another uncle, Colomb Gengembre, was at this time a partner in the firm of Bryan Donkin & Co., which he had joined in 1847, retiring in 1881. In association with Bryan Donkin, Junior (see below, n. 2), he carried out a long series of experiments to ascertain the respective performance of compound and single-cylinder steam engines, accounts of which were published over a period of years in the journal *Engineering*. Farey patented a number of inventions and various machines designed by him were successfully manufactured by the firm. See Harry J. Donkin, *Bryan Donkin & Co., some notes on the history of an engineering firm during the last century, 1803–1903* (1912).

[2] Bryan Donkin, Junior, son of Bryan Donkin, F.R.S., the founder of the engineering firm which

requests me to send you another applying to this country; the one referred to being for Russia only.

I have now the pleasure of enclosing one applicable to this country simply remarking that you are at liberty to make use in any way of the whole or part as you may find requisite for your purpose.

I take the liberty also of enclosing a sketch[3] of an apparatus for testing the steam used by a steam Engine, and which if thoroughly understood would enable owners of steam Engines to ascertain cheaply, and easily the performances of their Engines.

The want of some such test has I believe been the cause of so much coal being uselessly consumed.

An experiment upon coal used, and water evaporated is too expensive, and I may say almost impossible in most cases: besides bringing into the question other matters, such as the efficiency of the boiler, and quality of the coal, as well as leaks and priming, all of which have nothing to do with the question as to what quantity of steam is passing through the Engine for a given power.

Mr. B. Donkin Jun[r.] has been testing by this apparatus many steam Engines in Russia, and the results confirm the data given in the enclosed paper.[4]

With reference to the sketch enclosed, the Photographic apparatus is required only for scientific experiments but for testing steam Engines nothing more is required than the wooden box, and a thermometer. I intend as soon as time will permit publishing something having reference to this subject in one of the scientific papers.

I understand that you purpose delivering a lecture on 'coal' at Newcastle.[5] May I ask you to kindly inform me when it will take place.

I am, Dr Sir,
Yours truly
B. W. Farey[6]

---

bore his name; the son entered the firm in 1828 and became a partner in 1840; well known for his experiments on steam consumption and related subjects.

[3] The paper is reproduced as an appendix to this letter but the sketch has not survived.

[4] Both Farey and Donkin had long and extensive connections with Russia. It was in Russia in 1819 that Farey's uncle had first seen a steam-engine indicator in use and on his return to England had instituted their manufacture. In 1858 the firm of Bryan Donkin & Co. had secured a contract from the Russian government to build a complete paper mill, including a 2000-h.p. steam engine, at St Petersburg (Harry J. Donkin, loc. cit., p. 15).

[5] See below, Letter 307, p. 195.

[6] The original letter is signed by Farey, but written by a clerk on notepaper with a printed letterhead.

Estimate of the annual cost of a horse power exerted by a Steam Engine

---

Practically 25lbs of water made into steam of 40 lbs pressure is required per horse power per hour by the most economical Engines now known; a good boiler would evaporate this 25lbs of water with 2½lbs of best Welsh coal; thus in 24 hours 60 lbs. of coals would be burnt or 360 lbs. in a week of 6 days and in one year of 52 weeks 18720 lbs equal to say 8 tons which at 25/- per ton for best Welsh coals gives £10 as the expense of fuel for one horse power.

The "horse-power" referred to is what is termed "indicated" so that an Engine indicating 100 horses would cost under the most favo[u]rable circumstances £1.000 per annum for fuel alone.

If inferior fuel is used less water would be evaporated and according to experiments the Welsh coals even at 25/0 per ton is cheaper for boiler purposes in London than any other coals or at any rate as cheap.

A good condensing steam Engine of the ordinary construction would require under the *best* circumstances 40lbs. of water per horse power and by the same calculation as above would cost £16 per annum for fuel per horse power, or for 100 horses power £1600.

The cost of one of our Horizontal Patent Steam Engines is about £17 per indicated horse power; the fixing, foundations, and connections would cost about £4 per indicated horse power, making a total of say £21 per indicated horse power, and this Engine would require but 25lbs. of water converted into steam of 40lbs pressure per indicated horse power per hour whereas a *good* steam Engine of the ordinary construction would require *40 lbs.* of water converted into steam of 40 lbs. pressure per indicated horse power per hour, and would cost at least £11 per indicated horse power, the fixing, foundations and connections would cost the same as our Engines making a total of £15 per indicated horse power so that by an extra outlay of £6 per indicated horse, £6 per annum would be saved without taking into consideration, the wear and tear of boilers, cost of extra stoking and extra repairs necessary from inferior design, workmanship &c.

In a Mill of 300 indicated horses power £1800 worth of fuel would be saved for an extra first outlay of £1800 (and taking 5% for interest of money upon the extra outlay) a clear annual saving of £1710 would be effected or £427. 10. 0. per quarter. If this sum were invested quarterly at 5% (instead of being paid away for fuel it would accumulate at compound interest in 10 years in round numbers to £22,000, in 20 years to £57,700 and in 30 years to £117,700; but as in most cases even what are termed good condensing Engines require 55 lbs of water per indicated horse power per hour, the saving over this description of Steam Engine would in fact be double, amounting in 10 years to £44,000, 20 years, £115,400 and in 30 years to £235,400.

304.   R. GRIFFITH[1] TO W. S. JEVONS
        [WM]

Munster Bank,
Bandon.
Oct. 8, 1868

Dear Sir,

I was away from this for a couple of days or I would have replied earlier to your favour of the 2nd inst.

From what I can recollect I believe about 8 or 9 years ago the Irish Banks began more or less stringently to charge on all light coins, according to instructions received from their Head offices, the sums sent over by these to the Bank of England at that time being charged accordingly as they were under weight. It being usual up to that period to receive gold irrespective of weight, of course the Irish Banks when the charge was put on lost a good deal in their first remittances. I don't think that for some years past there has been the same particularity with regard to the *weight* of the coins either on the part of the Banks or the general public, and as you are aware the circulation of gold in this country is comparatively limited the £1 note having almost completely taken the place of the sovereign. The Irish Banks held their gold, a great deal of which by the above rule was of very questionable weight, finding that it answered their purpose as well as the best, for whenever the public demanded gold they took it as such. During and a good time before you last wrote me the disturbed state of the country[2] caused a great panic on the part of small tradesmen and the farming class and there was a general run for gold.[3] An immensity was thus set afloat which had not before seen the light for years, but I feel certain that very nearly the whole has again found its way back to the Banks, and unless it was this old coin which was handed out by the Banks to the public, and which happened to be the coin circulating here and generally, instead of the nominal amount of

---

[1] Griffith, in common with H. W. Roberts and E. W. Johnson, whose letters are reproduced below (see Letters 305 and 308, pp. 191 and 195) appears to have been representative of the bank managers in England, Wales and Ireland to whom Jevons wrote in the course of his enquiry into the condition of the gold coinage. No biographical details of Griffith and Johnson have been traced.

[2] In consequence of the Fenian uprising of 1867.

[3] A number of private banks in Ireland, including the very old and respected La Touche's Bank, experienced difficulty in meeting their commitments at this period, and either closed down or were absorbed into larger joint-stock banks. See F. G. Hall, *The Bank of Ireland 1783–1946* (Dublin, 1948) pp. 245–58.

more modern coinage which for the general business of the country in this way is held always as floating cash, but which had become swamped by the sudden increased and protracted demand, I say, unless this accounts someway for the old character of the coinage referred to I am at a loss to conjecture the cause.

Should you think that the sovereigns that day examined may have been a deposit of some very old coin which may have found its way in then (as the mind of the public was very much disturbed at that time) I will at this more settled period again go into your particulars, should you wish it.

I have read your very able and concise paper on an "International Currency" with great pleasure, for which, I thank you.

Yours very truly,
R. Griffith

W. S. Jevons, Esq.

305. H. W. ROBERTS[1] TO W. S. JEVONS
[WM]

North and South Wales Bank
Holyhead.
8th October, 1868

Dear Sir,

I duly received your note of 3rd inst. Indisposition and the pressure of business prevented my replying to it earlier. In the meantime however, the subject of your enquiries has occupied a share of my thoughts and I now venture at your invitation to offer a few remarks bearing upon the circulation of money, more especially of gold coin, in this part of the Principality.

The glut of gold coin in North Wales may, I think, be accounted for broadly in this manner:—That whereas our imports are *paid for* practically in paper *we receive* an equivalent for a certain proportion of our exports *in Specie*.

To take our imports first I may enumerate them shortly as articles of Drapery and Grocery, Wines, Spirits and coals. The Dealers in these adjust their accounts with English Houses by remittances in Bank Drafts, cheques and, sometimes in notes, and also by direct payment in cash to the Representative of such Houses during their periodical visits. The Commercial Traveller, however, in these cases relieves himself of the specie (if not always of cheques and notes) by paying it into the first

---

[1] Hugh W. Roberts, Manager of the North and South Wales Bank Limited, 1865–76. The bank was established in 1836 and was finally absorbed into the London Joint City and Midland Bank Limited (now the Midland Bank Limited) in 1918 after a series of amalgamations.

convenient Bank on his journey receiving in exchange a Bank Draft which he remits to his principals. Even when the purchases are made in England by our Merchants and Tradesmen personally the goods are almost invariably paid for in *paper*. This system, it will be clearly seen, admits of no outlet for the precious metals (in the form of coin) and in a country chiefly agricultural and pastoral like North Wales it is not therefore surprising that a very moderate influx of gold when the flow is constant, produces as constant a plethora. To explain this more fully I must revert to the question of exports.

First of all in importance perhaps under this head will rank our Minerals, Stones and Slates but I need only just name these since the trade as between England and Wales in [?]² merchandise of this particular description is such as can only be carried on by means of paper payments. I refer then chiefly to our great staples, Cattle, Horses, Sheep, Pigs, Butter and agricultural produce generally. It is in exchange for these that specie flows into the country. The traffic in commodities of this nature cannot be conducted without the medium of gold and silver for the following reasons. Because (1st) The transactions *are small and numerous*. (2nd) The dealings are between stranger and stranger (3rd) The payment must be immediate, while, the bargains are often concluded in localities affording no facilities for exchanging money. And (4th) finally because the sellers are people of primitive habits and pursuits – a class which, in this, as in all other countries, invariably give a preference to "*hard cash*" over paper.

I do not mean to assert however that all this enormous traffic or even the bulk of it is done by means specie payments. On the contrary, I am perfectly aware that many of the leading English Cattle-Buyers draw their supplies of gold *in Wales* and that transactions of any magnitude, are usually adjusted through the medium of cheques or Bank notes; but it is equally within my knowledge that the Trade (especially in Horses) is represented also by a horde of dealers of lesser Note who might as well stop at home as come into Wales without first providing themselves with a supply of gold, for they would find a difficulty in obtaining it in this country even in exchange for Bank of England notes.

Moreover there remain the Welsh Dealers – a numerous body – who accompanying their merchandise to the English markets always return with a certain proportion of gold as the proceeds of their Sales. Add to this the stream of Coin pouring into the country during the summer months and springing from the visit of Travellers Tourists Excursionists and the numerous frequenters of our Watering-Places in search of health or pleasure and I think it will sufficiently account for that affluence of gold

---

² This word is indecipherable.

coin in North Wales which left unutilized by commercial or[3] manufacturing enterprise remains to be returned to England by the direct remittances of the Banking Houses.

> I am Dear Sir,
> Yours faithfully,
> H. W. Roberts.
> (Manager)

W. Stanley Jevons, Esq.,
Owen's College,
Manchester.

306.   W. MCKEWAN[1] TO W. S. JEVONS

> London & County Bank,
> 21 Lombard St.,
> London October 28 1868.[2]

W. S. Jevons Esq.,
    Owens College
        Manchester.

Dear Sir,

I have much pleasure in furnishing, so far as I am able, the information requested in your letter of 24th inst.

1.   The actual loss *paid* by us in the year ending 30 September last on light gold was £6716. – but this is irrespective of a large loss in interest on the stock we keep, so as to avail ourselves of any opportunity of placing the coin in circulation.

2.   The proportion of light gold coin in circulation in London is, according to our experience, from 35 to 40 per cent, and in the country from 40 to 50 per cent – this higher proportion being occasioned by the universal course adopted of selecting the heavy coin for transmission to London and keeping the light in circulation.

3.   I am not aware of any other inconvenience arising from the lightness of the coin than the money loss referred to and the constant labour in selecting the coin so as to lessen the loss as far as possible.

The total amount of gold and silver coin received at this office during

---

[3] 'of' in the original manuscript.

[1] William McKewan (1820–1909), joined the London and County Banking Company in 1839; General Manager, 1867–90; Vice-President of the Institute of Bankers, 1885–90. The bank was established in 1836 and was finally absorbed into the Westminster Bank Limited in 1923, after a series of amalgamations.

[2] The original manuscript of this letter is now in the possession of the Royal Statistical Society, London.

the year ending 30th September was £8,811,000 of which £6,668,600 was received from our Branches in the country or in the suburbs of London. I am not able to distinguish gold from silver, the latter would probably amount to about 5 or 6 per cent.

The total amount of coin sent by us into the Bank of England during the period referred to was £4,459,000 – deducting £182,000 as the approximate amount of silver=£4,277,000 of gold coin, the loss on which, £6,716 – is equal to 1.571 per Mille or $3/\frac{14}{100}$ per cent, the average loss on the portion light being 1.363 per cent as ascertained by the actual sale of about £10,000 during the month – for which we obtained from dealers £3. 17. 7 per oz – the Bank paying only £3. 17. 6½ per oz.

The state of the gold coinage generally is very discreditable to us as a nation and its deficiency is, I believe, mainly attributable to the softness of the alloy used at the Mint – indeed the whole question of the management of the Mint deserves and will, I trust, receive some notice by the next parliament.

You are quite at liberty to use the statistics I have given if they are available for your purpose, though I do not wish reference to be made to the name of the Bank.

I am,

Dear Sir,

Yours faithfully,

W. McKewan.

General Manager.

P.S. Mr. E. Seyd[3] of Princes Street, who has recently published a Comprehensive Work on Bullion and Foreign Exchanges,[4] can give you much valuable information on the subject of the Coinage and will I am sure with pleasure do so.

---

[3] Ernest Seyd (1833–81), a German merchant in San Francisco who settled in England and became a banker in the City of London from 1861 until his death; a member of the council of the [Royal] Statistical Society, 1870–80. Cf. below, Letters 309 and 310, pp. 198 and 200.

[4] *Bullion and Foreign Exchanges Theoretically and Practically Considered, followed by a Defence of the Double Valuation* . . . (1868). Seyd's other principal works included: *California and its Resources* (1858); *The Fall in the Price of Silver: its causes, its consequences* . . . (1876); *The Wealth and Commerce of Nations* . . . (1878) and *The Decline of Prosperity; its insidious cause and obvious remedy* (1879).

307.   W. S. JEVONS TO HERBERT JEVONS
       [LJN, 245]

Parsonage Road, Withington,
Manchester, 20th November 1868

. . . I have just been one of my journeys to London, to read a paper to
the Statistical Society on the Gold Currency.[1] It is the result of a rather
elaborate inquiry during the past nine months, which has proved rather
successful, and is likely to prove useful, I think. I have some hope that
when Mr. Gladstone is Premier, with a great majority at his back, he may
give some attention to the subject.

. . . These journeys rather knock me up. I had three classes on
Monday afternoon and evening, went to London on Tuesday morning,
read the paper in the evening, and back on Wednesday for two classes in
the evening. Now a thing of this sort knocks me up for the rest of the week.

About a month ago I gave two lectures,[2] on successive evenings, at
Newcastle, on coal, with fair audiences, but this thoroughly knocked me
up. I cannot say my health is bad, but I have to take great care of myself,
drink port wine occasionally, and take things as easily as possible. I never
hear any complaints from you now, and hope that your health is stronger.

I cannot tell you how happy Harriet and I are together . . . so that I
am altogether better off than I had any right to expect in this world. . . .

308.   E. W. JOHNSON TO W. S. JEVONS
       [WM]

National Provincial Bank of England
South Molton.
25th Nov. 1868

Dear Sir,

I have been absent from this a month during which time your letter of
3rd Oct. arrived and I regret not sooner giving it my attention.

In reply to the first question as to how new gold is circulated, it
undoubtedly is drawn from the Bank of England to supply (as you
suggest) the manufacturing and mining districts or large seaports and a
further *large supply* is drawn by local Bankers in Agricultural Districts
from June to August to meet the requirements of farmers for the
ingathering of hay and corn. Moreover I think you will find that the Bank

---

[1] See above, Letter 281, n. 2, p. 159.
[2] 'The Exhaustion of Coal', two lectures to the Newcastle Literary and Philosophical Society,
delivered on 15 and 16 October 1868.

Returns at this period of the year show a decrease in the Gold and Silver Coin. Now we come to the question of Surplus, in my former remarks I ought to have said "in all Agricultural Districts a Surplus of Gold exists at certain periods of the year generally between Michaelmas and Christmas when the Gold circulated during harvest finds its way back to the Banks. As to Banks retaining its light Gold rather than remitting it at a loss – as a practical man seeing after Harvest the gold was accumulating I should keep all *new sovereigns* and issue all light ones so as to be in a position to remit without loss. I have however known Banks deterred from remitting gold to the Bank of England in consequence of its lightness, still I think by the above system loss could be avoided although this cannot last for ever. A Bank having more gold than it required would as a matter of course keep less Bank paper.

Many thanks for your interesting Pamphlet. I think with you government ought to bear the loss by the deterioration of the Coinage and if once agreed upon all Bankers would be glad to assist in collecting the old coinage.

The Royal Commission on International Coinage will not recommend an alteration of the pound sterling.

Believe me
Yours truly
Edwd. Wales Johnson

309.   LOUIS WOLOWSKI[1] TO W. S. JEVONS

Paris, 7 Decembre [1868]
45 rue de Clichy

Mon cher collègue,

Avez Vs reçu mes notes *sur la question monétaire* et mon *mémoire sur l'or et l'argent,* lu à l'Institut?[2] J'ai eu le courage d'attaquer la formule que je considère comme surannée et fausse, de *l'étalon unique,* sans être le defenseur du *double étalon,* denomination vicieuse qui a jeté la confusion dans le débat. La valeur n'admet aucun étalon c'est la verité économique proclamée par nos maitres à laquelle je me rattache forcement. On ne peut rencontrer ici qu'une mesure imparfaite et variable, car ce sera toujours une substance materielle qui servira de terme commun de comparaison, *tertium comparationis.* La monnaie n'est pas autre chose; les

---

[1] Louis Francois Raymond Wolowski (1810–76) French economist of Polish birth. Professeur de legislation industrielle at the Conservatoire des Arts et Métiers, 1839; director of the Banque Foncière, 1852; membre de l'Academie des sciences morales et politiques, 1855.

[2] *La Question Monétaire à la Société d'Économie Politique de Paris, Reunion du 1er juin 1867; L'Or et l'Argent – memoire lu le 7 Octobre 1868 à la Séance des Cinq Académies de l'Institut Imperial de France;* both reprinted in Wolowski's *L'Or et l'Argent* (1870).

peuples civilisés ont appelé les metaux précieux a cet office, parce qu'ils varient moins que les autres objets, dans la période assignée d'ordinaire aux transactions humaines. Ils les ont employés tous les deux, a fin que l'action solidaire et l'influence réciproque de l'or et de l'argent amortit les oscillations, en fondant dans la masse les changements survenus dans l'approvisionnement de l'un ou de l'autre.

Pour fortifier cette solidarité, la loi de germinal an XI a établi un taux fixè de change légal pour les monnaies frappées avec les deux metaux, alors qu'il s'agit d'offres legales ou de paiements au tresor public. C'est à cela que se réduit ce que l'on a mal appelé le *double étalon* en amenant la confusion dans les idées par la confusion des termes.

Quand les deux metaux remplissent [*sic*] le même but suivant un change fixè, toute oscillation grave devient impossible, si l'un faiblit de prix, la demande se porte immédiatement de ce côté, sert de parachute et relève le taux — ce mouvement alternatif et inévitable entretient la stabilité de la monnaie sur laquelle repose tout l'echaffaudage du crédit et des relations humaines, ainsi que le sens de tous les contrats.

Ma doctrine a déja rencontré des adhesions éclatantes à la société des economistes de Berlin (séance du 31 Octobre — Prince Smith,[3] docteur Wiss,[4] Michaelis,[5] professeur Schmoller de Halle[6]) elle a converté M. de Laveleye,[7] professeur d'écon. pol. a Liège, qui s'etait prononcé par écrit en sens contraire. Elle m'a valu hier une lettre d'approbation complète du venérable professeur Rau de Heidelberg, le Jean-Baptiste Say de l'Allemagne.[8] Je serais heureux de connaitre Votre opinion le plus promptement possible, aussi je sollicite une réponse immediate. Je me feliciterai fort si elle est favorable, mais comme avant tout j'aime la

[3] John Prince Smith (1809–74), London-born political economist who settled in Prussia; one of the leaders of the freetrade movement in Germany. Member of the Prussian Lower House, 1862–6 and of the Reichstag, 1870; President of the Society of Economists at Berlin, 1870. His publications included *The English Coinage Question* (Cobden Club Essays, 2nd series, 1871–2).

[4] Georg Eduard Wiss (1822–87), editor of *Vierteljahrsschrift für Volkswirtschaft und Kulturgeschichte*, published in Berlin from 1863; author of *Ueber die Wahrungsfrage in Deutschland* (1872).

[5] Otto Michaelis (1826–90), studied law in Bonn and Berlin but turned to journalism after 1848. Member of the Prussian lower house, 1861, and of the North German Reichstag, 1867. Director of the Finance Division of the German Imperial Chancellors Department, 1877; took over the administration of national insurance funds in 1879.

[6] Gustav Schmoller (1838–1917), Professor of Political Economy at Halle, 1864–72; at Strasbourg, 1872–82; and at Berlin from 1882. Prominent in the Verein für Sozialpolitik from its foundation in 1872 and acknowledged as leader of the 'younger' historical school. His many publications included *Geschichte der deutschen Kleingewerbe im 19. Jahrhundert* (1870), *Grundfragen der Sozialpolitik und Volkswirlschaftslehre* (1898) and *Grundriss der Allgemeinen Volkswirtchaftslehre* (1900–4).

[7] Emile Louis Victor de Laveleye (1822–92), Belgian economist and publicist. Joined the staff of *Revue de Deux Mondes*, 1858; Professor of Political Economy at the University of Liège, 1864–92. A follower of the historical school, his best-known work was *De la propriété et de ses formes primitives* (1874).

[8] Karl Heinrich Rau (1792–1870), Professor of Political Economy at Erlangen, 1816–22, and at Heidelberg, 1822–70. Wolowski's description probably refers to the dominant position which Rau's *Lehrbuch der politischen Ökonomie* (3 vols, 1826–37) occupied in the teaching of economics in Germany for some fifty years.

discussion avec des hommes éminents, si Vs me combattez dites-moi Vos raisons, je crois etre en mesure de repondre. Je voudrais une monnaie internationale et ne crois possible de l'etablir que sur la base de l'or et de l'argent reliés partout par un change légal uniforme, qui empecherais toute commotion violente. Supprimer l'argent, comme Vs l'avez fait en Angleterre, cela peut être bon pour un pays, ce serait funeste pour le marché universel, la contraction de l'outillage monetaire entrainerait un désastre véritable. M. Ernest Seyd l'a prouvé dans un livre récent *On Bullion and Foreign Exchange.* [9] Le connaissez Vs?

Agréer l'expression de mes sentiments les plus distingués

L. Wolowski

Je prends la liberté d'insister pour une prompte réponse.

Jevons replied to Wolowski in a letter dated 12 December 1868, the full text of which is included in *Investigations* under the title 'Gold and Silver' (first edition, pp. 303–6). He thus summarised his views in the concluding paragraph: 'Though far from feeling confident in anything which I say upon this subject, I must acknowledge that *in theory* you and the other defenders of what may be called the *alternative standard* are right. But in the *practical aspect* the subject looks very different, and I am inclined to hope for the extension of the *single gold standard*.'

Wolowski translated and published part of Jevons's letter in his book *L'Or et l'Argent* (Paris, 1870) pp. 62–4.

310.   LOUIS WOLOWSKI TO W. S. JEVONS

Paris, 18 Decembre/1868/
45 rue de Clichy

Mon cher collègue,

Je Vs remercie de Votre excellente lettre qui renferme tant de preuves de Votre conscience sciéntifique. Vous declarez que Vs inclineriez de mon côté en théorie, mais que le côté pratique Vs arrete. C'est ce côté qui me détermine – L'outillage monétaire du monde peut être affecté de deux manières: 1° par une expansion qui correspond à l'acroissement de la production et à la multiplication des relations; loin d'être un mal, elle est un bien, elle facilite une transformation heureuse. Il reste encore de ce

---

[9] See above, Letter 306, n. 4, p. 194.

côté des nombreuses lacunes à remplir. La plaie du papier-monnaie existe dans de nombreux pays, desireux de s'enguérir [*sic*]. L'Italie va supprimer le cours forcé; il faut espérer que les États-Unis renonceront bientôt aux *greenbacks*; l'Autriche travaille a retablir la monnaie réelle et la Russie le desire. Il y a de quoi employer des milliards d'or et d'argent nouveau rien que pour satisfaire a cette nécessite première. D'ailleurs la population croît, l'aisance augmente, les besoins du luxe descendent dans les couches inférieures et par consequent plus larges de la pyramide humaine: un montre d'or, une alliance, des chaines, des bijoux vulgaires, la vaisselle plate, les couverts d'argent offrent un vaste champ a l'emploi des nouveaux arrivages d'or et d'argent. Enfin moi qui suis *Bullionist*, je vois avec plaisir que la base étroite sur laquelle s'elève le colossal echaffaudage du crédit et des compensations, s'affermisse, que la monnaie qui traduit toutes les conventions, vacille moins qu'elle ne le fait. Avec un seul métal, elle est exposée à des secousses sensibles, car rien ne balance l'effet de l'accroissement ou de la diminution du *stock* progressif; avec les deux métaux qui se combinent dans une action commune, qui servent tous deux de *legal tenders* on évite les commotions, on ménage les transitions – C'est l'or, unique instrument, de droit chez vous, de fait chez nous qui a provoqué les brusques exhaussements de l'escompte.

Si au contraire l'outillage metallique se contracte, si la masse diminue, si la suppression successive de l'argent, par suite de conventions internationales, deplace les rapports actuels, la baisse des prix s'en suivra, l'aggravation de la dette publique et des dettes privées s'alourdira; tout ira en sens inverse de ce que commande l'equité et l'interêt bien entendu des nations.

Vs êtes dominé par la crainte d'un avilissement de l'or – Je crains que Vous ne pench[iez trop?][1] de ce côté; mais s'il fallait choisir entre deux maux, je preferais la diminution du prix de l'or a son renchérissement. Je ne désire en aucune manière porter prejudice aux exportateurs, mais je les crois moins a plaindre que les débiteurs.

Quant a la question de *l'étalon unique,* permettez moi de m'exprimer avec une rude franchise: c'est une chimère surannée. Qu'on trouve plus d'avantage à employer l'or, il faut pour cela d'autres motifs que celui *de l'unité pretendue de la mesure de la valeur,* car tout se reduit ici à une *offre legale de paiement (legal tender* – Währung en allemand: les Anglais et les Allemands sont heureux d'échapper par une langue plus précise sur ce point, à l'équivoque captieuse de *l'étalon*). *L'offre légale* sera d'autant plus juste que la substance sur laquelle elle porte variera moins, et retiendra d'une manière plus fidèle, la veritable portée de *la puissance d'acquérir.* La monnaie n'est que le gage matériel de l'exercice différé du *pouvoir*

---

[1] Part of the original manuscript is blotted out at this point.

d'acquérir, obtenu en échange du produit cedé ou du service rendu. Il importe que cet *equivalent potestatif* demeure aussi stable que possible; on y arrive par l'emploi alternatif ou annulé de l'or et de l'argent. Je travaille au [volu]me[1] qui mettra pleinement cette verite en lumière.

Votre bien devoué

L. Wolowski

[Pouve]z[1] Vs me dire qui est [M. Er][1]nest Seyd – auteur du livre nouveau: *On Bullion and foreign exchange?*

Veuillez m'envoyer l'adresse de M. le professeur Cairns dont j'ai eu le plaisir de faire la connaissance a Londres. En attendant que je lui écris, ne pourriez Vs pas lui communiquer ma correspondance? A-t-il reçu mes deux brochures?[2]

311.   G. WALKER[1] TO W. S. JEVONS

Third National Bank,
Springfield, Mass.
Dec. 28, 1868.

Professor Stanley Jevons,
London.

Dear Sir,

I have just seen in the Economist of the 12th inst. notice of a paper read by you at a late meeting of the Statistical Society on the amount and condition of the existing gold coinage of Great Britain. The part which particularly interested me, though quite aside, I presume, from the main purpose of your enquiry, was your estimate of the total circulating medium of the United Kingdom, – at the request of my friend Honble. David A. Wells,[2] Special Comm[r.] of the Revenue, I have lately addressed

---

[1] Part of the original manuscript is blotted out at this point.

[2] Wolowski wrote a further postscript on a corner of the first sheet of the letter; parts of this are also blotted, but the remainder reads:

'. . . de mon affreux griffonage, une fois la plume . . . je ne peux bientôt plus la retenir, car elle est tres lente au gré de la pensée et je suis trop paresseux pour récopier ce que j'écris.' Jevons apparently found Wolowski's 'affreux griffonage' difficult to decipher, for the letters are accompanied by a transcription in another hand of the text of the letter of 18 December. The transcriber (possibly Hermann Breymann?) was also unable to identify a number of words in Wolowski's manuscript.

[1] George Walker (1824–88), president of the Third National Bank of Springfield, Massachusetts, and of the Bank Commissioners of that state; known as an opponent of greenbacks and an advocate of 'hard money'. See Dorfman, *The Economic Mind in American Civilisation* (1947) III, 6.

[2] David Ames Wells (1828–98), also of Springfield, Mass., began life as a journalist. Became interested in financial questions in 1863 and wrote *Our Burden and our Strength, A Comparative Examination of the Debts and Resources of the Country, Present and Prospective.* This attracted the attention of Lincoln, who appointed a commission on the revenue and in 1865 made Wells its Chairman. From 1866 to 1870 Wells acted as Special Commissioner of the Revenue and later as Chairman of the New

him a letter, to be printed with his forthcoming report, on the "currencies of Great Britain France and the United States". I now send you a copy of this paper. I regret that I had not seen your paper before writing my own, for as you will observe, I have put the metallic circulation of Great Britain considerably below your estimate. Taking the estimate of Dr. Lees[3] (Drain of Silver to the East etc. Lond. 1864) I have called it £80,000,000 gold & silver – *including the amount in bank*. You make it 110 mil. I suppose the estimate of gold and silver coinage covers the amt. in bank and therefore deduct the amt. estimated in Scotch and Irish and Eng. provincial banks – w$^{\underline{d}}$. it not cover any coin in the two depts. of the Bk. of England. A later private letter from Mr. Newmarch (addressed to a friend) says the British currency consists of "about 100 millions of gold and silver and 40 millions of bank notes". Chevalier in 1853 (Dic d'Econ. Pol.) estimated it at £60,000,000 *including* the coin and bullion in the Bk of England. Rosung (Metaux Precieux p. 173) sets down the amount of "specie – gold and silver coined" in England in 1856 at 1,665 mil. fr. $= 66\frac{6}{10}$ mils. l stg. Your judgment in the matter, for which your previous publications would lead me to entertain the highest respect would indicate that the English authorities whom I have consulted, do not include the money in bank in these estimates, and I wonder that Mr. Goschen (my quotation from whom was, I regret to say, from memory,) refers to estimates of the *present* circulation of *sovereigns* only. Whatever mistake I may have made in estimating the metallic circulation of Great Britain, it will not, I think, impugn the general conclusions of my paper – that the United States has not suffered in comparison with European nations from any inadequacy of the circulating medium but rather from its inferior quality and over abundance such as it was. I meant my communication to correct the false impressions which prevail here as to the amount of foreign currencies and as to the proper function of money in the economy of society. I regret, therefore, that it should be open to the charge of inaccuracy, even where accuracy is so difficult to arrive at.

As you probably know, we have a large and influential body of public men – and with them a few economists at the head of whom is Mr. Carey[4] who think it for their advantage just now to preach up the virtues of paper money and an expanded circulation.

York State Tax Commission. At first a protectionist he later became a strong advocate of free trade, but always favoured 'sound money', opposing the issue of paper money by the Federal Government. See F. B. Joyner, *David Ames Wells, Champion of Free Trade* (Cedar Rapids, 1939).

[3] William Nassau Lees, *The Drain of Silver to the East and the Currency of India* (1863).

[4] Henry C. Carey (1793–1879), Philadelphia publisher, company promoter and pamphleteer; advocate of protection and a managed currency. Dorfman, op. cit., II, 789–804.

If your paper before the Statistical Society is separately printed I shall be greatly obliged to you for a copy.

I have the honor to be
With high respect
Your obedient servant
George Walker.

312.   G. WALKER TO W. S. JEVONS

Washington,
March 1. 1869.

My dear Sir,

I have to acknowledge the receipt of your obliging letter of the 15th of January, as well as of your paper read before the Statistical Society in Nov. both of which I found on a recent visit to my home in Mass. I am very glad to find that you approve of the general tenor of my remarks on the currency, in my recent letter to Mr. Wells. They meet with a more ready acquiescence in an old country like England, than in this country, & especially among the trading classes, & in the new states. But they are gaining ground, and will vindicate themselves more fully after a return to specie payments, when the currency of this country becomes once more subject to natural laws.

A perusal of your paper encourages me to believe, that my estimate of the metallic circulation of Great Britain was not, after all, far out of the way. Will you permit me to say, that I think you do not make allowance enough for the exportation & melting of recent coins, & that thus your basis of estimate of the actual circulation is too large. To arrive at the actual amount of existing sovereigns of '63 & 4, on which the whole estimate depends, you assume that they have constituted only 1/5 of the export, because they constitute only 1/5 of the circulation remaining. Is this a justifiable conclusion, in view of the known fact, which you elsewhere state, that only coins of full weight are either exported or melted? Now, if I understand the matter rightly, exporters & melters draw their coin from the Bank, and on page 457 it appears, that of sovereigns in Bank, 69% are of late coinages ('60–67). Is it not therefore, probable that 1/2 the exports are of dates as late as '60? Putting 1/3 of the exports (8,664,653) as of coins of '63 & 4 and the total, instead of £1,750,000 w$^{d.}$ be £2,890,000. Besides this, in view of the large operations of bullion dealers, and of the use of gold in the arts, is it not reasonable to suppose that the melting would deduct £1,110,000, so as to make a round sum of £4,000,000 to be deducted? This w$^{d.}$ leave

£10,000,000 of sovereigns of '63 & 4 which x by 5.356 = 53,560,000 sovereigns.

add ½ sovs.	12,000,000
add new coin in Bk.	3,500,000

	69,060,000
or, as no deduction is made from half sovereigns, say	69,000,000
add silver	14,000,000
copper	1,000,000
Total Metallic Cir.	£84,000,000
add Bullion	15,
" notes and security	15,
" net English bank notes	3,500,000
" " Scotch & Irish "	5,500,000
	£123,000,000

Now to make a proper comparison with the circulation of the U.S.,° where the banks return only the notes actually outstanding in the hands of the people, it is necessary to deduct £9,000,000, being the average reserve of notes in the Banking Dept. of the B. of E. say 123,000,000 − 9,000,000 = 114,000,000 as the actual outstanding circulation. Say estimate was £110,000,000.

Perfect accuracy in this matter is not only unattainable, but of no great consequence, but I am glad to believe that I do not widely differ from so competent an authority as yourself. Actual money is now so inconsiderable a vehicle in the exchanges, that the real question has come to be more of *quality* than anything else. It is important far more as a measure of value, than as an instrument of exchange. This consideration is fast leading me towards a desire for a purely metallic, or merely representative money. I have requested my friend Prof. Blake[1] of California (now here in employ of the State Dept.) to send you a valuable report on the precious metals which he is finishing.[2] I shall also ask the Director of the Mint (which I have recently visited as one of the annual commission of assay) to send you his recent reports and other papers. I have sent you Mr. Wells full report.[3]

[1] William Phipps Blake (1825–1910), geologist and mining engineer; Professor of Mineralogy and Geology at the College of California, 1863–95; Professor of Geology and Mining, University of Arizona, 1895–1905; Commissioner for California at the Paris Exposition of 1867.

[2] *The production of the precious metals: or, statistical notices of the principal gold and silver producing regions of the world; with a chapter on the unification of gold and silver coinage* (New York, 1869).

[3] *Report of the Special Commissioner of the Revenue upon the industry, trade, commerce, etc., of the United States for the year 1868* (Washington, D.C., 1869).

If I can at any time aid your enquiries into American statistics I beg you will command me freely. My address is as before at Springfield Mass.

> I am dear Sir,
> Very faithfully,
> Yours
> George Walker

Prof. W. S. Jevons
Owens College,
MANCHESTER.

313. W. S. JEVONS TO HERBERT JEVONS

> Withington
> 23 March 69.

My dear Herbert

I posted a letter to you by the mail via Southampton containing a duplicate of the letter of credit for £80 on the Dunedin Office of B of N S W. A few days afterwards I heard from Henry that Roscoe was ill of a bad cold, and the next day but one we heard that he was dead. Henry on hearing that he was ill went to see him at once, and ordered him to have a nurse & everything requisite if he should become worse. The physician of the Hospital Dr Inman also visited him and the doctors thought his lungs were not sound. But on Thursday 18th March he seems to have rapidly grown worse and died at 6.30 pm probably of an effusion of serum on the lungs. As I anticipated that the illness would in any case be a very slow one I did not immediately go over & thus did not again see him alive. On Saturday 19th, having heard of his death the previous evening, I went over to Lpool, to assist Henry in arranging for the funeral. I saw what remained of poor Roscoe at the Asylum where he lay at last calm and placid and with signs of peace & rest upon a face which has so often distressed me.

It seems that there was no return of anything like reason, and we have only to be thankful that his illness was short, being only a week from the beginning of his cold, and that it was not a particularly painful one.

I was this morning at his funeral in the Park Chapel Yard, the Renshaw Street one being closed. For my own part I preferred the Park to any other & chose a grave there myself near those of some others of the Jevons family & also close to the Daulbys'[1] grave. The funeral was exceedingly quiet & consisted of only a single carriage into which we got out of the street – opposite the Asylum. Henry, Will & myself alone

---

[1] See Vol. I, p. 59, n. 5.

followed the hearse, but at the Chapel were Henny, Mary Catharine,[2] & Uncle Timothy, besides Mary Bentley,[3] George Edge[4] & another or two. Mr Upton[5] a College fellow of mine & the present minister of the Chapel read the service very pleasingly and altogether it was done agreably* to my own feelings.

This will remove a sad weight from our minds and though it must revive many painful memories we need not hesitate now to dismiss them as far as possible for the future. From what Lucy now writes to me she seems to have been filled with unhappy remembrances of Roscoes illness more than I had supposed and you will doubtless also remember more than I do, though I can remember enough that is painful.

Mary Bentley tells me that my mother seemed aware of Roscoes danger, for she said one day "Poor Roscoe, I fear he will have much to suffer" & we know that few have suffered what to us seems worse.[6]

Henry has acted very kindly in this as in all other things & I think it is time we made him some slight acknowledgement. I propose therefore to make him a very handsome present of something costing under £50, sharing the expense between Tom, you, & me. I think I may take the liberty of charging you on account of it something not exceeding £10 & Tom who consented to the notion, if he did not himself propose it, will doubtless divide the rest whatever it may be with me. I am thinking of getting him some handsome work of art or a picture.

I have been thinking a good deal about you, and am very much afraid you may lose all your savings in quartz-mining. John Hutton has almost ruined himself in like manner, and I do wish you would do anything with your money rather than put it into such hazardous speculations.

This afternoon Henry, James Thornely,[7] William Jevons[8] and I had a regular Consultation over Lucy's affairs, and I hope we shall get the remainder of Johns property safely settled upon her, & I am likely to be one trustee with Richard Hutton for the other, but it is a complicated matter & the property after all is worth but little.

I am going to see them at Ludlow the day after tomorrow & will tell you by next mail how Lucy is getting on. She was not strong or well enough to undertake a journey to join us at the funeral.

[2] See Vol. I, p. 56, n. 8.

[3] See Vol. II, Letter 20, n. 4, p. 36.

[4] It has proved impossible to obtain any biographical information about George Edge, who seems likely to have been a former servant or employee of the Jevons family.

[5] Charles Upton (1831–1920), Unitarian minister; student in the Faculty of Arts and Laws, University College London, 1853–7; studied for the ministry at Manchester New College, London, 1853–63; minister of the Ancient Chapel, Toxteth Park, Liverpool, 1867–75; then joined the staff of Manchester New College, which was moved to Oxford in 1889; Professor Emeritus from 1903 until his death. Joint author with James Drummond of *The Life and Letters of James Martineau*, 2 vols (1902).

[6] See Vol. I, pp. 7–9, 212.

[7] See Vol. II, Letter 59, n. 3, p. 141.

[8] i.e. William Alfred Jevons. See Vol. II, Letter 143, n. 5, p. 405.

This letter tells you the end of a sad chapter in our history & now I hope we may close our minds to its memory.

Hoping to hear from you often

Your affectionate Brother

W. Stanley Jevons.

314.   E. HELM[1] TO W. S. JEVONS

5 Clarendon Road,
High Street,
Chorlton on Medlock.
6 April 1869.

My Dear Sir,

Further examination leads me to estimate the quantity of wheaten flour used in Cotton Manufacture in this country as follows:—

In sizing yarn for weaving	105,000,000 lbs.
In finishing bleached, printed and dyed goods	25,000,000
	130,000,000

Other substances containing starch and gluten are also used, as sago, rice and potatoes but I have excluded these in the above rough estimate.

Believe me,

Yours faithfully,
Elijah Helm.

W. S. Jevons, Esq.

315.   J. E. CAIRNES TO W. S. JEVONS

Villa Conte,
Nice.
15 April 1869.

Dear Professor Jevons,

I trust it is not too late to thank you for your pamphlet on the "Metallic Currency of the United Kingdom", which you did me the favour to send to my address in London, but which only reached me here within a few weeks.[1] I have just read it, and am greatly pleased and interested with the

---

[1] Elijah Helm (1837–1904), authority on the history and economics of the cotton trade. A student in Jevons's evening classes at Owens College, he later became Cobden Lecturer on Political Economy himself; President of Manchester Statistical Society, 1879–81; Secretary of Manchester Chamber of Commerce, 1889–1904.

[1] Apparently an offprint of 'On the Condition of the Metallic Currency of the United Kingdom with reference to the Question of International Coinage'. See above, Letter 281, n. 2, p. 159.

very curious and valuable information which you have brought together. I confess the revelations it makes as to the condition of our metallic currency take me by surprise and I trust will lead to the adoption of the practical measures which the pamphlet recommends. Having been absent from England (with the exception of a few months last summer) for more than two years, owing to ill health, I am not at present au courant with the state of the controversy, and have not read the report of the Royal Commission. I am not quite certain that I apprehend the purport of your reply to the passage quoted at pp. 431–2,[2] but, as I understand it, you accept the first horn of the dilemma propounded, and you contend that, while the proposed sovereign, containing less gold, wd. by the imposition of a seignorage, retain its equality with the present sovereign it would nevertheless lose the superiority possessed by the present sovereign over 25 francs; the comparison under the existing state of things lying between the *gold* in the sovereign and the *gold* in 25 francs; whereas under the proposed arrangement it wd. lie between the gold *plus* the seignorage in each coin.

I hope you find the study of Political Economy progressing in Manchester, and thanking you again for your kindness in sending me your pamphlet.

I remain,

Dear Professor Jevons,
very truly yours,
J. E. Cairnes.

---

[2] The passage quoted by Jevons on pp. 431–2 was as follows: 'If the new sovereign, containing only 112 grains of fine gold, retains, in consequence of the imposition of a seigniorage, the value of the old sovereign, it would retain its superiority in value over 25frs. If it is equal in value to 25frs. of the present French currency, it would not be equal in value to the existing sovereign.'

On which Jevons commented: 'But it is apparent that at present, in the absence of an international currency, we measure only the gold in our sovereign against the gold in 25frs. and in calculating the par, no account is taken of the mint charge in France, which is an uncertain amount. The fact has even come out during the discussion, that the true pars of exchange are not accurately ascertainable in the absence of precise information concerning the mint charge in different countries. No exact comparison can at present be made between the value of the franc *plus* a mint charge, with the sovereign without a mint charge. But it is indisputable that if both coins and mint charges are exactly assimilated there will be no difference in value possible between the currencies of France & England, but such as may arise from the natural variation of the exchanges, and this will be restricted within the very small cost incurred by the transmission of specie.'

316.   M. CHEVALIER[1] TO W. S. JEVONS

Paris, 27 Avenue de
l'Impératrice
31 Mai 1869

Monsieur,

J'ai remarqué, dans *l'Economist* du 8 de ce mois, un article qui porte votre signature et qui traite de *la depreciation de l'or*.[2] La question est discutée avec cette distinction et cette lucidité qui vous sont familières. Si donc je prends la liberté de vous écrire, ce n'est aucunement pour contredire l'opinion que vous avez exprimée.

Je voudrais soumettre à l'appréciation de votre excellent esprit un fait qui me semble considerable, et qui a du contribuer, ce me semble, dans une proportion pas commune, à renverser la prédiction que je m'étais permise, d'une forte dépréciation de l'or.[3]

Ce fait, c'est que des évènements imprévus et énormes ont determiné l'exportation de l'Europe d'une grande masse d'argent, à destination de l'Asie, d'où il est resulté que, malgré d'immenses arrivages d'or, fournis par la Californie et l' Australie, sans parler de la Sibérie, la quantité de monnaie n'a pas augmenté en Europe dans une très grande proportion; et comme, pendant le même temps, le développement de l'industrie et du commerce, et le progrès du bien-être parmi les populations ouvrières etaient très marqués, il est arrivé que la hausse des prix a dû être très limitée.

Les évènements dont je viens de parler sont 1° la guerre occasionée dans l'Inde par la rébellion des troupes indigènes; 2° L'exécution des chemins de fer et autres travaux publics dans l'Inde; 3° La guerre de la Sécession en Amérique, qui a déterminé l'achat, par l'Europe, d'une très grande quantité de cotons dans l'Inde; 4° La maladie du ver à soie qui oblige l'Europe a acheter de la soie pour une somme importante en Chine et au Japon.

Des calculs, que je me suis appliqué à rendre aussi peu incertains que

---

[1] Michel Chevalier (1816–79), Professor of Political Economy at the Collège de France, 1850. Champion of free trade and architect, with Cobden, of the Anglo-French commercial treaty of 1860. At the time of the Californian and Australian gold discoveries he anticipated a rapid depreciation of gold and advocated a silver standard, but in later years he opposed bimetallism.

[2] 'The Depreciation of Gold,' *Economist*, 8 May 1869, pp. 530–2; reprinted in *JRSS*, 32 (1869) 445–9, and *Investigations*, pp. 151–9.

[3] In his letter to *The Economist* Jevons argued that his predictions of a fall in the value of gold had been largely vindicated – 'I believe it is wholly beyond doubt that the expected result has been manifested, but not in the mode predicted. Many eminent men, especially Chevalier, looked upon the depreciation of gold as a revolutionary event which would happen in the course of time, and yet I believe that when Chevalier was writing the most sudden and serious part of the effect had already been produced.' Cf. Chevalier, *De la Baisse Probable de l'Or* (Paris, 1858, English translation by Richard Cobden, Manchester, 1859).

possible, m'ont donné ce résultat que, en seize ans, du 1er janvier 1849 au 1er janvier 1865, l'approvisionnement de la civilisation occidentale (Europe et Amerique) en or et en argent, les deux ensemble, ce serait accru seulement de 5,379,000,000 francs (difference entre 39,583,000,000 et 34,204,000,000 fr.). Cet accroissement n'est guère que d'un septième de la masse preéxistente (34,204,000,000 fr.) ou en moyenne de 1 pour cent par an. C'en est assez, ce me semble, pour expliquer comment les prix n'ont pas éprouvé une plus forte hausse.

Les calculs dont je parle ont été continués dans la seconde édition de mon *Traité de la Monnaie*, publiée en 1856,[1] édition

---

[1] pages 569 et suivantes[4]

---

très différente de la première.

Si vous n'avez pas cette second edition de mon *Traité de la Monnaie*, je serai heureux de vous l'offrir personellement.

J'ai été chargé par la Commission Impériale de l'Exposition du soin de diriger et de publier le rapport du . . . sur cette solemnité de 1867. Le rapport forme treize volumes.[5] Je serais charme de le presenter au College d'Owen, dont vous êtes un des eminents professeurs, pour sa bibliothèque. Si le Collège avait un correspondent ou agent à Paris je vous serais obligé de me le faire connaitre. Dans le cas contraire, je prierais Lord Lyons[6] de vouloir l'en charger. Dans l'Introduction de ce rapport, j'ai traité diverses questions d'Economie Politique générale et appliquée.

Croyez, Monsieur, à mes sentiments les plus distingués.

Michel Chevalier

317.   W. S. JEVONS TO HERBERT JEVONS
       [LJP, 248]

Keppel Street London
7 July 1869.

My dear Herbert

We have now been nearly three weeks on a visit to London lodging in pretty comfortable rooms. The day after tomorrow we shall probably start for the Continent on a tour of 4 or 5 weeks & before going I will write what I have to say.

[4] Chevalier was referring to the third volume of the second enlarged edition of his *Cours d'économie politique fait au Collège de France* . . . 3 vols (1855–6), which was entitled *La Monnaie*. The footnote supplying the page reference was inserted by Chevalier himself.

[5] *Exposition universelle de 1867 à Paris. Rapports du jury international, publiés sous la direction de M. Michel Chevalier* (1868).

[6] Richard Bickerton, first Viscount Lyons (1817–87), British Ambassador at Paris, 1867–87.

... Tom & I agreed that we ought to give Henry some present in acknowledgment of his great attention to our trust affairs and his constant care of Roscoe. We thought that after Roscoe's death it was a suitable time to carry out the idea and I therefore sent him a beautiful electro plate silver tea urn and four dishes for dinner which seem to have pleased him pretty well. They were of the best design & workmanship & cost altogether about £31. 10. I shall be glad to know whether you will like to join in the present say to the extent of 1/5 or about £6. 6. 0.

... I have posted you a copy of my new little Logical book, also a number of newspapers which we have had in London.

We have been chiefly occupied in pleasure in London, but I have been rather done up these last few days. Both Harriet & I needed a little change to turn our thoughts from the distressing time we had not long ago. It has given us all a sorrow which can hardly ever be removed. But however distressing it must be to you & Lucy & Tom, you have been spared the painful times impressed upon our memories.

... My sovereign research has been more successful than I expected. The Chancellor of the Exchequer has adopted the notion & quoted one of my figures in the House of Commons lately,[1] & he has had a report prepared partly based upon my figures.[2] I do not know whether he will succeed in carrying any change through but I should not wonder if he makes some attempt next session. At present the Irish Church stops the way. I was much pleased to get the return of New Zealand sovereigns which you prepared.

... I hope you will prosper with your banking business and avoid mines which are in my opinion a sure way of coming to grief. We have had enough of John's Copper mine and though I dare say gold mines are better things they have my hearty abhorrence.

Tom is according to late letters as flourishing as usual and Lucy is as far as I know pretty well though I fear bothered by business.

Believe me
Your affectionate Brother
W. S. Jevons

---

[1] In a debate on the Money Laws (Ireland) Bill in the House of Commons on 23 June 1869, Lowe quoted figures of the proportion of light gold coins in the total gold circulation: these figures were taken from Jevons's paper 'On the condition of the Gold Coinage of the United Kingdom', although Lowe described them as 'given to me by the responsible officers of the Government'. Cf. *The Times*, 24 June 1869, p. 6, and *Investigations*, pp. 286 and 294.

[2] Report addressed to the Chancellor of the Exchequer by the Master of the Mint and Colonel J. T. Smith, late Master of the Calcutta Mint, on the Mintage necessary to cover the expense of establishing and maintaining the Gold Currency. *Parl. Papers*, 1868–9 (285) XXXIV, 275.

This report was presented to the House of Commons on 28 June 1869 – *Commons Journals, 1868–69*, p. 286.

The Gold Coinage Controversy of 1869

The ensuing letters 318–321 are indicative of the part which Jevons played in a controversy on gold, seignorage and international coinage which occupied considerable space in the columns of *The Times* and other papers during August and September 1869.

This controversy arose from a speech made by Robert Lowe in the Commons on 6 August 1869, in reply to questions from J. B. Smith and G. Sclater-Booth (*Hansard*, third series, CXCVIII, 1408–22). In the course of this speech Lowe reiterated Jevons's figures of the proportions of the gold coinage which had become light-weight through wear and tear (cf. above, Letter 317, n. 1, p. 210); he then went on to argue that a seignorage to meet the cost of the necessary recoinage was justifiable and to point out that a 1 per cent seignorage, as recommended by the Paris Monetary Conference of 1867, would enable Britain to assimilate her coinage to that of the Latin Monetary Union and so gain the advantages of an international coinage. (Cf. 'On the International Monetary Convention and the Introduction of an International Currency into this Kingdom', Vol. VII, Part I.)

J. G. Hubbard (afterwards Lord Addington) took up the position that while a small premium to cover the cost of coinage was not objectionable, any reduction of the amount of gold in the sovereign would be. In this he was supported by Thomson Hankey, Ernest Seyd, Sir John Herschel and Lord Overstone – whose view was 'that Bobby Lowe will get himself and the country into a serious mess with his rash theories'. (Overstone to G. W. Norman, *Correspondence of Lord Overstone*, edited by D. P. O'Brien, III, 1178.)

In the opinion of this group, a mintage charge was allowable, but a seignorage was not, because, as Overstone put it, 'the quantity of Gold to which the Creditor is entitled is absolute'. Jevons, J. B. Smith, Colonel J. T. Smith, Leone Levi and Frederick Hendricks, on the other hand, felt that the advantages of securing a sound coinage, adjusted so as to give it international acceptability, far outweighed any inconvenience which might result to debtors and creditors from a small variation of the monetary standard. Their contention was that the imposition of a seignorage might alter the quantity of gold in a sovereign but would not alter its purchasing power, and they shared the view expressed by Jevons 'that there is no such thing as value intrinsic in any commodity' ('On the Condition of the Gold Coinage', *Investigations*, p. 251).

The controversy continued, in the columns of *The Times* and other papers, from August to November 1869; most of the contributions were reproduced in a volume entitled *Speeches, Letters, Articles etc. on the Gold*

Coinage Controversy of 1869 printed by the Bank of England for private circulation in 1870. Lowe's proposal met with considerably more opposition than support and he proceeded no further with it. For Jevons's views on the controversy and its results, see below, Letter 329, p. 232.

318.   W. S. JEVONS TO THE EDITOR OF *THE TIMES*[1]

Sir,

Mr. Hubbard, in *The Times* of Friday last, has assailed certain calculations of mine in the hope of thereby refuting the arguments of the Chancellor of the Exchequer in favour of a modification of our Mint regulations. As you truly remark in your article of the same day, those calculations have little or no relevancy to the scheme in question. Mr. Lowe proposes to reduce very slightly the weight of the sovereign in order that our coin may be exchangeable with that of the International Monetary Convention, and that, at the same time, the cost of coining may not fall needlessly upon the nation. My calculations were directed simply to ascertaining the amount and condition of our present gold coinage, which has only a collateral bearing upon the question at issue.

To trace the precise paternity of the scheme which Mr. Lowe has so clearly put forward would be a long and needless task. That scheme is in reality the natural result of the establishment of an international currency in Western Europe, and it may be said to be forced upon us by a remarkable conjuncture of circumstances. After prolonged discussion, it has become at last apparent that one grain of gold in 123 grains is all that prevents us from securing some three or four great improvements, in our circulating medium. This scheme, far from being due to any one person, is in reality the outcome of the efforts of several Statistical Congresses, of two International Conventions (in 1865 and 1867), and of one Royal Commission, of which Mr. Hubbard was himself a member. The eminent Continental economists who have successfully established an international money in France, Italy, Belgium, Switzerland, and elsewhere, clearly saw that the trifling reduction of the sovereign must be the concession asked from us. So far as I am aware, this view was first distinctly laid before Englishmen by the eminent actuary Mr. Hendriks, in a most able pamphlet on decimal coinage, which was privately printed, and therefore not so readily accessible as it ought to be. The scheme was also most clearly discussed in the official report drawn up by the Master of the Mint and Mr. Rivers Wilson, of the Treasury, after

---

[1] Published in the issue of 24 August 1869.

their return from the International Monetary Convention of 1867, at which they officially represented the British Government. No one who has looked into the report of the International Coinage Commission can be ignorant of the able and, to my mind, conclusive manner in which the scheme was advocated by Colonel J. T. Smith, Mr. Hendriks, and Mr. S. Brown. Moreover, that Commission published a correspondence which Sir John Herschel, then Master of the Mint, held with the Treasury and the Bank so long ago as the year 1852. It is clearly shown by Sir John that our present law of free coinage works chiefly to the advantage of the Bank and a few great bullion dealers, and that a small seigniorage is a most sound and rational measure.

I must confess that until the last few years I entirely shared the prejudice in favour of free coinage which Mr. Hubbard so strongly represents; but when independently engaged in inquiring into the amount and condition of our gold coinage, I met with facts which unmistakably showed the faulty working of our present law. Mr. Hendriks' pamphlet happened at that time to come into my hands, and seemed to me at once to point out the true remedy. It was no hastily concocted scheme, then, that Mr. Lowe set forth with so much force and completeness. The main features of the plan have been under discussion for years past, and it is only a detail or two that any single person could have added to a measure which is truly remarkable from the manifold advantages likely to flow from a very slight cause.

But even if my calculations had any important bearing on the scheme, I am not prepared to admit that Mr. Hubbard has in the least degree shaken those calculations. Mr. Hubbard, as you yourself point out, has entirely missed the point and purpose of my method, and his letter is therefore full of mistakes. My purpose was to circumvent, if possible, the difficulty that we do not know how many sovereigns have in past years been exported, melted, lost, or otherwise withdrawn from circulation. It seemed obvious that these causes must have operated least upon the coinages of recent years, and that we might consequently take the proportion which those coinages appear to form of the whole circulation as a means of arriving at the total amount of that circulation. From inquiries which you have already described, it was ascertained that the coinages of 1863–4 formed rather more than one-fifth part of the circulation. I concluded, then, that the circulation could not exceed about five times the whole coinage of 1863–4. Mr. Hubbard says that I made a purely arbitrary selection of those years, and that other years, for instance 1852–3, would have given totally different results. Certainly they would, because the coinages of those years have suffered during 16 or 17 years from the destructive influences the effects of which I was trying to eliminate from the calculation. The same may be said of any other early years. My purpose was to select that part of the coinage which had suffered least as a measure of the whole, and I selected the years 1863–4 not by mere caprice, but because they were the best. The coinage of those years was very large in amount (14,578,000*l.*), and had got thoroughly well into circulation, so as to form one-fifth of the whole circulation. Mr. Hubbard is no doubt right in saying that the years 1865–6 might have been taken, but they were less suitable, because the coins of those years formed only 1-25th part of the circulation. I took the utmost care in the paper to explain emphatically that I did not pretend to define the exact amount of the circulation, but only to ascertain a quantity (68,000,000*l.*) in sovereigns, and 12,000,000*l.* in half-sovereigns) below which the truth certainly lay. If I have erred at all, it is on the side of caution, as a careful reader of the paper will allow, and if Mr. Hubbard could really show my estimate to be worthless and meaningless, it could only be by establishing another and lower estimate, which would only the more strengthen Mr. Lowe's assertion concerning the needless destruction of good new sovereigns.

In the latter part of his letter Mr. Hubbard shows that he does not understand the Rule of Three. He makes the extraordinary assertion that my method of calculation is fallacious, and the conclusions derived from it utterly worthless, because the first and third terms of a proportion are not of one kind. That there may be no mistake I give his words:—

"If I may presume to criticize the calculations of a Professor of Political Economy, I would say that his formula is essentially defective, inasmuch as his first and third terms are not of one kind."

I need hardly remind your readers that, so far is the Rule of Three from requiring the first and third terms to be of one kind, the rule, as given by Colenso and other eminent successors of Cocker, directs the learner to select as the third term that which is of the same kind as the answer, implying that, in the vast majority of cases it will differ in kind from the first two. When an ordinary schoolboy has to work such a sum as this – If 100 workmen can do a piece of work in 12 days, how many men can do the work in eight days? he at once selects 100 workmen as the third term *because it is not of the same kind as the other two.*

But with a curious propensity to error, which I know not how to characterize, Mr. Hubbard has falsified at once the Rule of Three and the facts of the case. My Rule of Three happens to be one of those comparatively rare cases where the terms are all of one kind. All the terms consist of numbers of coins, as witness the "formula" stated in Mr. Hubbard's own words, "as 18,671 (examined sovereigns dated 1863 and 1864): 100,000 (the aggregate of examined sovereigns): 14,000,000 (the issued coins of 1863 and 1864): the whole circulation."

Nothing could have driven me to trouble your readers with such matters, had not Mr. Hubbard asserted that an important State measure rested on my figures, and that my figures were utterly fallacious. Your readers must judge to which side the charge of putting forth worthless fallacies will finally attach.

I am, Sir, yours obediently,
W. Stanley Jevons.

Owens College, Manchester, Aug. 21

319. J. T. SMITH[1] TO W. S. JEVONS

8 Queen Street Place,
London.
31st August, 1869.

Dear Sir,

I am exceedingly obliged to you for your kind and friendly letter received yesterday, and I should not think of troubling you again, had you not asked me to notice any particular in which I might think you mistaken. What I have now to say is, merely, that previously to my becoming acquainted with Mr. Hendriks, he by no means approved of a seignorage of 1 per cent, and recommended the sacrifice of the difference of intrinsic value between our present and the proposed new coins, by coining the new ounce of gold into £3. 17s. 1½d. instead of £3. 16s. 5½d. but he adopted my proposal after discussing the matter fully with me.

Messrs. Graham and Wilson[2] although they discuss the propriety of a small *mint charge* did not speak of it as restoring the value to be taken out of the sovereign altogether; but only as I understand them, on the same principle as the French Mint charge is made, vizt. as an equivalent to the charge for *first* or *immediate* coinage. I think, myself, that they did not contemplate or think of proposing as high a charge as 1 per cent.

My argument, therefore, is that the whole merit of the plan consists in the combination of the principles 1st of the additional value given to a coin to the full extent required by a Mint charge (still stoutly denied by some authorities) – 2ndly the fact that that charge does *not* fall on the merchant or importer and 3rdly of the necessity for the reduction of intrinsic value of our coins to bring about uniformity – which combination was, I think, not publicly proposed previously to my publication.

---

[1] John Thomas Smith (1805–82), F.R.S., Colonel of Engineers; Mint Master of Madras, 1840, and of Calcutta, 1855; Member of Consulting Committee, Military Fund Department, India Office, 1866–80; author of *Observations on the Management of Mints* (1848); *Remarks on a Gold Currency for India* (1868).

[2] In their report on the International Monetary Conference, Paris, June 1867. *Parl. Papers*, 1867–8 (4021) XXVII.

It is followed by the justification of the charge in the form of seignorage contained in Mr. Graham's and my joint report;[3] and by the arguments to be used with the French Government which have already been privately submitted.

Pray excuse my troubling you again in this matter. I do not ask you to reply.

Believe me,

Sincerely yours,

J. T. Smith.

Prof.ʳ Jevons, M.A.
    Ec. Ec.

320.   SIR JOHN F. W. HERSCHEL TO W. S. JEVONS

Collingwood[1]

Dear Sir,

I am not aware of any experiments such as you suggest having been tried, to ascertain the amount of *absolute* personal error in the estimate of the time of a star-transit – but there may have been such without coming to my knowledge. The thing seems feasible and seems worth trying.[2]

I am so far opposed to Mr. Lowe's proposal as it shall (when it is known *what* is intended in all its details, and with what *Legislative enactment* accompanied) imperil *the pound sterling*. If we are to have a sovereign to pass for a pound sterling let us be secured *by law* and *positive right* without the necessity of haggling in any market that we can get 113 grains of pure gold for it – or at all events that for 100 of them we can obtain (by simply

---

³ See above, Letter 317, n. 2, p. 210.

¹ The original manuscript of this letter bears no date, but from internal evidence it can be inferred that it was almost certainly written during September 1869, shortly after a letter on the gold coinage controversy, written by Herschel on 30 August 1869, had been published in *The Times* of 2 September.

² The experiment here referred to was thus described in a letter signed 'J.' and published in *Nature*, 18 November 1869, p. 85:

'Imagine an artificial star, formed by a minute electrical spark, placed at a considerable distance, say three miles, and made to move across the field of a transit instrument at a rate not very different from the average apparent rate of stars observed (say nine inches per second): very simple mechanism might be devised to register upon the chronograph of the observatory the exact moment at which the star is absolutely upon each of the cross wires of the telescope. At the same time the observer, whose error is to be determined, should endeavour to record in the ordinary way the passage of the star, and the difference of time, as shown on the chronograph, would give the required error. Every observer might thus be put through a kind of exercise, which would inevitably show the degree of his proficiency, or detect any change in his habits of observation.'

Subsequent letters indicated that this method had already been employed in observatories at Paris, Leiden and Neuchâtel. In the *Principles of Science* (second edition, p. 348) Jevons indicated that he was the author of the letter signed 'J'.

presenting them at some office or bank) 11,300 grains of gold pure – or 12,327.4 standard gold ($\frac{11}{12}$ fine) for them as we can do for 100 £ Bank Note.

That secured, I withdraw the accusation of confiscation[3] though still I should not think the advantages proposed worth the disturbance of a system that has worked well for so long a period. And I would never admit the *gramme* of gold as the legal weight of a British coin.

Of course I speak of a *Coin* as it issues from the Mint – if people choose to wear it down or scrape it light beyond "remedy" it ceases to be a Coin. – Our coin as it issues from our Mint (whatever Mr. Seyd may say) is *exact* in weight and fineness[4] – Moreover in getting sovereigns for notes from the bank it has to be remembered—

1st that the bank never reissue light sovereigns (i.e. below the remedy)

2nd that they *do* issue in payment (of demands for pounds sterling) *every individual new sovereign* which is struck at the Mint (amounting at 5,000,000 per annum since 1851 to somewhere about 90,000,000) so that the bearer of a 100 £ note to the bank may reckon to a certainty to receive 12,327.4 grains standard gold within a fraction *very much* less than the *aggregate remedy*.

> I remain, Dear Sir,
> Yours very truly,
> J. F. W. Herschel.

321. W. S. JEVONS TO THE EDITOR OF *THE TIMES*[1]

Sir,

The *Economist* of last Saturday remarks that no complete answer has been given to the letter of Mr. Ernest Seyd in *The Times* of August 30, impugning the goodness of our gold coin, and showing apparently that loss must follow from its melting or exportation. You will, perhaps, allow me, therefore, to point out that, though Mr. Seyd's facts and figures may be accurate in themselves, they will not in the least bear the construction which he puts upon them.

---

[3] In his letter to *The Times* Herschel had indicated that while he supported the idea of a 'Mint charge' to cover the cost of coinage, he was strongly opposed to a seignorage 'as a reduction in the intrinsic value of the pound sterling; that is to say, in plain terms, as being equivalent to a confiscation to the extent of the proposed per-centage on the total claims of the national creditor'.

[4] Ernest Seyd, in letters published in *The Times* of 20 and 30 August 1869, had argued 'that British gold coin is less "identical" with bullion than other coinages, and that consequently it is less liable to be exported'. Herschel, in a postscript to his own letter, attacked these 'allegations . . . against the purity of the British coinage'. Cf. below, Letter 312.

[1] Published in the issue of 10 September 1869.

To show the quality of the gold coinage, Mr. Seyd quotes the assays of ten bars of gold composed of 10,000 sovereigns "cut" by the Bank and melted by Messrs. Sillar and Co. in 1866. The average fineness of the gold was 915.2, instead of 916.6, as it should have been. These numbers I am perfectly prepared to accept; but if he implies that they reflect upon the conduct of the Mint, I may point out that at p.390 of his own recent work on bullion Mr. Seyd himself calculates the value of new British sovereigns at a very different figure, – namely, 916. Mr. Seyd ought to be aware, after reading the letter of "Monetarius," if not before, that there is a difference in fineness between sovereigns coined before and those coined since 1851. In that year a reform of the Mint was made, and the management of the coining, as well as of the assaying, was placed in the hands of the most eminent scientific men. The change effected is thus referred to in the letter of the Director of the United States' Mint to the Secretary of the Treasury, dated the 28th of January, 1854, and published in the proceedings of the 33d Congress (1st Sess. Ex. Doc., No. 68):—

"The law provides that 'gold coins of Great Britain, not less than $915\frac{1}{2}$ thousandths fine, shall be received at 94 6-10ths cents per pennyweight.' In a long series of years, and operating at times upon large quantities of such coin, we have not been able to find a higher average result than $915\frac{1}{2}$, and it was upon this basis that the enactment was framed. But under the present management of the British Mint, and of its assay department, beginning fairly with the year 1852, there is an upward tendency more strictly conforming with the legal standard of 916 2-3ds. The assay of a few pieces of 1852 and 1853 (the course of trade preventing the receipt of large quantities here) gives an average of $916\frac{1}{2}$, and the consequent rate would be 94 7-10ths cents per pennyweight. But it will evidently require a large emission at this rate to make a perceptible improvement in any promiscuous parcel."

As the sovereigns melted by Messrs. Sillar were all cut for lightness by the Bank, they would for the most part be old ones coined before 1851, and Mr. Seyd's facts therefore have not the least reference to the conduct of the Mint since that year. Nor do they at all affect the good faith of the previous management. The art of assaying is a very ancient one, and the assayers of the old Mint Company performed it faithfully in the traditional manner. But the progress of chymical science showed that what had previously been esteemed pure gold was not perfectly pure. The analysis of the gold and its alloy had been imperfectly accomplished, and about the year 1851 Mr. Graham and Dr. Allen Miller brought the coinage up to its true fineness by the employment of more scientific methods. With these facts I happen to be familiar, owing to my former connexion with the Sydney branch of the Royal Mint.

The more recent reports of the Director of the United States' Mint contain an official table of the weight and fineness of foreign coins, prepared according to the law of the United States of the year 1857. On looking over these we find that up to the year 1863 the sovereign is quoted as follows:—

"England. –   Pound or sovereign, new   ...   916.5
               Pound or sovereign, average   ...   915.5"

But beginning with the year 1864, we find:—

"England. –   Pound or sovereign, new   ...   916.5
               Pound or sovereign, average   ...   916.0"

The exact theoretical standard fineness of our coin is 916.66, and the American assayers certify that it comes within from one to two parts in 10,000 of the truth. I may add, however, that when the question comes to these very small fractions it becomes purely a matter of opinion. The gold assay process even now does not admit of certain accuracy to one or two parts in 10,000. Under these circumstances we can surely rest satisfied with the fact that three of the most eminent English chymists are concerned in the production of the English sovereign, and that M. Stas, who is, I believe, esteemed above all other living chymists for the extreme accuracy of his analytical determinations, has certified the fineness of the British sovereign to be 916.66.

The French gold coin is quoted by the American assayers at 899 in their recent report in 1868, or just ten parts in 10,000 below the true standard. The Russian coin is quoted at 916, or about six parts in 10,000 too low. So much for the accuracy of Mr. Seyd's statement that "in reality the British gold coin falls much more below its standard fineness than French, American, and Russian coin."

Mr. Seyd, again, adduces figures to show that sovereigns cannot be profitably picked and melted in the way asserted by Mr. Lowe. Such arguments are not calculated to meet the fact that they are or have not been so picked and melted; but I think it is not difficult to show how Mr. Seyd puts a completely wrong construction on his figures. If Mr. Seyd proves anything he proves that sovereigns cannot be profitably exported at all, and that, owing to the supposed want of fineness, and the costs of the operation, exportation must leave a loss. How is this to be reconciled with the fact that from 1858 to 1866 the acknowledged and registered exports of British gold coin averaged 4,300,000l. a year (Report of Royal Commission on International Coinage, p. 341), not including what is sent unregistered at the Custom-house, or what is first melted in London and then exported as bullion? In order that such large quantities of coin may be sent it must pay to send them, and it is of course the state of the foreign exchanges which enables the exporter to bear all the expenses and yet make a profit.

Now, the question which Mr. Seyd has not really touched is this:—
When sovereigns are actually going to be exported is it profitable or not to
pick out the heaviest? It is a secondary and unimportant question
whether the expense of melting be incurred in this country or not, for it is
universally allowed that at present, when our sovereigns are not current
on the Continent, they there become mere bullion, and are bought and
sold by weight. The real point, disentangled from irrelevant considerations, is this – Can the operation of weighing and picking out the
heaviest sovereigns be profitably performed?

According to Mr. Seyd's own figures there will clearly be a profit. He
supposes 20,000 sovereigns of an average weight of 123.531 grains each to
be picked by weighing out of a mass of 100,000 l., the cost being as
follows:— Weighing 100,000 sovereigns at 6d. per 500, 5 l.; interest at 5
per cent., 13 l. 14s. – total. 18 l. 14s. Now, the excess of weight of the
sovereigns above the standard weight (123.274 grains) is .257 grain per
sovereign, or in all 5,140 grains of standard gold, worth at 77s. 9d. per oz.
41 l. 12s. 6d.

Subtracting the expenses there remains a net profit on the operation
of 22 l. 18s. 6d.

It is by no means clear, however, that we ought to debit the operation
with interest at 5 per cent., for money can often be borrowed for a few
days at a very low rate of interest, and it is possible that the operation
might sometimes be carried out upon sovereigns which are temporarily
detained for some other cause. If we throw out of account this very
doubtful item of interest there remains a profit of 36 l. 12s. 6d.

The reader will clearly understand that this is not the whole profit
which may arise from remitting sovereigns abroad. It is merely the
accessory and incidental profit which that bullion-broker will make who
can carry out this picking operation. Mr. Seyd confuses the whole matter
when he implies that the excess of weight of some sovereigns is not only to
pay all the expenses, but it is to be the motive for melting and exporting
the coin. That sovereigns are exported to countries where they are bought
and sold by weight cannot be doubted, and Mr. Seyd's own data, I
repeat, show that when sovereigns are about to be exported it will pay to
pick out the heaviest.

This practice of picking might, no doubt, be prevented by issuing none
but sovereigns close to the standard weight, but this would increase the
cost of coining. A larger proportion of blanks and coined sovereigns
would have to be turned back and remelted. The true remedy is so to fit
the sovereign for currency abroad that it would be valued there as here,
by tale, and not by weight. All motive for melting or picking would thus
be done away with, because the gold would, abroad as well as at home, be
more valuable as coin than as bullion.

I wish to add to my last letter that though the reduction of the sovereign and the imposition of a Mint charge have been discussed in various quarters during several years past, the scheme stated by Mr. Lowe was first put forth with all its main features in Colonel Smith's work, entitled *Remarks on a Gold Currency for India*. This book was published early in 1868, and at the end is given "A Suggestion regarding International Coinage," in which the peculiar feature of the scheme – namely, the exact equivalence of the Mint charge and the gold subtracted from the sovereign – is clearly explained. This equivalence is the turning point of the whole matter, since it enables us to avoid altogether any disturbance of the standard of value.

I should be trifling with your readers' patience if I noticed again at any length the difference of opinion on an arithmetical point which still exists between Mr. Hubbard and myself. He demolished all my calculations by pointing out the fact (which, by the way, happened not to be the fact) that the first and third terms of a proportion were not of the same kind. In his latest utterance Mr. Hubbard says of me:—

"He retorted with a quibble about the Rule of Three, wholly irrelevant to the purpose, for it was to a given formula framed in the olden fashion, and not in that of Colenso, that I applied a criticism sanctioned by standard works on arithmetic, not the less accurate because they are of the last generation."

If I can extract any meaning from this almost unintelligible sentence, it is that Colenso's heresies are not confined to the numbers of the Old Testament, but that he has corrupted the principles of arithmetic accepted by a past generation, of which Mr. Hubbard is the living representative.

I am, Sir, yours obediently,

W. Stanley Jevons

Owen's College, Sept. 7

322.   H. W. FIELD[1] TO W. S. JEVONS
    [WM]
To W. Stanley Jevons Esq.   Her Majesty's Mint
    &c. &c.   13 Sep. 69

Sir,

From the interest you take on the subject of the coinage of this country I feel sure you will excuse a few remarks on your last letter[2] in the

---

[1] Henry William Field (1803–88), entered the service of the Royal Mint in 1815; probationer assayer, 1836; Queen's Assay Master, 1850–71.

[2] See above, Letter 321; p. 217.

"Times" of the 10th inst; the former I regret to say I have not seen having been rather locomotive the last few weeks.

Since the year 1828 I have been attached to the Chief Assay Office, in fact a large portion of the operations have been conducted by me, hence my assurance in addressing you, though until 1850 I was only the "Probationer".

My remarks have reference merely to the Standard of the Coin – previous to 1851 the Mint in accordance with the Act 56 Geo: 3rd c.68[3] was compelled to conduct all its operations under the Authority of an Indenture (a system adopted from the reign of Edwd. 3d.) the last Indenture made between the King & the Master of the Mint is dated 6th Feb. 1817, by that instrument, inter alia, the Assayers had to regulate the Standd. of the Country by "Trial Plates" the last Plates have engraved thereon 31 Oct. 1829, these plates agreeably to precedent were made & commixed by the Assayers & Members of the Goldsmiths Compy. but subject to & sanctioned as to correctness by the Assayers attached to the Royal Mint, whose superior skill, from long practice, at that time entitled them to greater credit, these Plates are referred to in the House of Commons report 30 June 1837 p: 78 to 80.[4]

These gold plates however modern science acknowledges to be slightly incorrect & when Sir J. Herschell [sic] became Master in Dec. 1850 & Captain Harness previously Deputy, the Mint Indenture was superceded – Sir J. Herschell desired me, then appointed the "Queen's Assay Master" (though you may observe called Resident assayer in contradistinction to a new class called "nonresident assayers") to pay no regard to the said Trial Plates, but to use such means as I should deem best, in order to approach as nigh as possible, if not to actual mathematical precision, to the Standd. of 11/12th fine 1/12th Alloy, I replied it would not be possible to attain *such* precision, but that I could work considerably nearer than the plates indicated.

To this end I prepared Chemically pure Gold & made alterations in the "Modus operandi" by the result of which the desired accuracy was attained, thus it may be said that the appointment of Sir J. Herschell & Captain Harness has led to the Coinage having been brought up in 1851 to the true fineness, by the employment [of][5] the pure Standard or test pieces &c.

It was at this time that Sir J. H. & Captn H. thought that if nonresident assayers were appointed it would be an additional check and more independt. in the eye of the Public. Two of the most eminent

---

[3] 56 Geo III, c. 68, An Act to provide for a new Silver Coinage, and to regulate the Currency of the Gold and Silver Coin of this Realm (22 June 1816).

[4] Report of Select Committee on the Establishment of the Royal Mint, *Parl. Papers*, 1837 (465) XVI.

[5] Omitted in the original manuscript.

Chemical & Scientific men were selected who from their skill might quickly bring their theoretical knowledge into practical utility, Sir J. H. in a note of the 7th April 1851 requested that they should be admitted into the assay offices to inspect the process therein practised – & on a visit (the 9th April), the question was put whether in their professional pursuits Gold Assaying came frequently before them, the reply made was "once in the course of the year to shew pupils."

May I not therefore say in reference to the latter part of the 4th paragh. of your letter,

"Palmam qui meruit ferat"—

The coin resulting from ingots of Gold melted under the calculations of the improved mode of Assay have since been assayed and checked not only by the Gentleman constituting the nonresidents but also by the Assay Masters of the Philadelphia Mint, who with the French & other assayers agree that our Coins "are up to the Mark" 916.66.

I may here state the reason why old Coin has been called under Standard.

The Indenture also authorised the use of a "Remedy" for fallacy of workmanship, both as to weight and Fineness – 12 Troy Grains in the lb. for weight 15 T.G. for Fineness you will therefore observe, that as long as the Assay Master found the Bars & Coin within the "Remedy" he could pass them, consequently as the Plate caused a depreciation of about 4 T.G^{n} in the lb. Troy (for such I have proved it to be by the analysis of a Portion) & the bars & Coin could be passed 15 T.G. above or below the Standd. Plate this large deviation of 19 T.G. would be legal, but I state as fact that the Assayers never availed themselves of that legality, – if at times the bars or coin turned out & were passed 3 or 4 grs. worse than the Plate, which no doubt sometimes happened, still there was the worseness on the Plate to add – the reason therefore is evident, how old coins before 1851 under that system, are now reported W$\frac{gr.}{6.}$ [*] [6]

I may state that the system & process I have alluded to & carried on since 1851 is such that the stoppage of any Bullion for remelting &c. as deviating from truth is of *the very rarest* occurence.

I can also confirm Sir J. H's suggestion in his P.S. – "many of the cut sov$\underline{ns}$ · may have never issued from the Mint at all & may have owed their lightness to the fraudulent use of inferior Gold". I have exam$\underline{in'd}$ such with the dates 1822.1849.1852 which have been of gold varying from Worse 2 Carats to Worse 6 Carats.

I am Sir,

Yours truly

Henry W. Field

Queen's Assay Master

[6] i.e. worse 6 grains.

I may say that my reports Sir J. H. called *o* & any diff^{ce}. on either side B or W by other assayers, was compensated to mine. Mr. Graham was appointed Master in 1855.

323.   H. W. FIELD TO W. S. JEVONS
      [WM]

Her Majesty's Mint
28 Sept 69.

Dear Sir,

Having been again from home, I have delayed ackg^g. your note of the 14th, permit me to thank you for your pamphlet[1] which I have hitherto been prevented reading in consequence of an accumulation of Public and private matter.

In your note you say you have not even unintentionally done me an injustice, certainly not in reference to the "Trial Plates," or the mode of assay previous to 1851 because I was until then obliged to follow the practice of my Predecessors.

I think you will admit that, (quite unintentionally) you have taken from me and I may say Sir J. Herschell (who liberated me from the bondage of Trial Plates and Remedies) the credit, if credit be due, of bringing the Coinage up to almost mathematical precision, by attributing the improved system to two gentlemen[2] who as I have already stated were in no way instrumental in effecting the change.

I have ever been unwilling to court notoriety though advised by Sir J. H. to have the foregoing and other improvements and minute peculiarities, that have arisen in practice, during my long career in the so called "art mysteries" of assaying, registered in one of the Chemical Publications of the day but I have refrained.

I appreciate the right feeling of gratitude you express towards one who was so kind in opening his Laboratory to you, but I think if you were to make enquiry you would find that the assay reports of Gold and silver issued *therefrom* both to the Mint and Bk. of England were such that the Bank withdrew the continuance of the whole or major part of their work and from this Establishment *some* notice was taken of their irregularity.

You must feel deep personal regret at the loss you have sustained in the death of your late friend whose departure, as well as his brother within the year,[3] leaves no doubt great blanks in the scientific world.

---

[1] Presumably a copy of Jevons's paper 'On the Condition of the Metallic Currency of the United Kingdom'.

[2] i.e. Professor Thomas Graham and Dr Allen Miller.

[3] Thomas Graham had died on 16 September 1869; his brother John on 22 February.

The Vacancy of Master is not yet filled up some good names are talked of but it is mere conjecture and no doubt some little time will elapse before the *right man* is put into the right place.

      I am,

            Dear Sir,

                    Yours sincerely,

                        Henry W. Field

To

W. S. Jevons, Esq.,

etc. etc. etc.

324. GEORGE WHITEHEAD[1] TO W. S. JEVONS

                              3, Richmond Terrace

                                  Charles Street,

                                        Hull.

                          November 5th 1869.

Dear Sir,

      If your time will admit I belive* a repetition from your pen of the letter you wrote to the "Economist" newspaper, in 1866 or '7[2] on the British Iron Trade, would do great service to masters and men, at this critical period. I do think the present agitation amongst my fellow-workmen, for an advance of wages and to avoid a strike, the apparent disposition of the masters, to meet them, by rising the price of iron, is most unwise, and unwarrantable policy, the present demand been* too fickle, and not sufficiently general to admit of this course. I am sure it is altogether unnecessary for me to remind you of the disastrous effects of this policy in the years 1865–6 and 7.

      I think a letter at this time and from your own disinterested pen, would not fail to have some effect on this subject. I would in conclusion apologise for this trespassing on your valuable time, and thank you for past favours, when employed at the Parkgate Iron Works, Rotherham.

                        Yours very truly,

                          Geo Whitehead.

Prof. Jevons, Manchester –

  [1] George Whitehead (b. 1842), recorded as living at 3 Richmond Terrace, Hull, from 1869 to 1873 and at various addresses in Hull until 1889; manager of the Parkgate Iron Works, Rotherham, and subsequently of the Hull Forge Co., establishing his own firm of iron and steel merchants in Hull in 1888. Cf. above, Letter 289, p. 166.

  [2] No letter from Jevons on the subject of the British Iron Trade was published in *The Economist* for 1866 or 1867. It seems probable that Whitehead had in mind the letter entitled 'Ironmasters and Ironworkers' which was published in *The Times* of 17 December 1866 (above, Letter 274, p. 141).

  In fact, as the letter from Henry Jevons (below, Letter 325, p. 226) makes clear the iron trade had moved from a state of depression in 1866 to expansion in 1869, largely as a result of changes in the demand for rails. In this situation it was not surprising that the trade union in the industry should seek to make use of their growing strength. Cf. Burn, *The Economic History of Steel-Making*, chapter 2.

325.   HENRY JEVONS TO W. S. JEVONS

L'pool 8 Nov 1869

My dear Stanley

I have your note of Saturday, to which I hasten to reply to the best of my ability, promising that my own personal opinion of the conduct of the Staffre Iron Masters is that they have made fools of themselves.—

It is necessary that I should revert to what took place some months ago in the Cleveland district, when as you will remember the men demanded an advance of 10% in their wages, but to avert a strike, an arbitration was resolved upon. Mr Rupert Kettle was the umpire selected, & he bearing in mind that the masters had all got considerable contracts on hand at low price, awarded the men 5% advance, or *half* what they asked, & attached the condition that the men must be satisfied with that advance for the whole of the present year. This decision, I believe, gave satisfaction to *both* parties.

It is beyond a doubt that for the last 12 months & more, the demand for Railroad Iron has been steadily improving, so that from a price of about £5.0.0. per ton, which I think was the lowest point touched, we now see the price about £7 - per ton in Wales! Bar Iron has not improved to so great an extent, but as it was never so depressed as Rails, so it has not as yet advanced so much. The rise in Bar Iron however is fully 20^s/- per ton during the last 18 months.

I have alluded to the matter of Rails, because as far as I know, this is the only branch of the Trade in which there has been a *marked* improvement, & the consequence has been to send numerous Rail orders into the North of England & into Staff^{re}., since *Wales*, the natural home of the Rail Trade, has not been able to meet the demand. In taking orders for Rails, the result has been that those makers who did so became more indifferent about orders for other kinds of Iron, & so gradually the whole Trade has indirectly participated in the improvement, though the real increase in the demand was, as I believe, for Rails only. This was the state of affairs when Quarter Day came round just a month ago. The men in South Staff^{re}. asked for 10% advance in their wages, which was *refused, the Trade not justifying any advance whatever*!!! It appears however that the managers of two concerns which happened to be better off than their neighbours agreed to give one class of their men a rise of 5%, viz the *puddlers*, intending to stave off all the other men without any advance. North Staff^{re}., which, being a newer & cheaper producing district had participated very much more in the improvement than South Staff^{re}. could do (this latter being in our view nearly played out), followed suit, & gave the men 5% advance, declaring the price of Iron 10^s/- per ton up.

Lord Ward[1] followed suit, until last Thursday the South Staffordshire Iron Masters, in solemn Conclave, decided to give the men the full advance they asked for, viz 10%, & advanced the price of Iron 20^s/- per ton, though a very short time before, they had declared that the state of the Trade would not justify *any* advance!!

It looks to us just like a piece of spite against North Staff^{re} & Lord Ward, for venturing to act upon an independent course. Of course it remains to be seen what the effect of this sudden rise is, but our opinion is very strong that it will kill the gradually returning confidence which the Trade was very slowly beginning to assume, & that before 3 months are over, we shall again have underselling going on. We *may* be wrong, but it appears to us that neither America, France, Italy, nor India will be willing to pay the advanced prices, & we look for an absolute *cessation* of demand for the present.

Now if the South Staffordshire Iron Masters had only been satisfied to pay 5% advance in wages, & put the price of Iron up 10^s/- per ton, there would have been a *chance* that the Trade would have stood it, & next year, if things went on well, they might have got the other 10^s/-, but as it is, we believe this sudden & large advance will be *very prejudicial* to the Trade, & probably bring back the state of affairs from which we fondly hoped we were just beginning to emerge. Your correspondent George Whitehead seems a most sensible sort of fellow & I wish there were more like him.

I am very glad to hear so good an account of Henny, & most sincerely do hope she may yet be restored to us all, sound in mind & body.—

My defeat was a disappointment on public grounds, but personally I do not know that there is much to regret. I should never have tried, but that I thought the new Constituency ought to have the opportunity of voting, & after all, very little more than half the electors took the trouble to vote. I have no copies of my speeches to send you, but they were neither long nor numerous.[2]

With love to your wife & yourself, I am

Ever yours affly

H. Jevons

P.S.   Please send me a copy of your letter if you write one to the papers on the matter herein referred to.

[1] William Ward (1817–85), first Earl of Dudley.

[2] In the municipal elections held in Liverpool on 1 November 1869 Henry Jevons stood as a Liberal candidate for the North Toxteth Ward. Out of an electorate of 3500, 2055 voted. Henry Jevons secured 815 votes, and his Conservative opponent, Lieutenant-Colonel Steble, 1250 (*Liverpool Mercury*, 2 November 1869, p. 7).

326.   GEORGE WHITEHEAD TO W. S. JEVONS

3, Richmond Terrace
Charles Street. Hull.
Novr 9th 1869.

Dear Sir,

I can quite understand your disposition to avoid a controversy, where your own interests are not at stake, at the same time, had the counsel you were pleased to give been taken by the parties concern'd in the British Iron Trade in 1866, great disasters which have already overtaken us might in all probability [have]¹ been avoided.

You ask if I have any remarks to make on the State of Trade. A few months ago a reaction set in, for rails chiefly, and I believe it is now affecting plates and angles for ships, and bridge building the former for the Tyne and Clyde, the latter for our Indian colonies—

I complain, on acc^t. of haste on the part of both men and masters manifested when the general trades, such as the engineering, hardware, and especially the larger staple trades are so very quiet, and also seen* the Bank interest on money is so very low, which is I think a safe guide to the pulse of Trade in general.

I may add the iron trade as* been the subject of another injustice, not commonly complain'd of. During the late panic the colliers have managed to keep up a very brisk agitation, and by some means although iron as* been sold at such ruinously low rates yet coal as* never been dearer, I believe in some instances it as* been sold as high as 8/s per ton @ the pit, whereas in former depressions, it as a rule, as* ebb'd and flow'd with the Iron Trade. I have known it as low as 5/6 per ton.

On the day I posted you my last letter the Staffordshire masters had decided to raise the price of iron 1£ per ton, in consequence of [which] Lord Wards agent in order to meet the dissatisfaction of his men raised the list of prices 10/s per ton, the other masters however called a special meeting of the trade, and determined to advance it 20/s per ton, although it was manifest the men seem'd to be satisfied with the former move. I believe these are the real facts. Lord Ward's brand is reliable and well in, and having his book pretty well stocked with orders, choose* the alternative of an advance rather than oppose his men under the circumstances. I only hope this concession will be properly understood by the men but my fear is they will not stay at this, hence my appeal that some pen that can make the lesson very plain may be induced @ this very critical period to furnish it for us. I do think you are right in stating, we are on the eve of an improvement if only properly managed. I was told

---

¹ Omitted in the original manuscript.

(confidentially) the Parkgate Iron C? and several other large firms including Bolckow & Vaughan,[2] &c are refusing to book orders for Spring delivery, for this very reason fearing the action of the workmen might be awkward rendering the speculation altogether unsafe—

We have had a Lecture in Hull last night from a gentleman from Lancashire, Preston. I believe his name is M? Chapman. I fancy he is connected with the Tories. I was very sorry to meet such impudent effrontery after such sacrifice and labour had been bestow'd upon us, he feigns to come to save the poor pauperised working men from "The present and long continued Stagnation of Trade" by a "Monster national Trades Union", and to return to the system of "Protection", on finish'd goods. I am very glad to say found it *"pretty hot"*, he had too much sound for sense, and I assure you he was properly snubb'd by a few Yorkshire working men, and should he or any of his party dare to come again to Hull, they will find it difficult to obtain a hearing.

excuse this disconnected letter and
believe me to remain
Yours gratefully
Geo Whitehead

Prof. Jevons M. A. Manchester

327. HENRY JEVONS TO W. S. JEVONS

L'pool, Saturday
[13 November 1869]

Dear Stanley

If you have not yet written your letter on the subject of the State of the Iron Trade & wages, I think a word of warning to the *men* against forcing up prices any further would not be misplaced. Already I hear rumours that having gained so easy a victory the other day, they are thinking of making still further demands upon their masters, which could only be injurious to the interests of the Trade in general. Your correspondent Whitehead seemed to hint at something of the kind, & I am sorry to say the report gains ground that the men will not be satisfied with what they have got.

I should like to hear what you are doing, & with love to Harriet & yourself, I am

Yours affly
H. Jevons

---

[2] Bolckow, Vaughan & Co., one of the leading iron firms in the Cleveland district. See Burn, *The Economic History of Steel-Making*, p.23.

I sent you a manufacturers letter to read a day or two ago, so that you might hear both sides.[1]

327A.   WILLIAM MILLINGTON & CO. TO JEVONS & CO.[1]

Summer Hill Iron Works
Tipton   Novr 10. 1869.

Messrs Jevons & C°
Liverpool

Order 4th inst.

Dear Sirs

We are in receipt of yours of the 9th & we really cannot do better for you relative to the above than is stated in ours of the 8th. 10/^s per ton commission is the most we can allow off the orders received & we will until further notice allow 7/6 per ton off all orders you may be pleased to favour us with. In reference to the advance we should have much rather preferred prices remaining unaltered till spring but as Trade seems to be improving in this district the men became uneasy they held meetings to arrange for a deputation in each works to wait upon the masters, and ask for an advance. The masters wished them to wait awhile, & promised them that as soon as Trade was in a state to advance Iron[2] that an advance would be declared & wages raised in proportion. The Puddlers upon that immediately gave notice for 1/s advance. The masters met & agreed to give them 6^d, & no advance upon Millmen. Then the Millmen gave notice for 10% advance. In the meantime Earl Dudley advanced his price of iron – then a meeting was called of the Trade & the only course open to pursue seemed to be 20% advance. Time alone will prove whether it was an improper step or not. Masters had no inclination to advance; it has been forced upon them by the men. It is generally thought that the advance will be maintained orders are now beginning to come in as it. [   ][3]

We hope to receive a good share from you & that neither firm will realise the dearth of orders to which you refer. We may name that our men are perfectly satisfied with their wages & had no interview with us at the time the agitation was going on.

Yours most respectfully
W^m. Millington & C°.

---

[1] See below, Letter 327A.

[1] Jevons evidently copied this letter and returned the original to his cousin: the manuscript now among the Jevons Papers is headed in his own handwriting, 'Copy'.

[2] i.e. the price of iron.

[3] A word appears to have been omitted here.

328.   W. S. JEVONS TO HARRIET JEVONS

Strand W.C.
3 Dec. 69.

Dearest Harriet,

I have just been with the great man[1] for about half an hour and found him very agreeable. We talked about all sorts of things chiefly great secrets – and I am very glad on the whole that I have seen him, but nothing particular comes of it in any way.[2]

I had a very quiet journey down as there were very few people in the train and I was alone except between Stockport and Crewe.

I hope I shall get back as comfortably. I do not think there will be anything to keep me beyond tomorrow here so you had better not think of going to Liverpool till next week; but if I should stay you must not be surprised. If I come it will be by the 5 p.m. train and I should be home shortly after 11 p.m.

I have no difficulty in posting this in time at the Charing Cross Central Post Office, where the mail closes at 6 p.m.

I hope you will be enjoying the soirée this evening. I do not the least know what I shall do. I sleep at the Euston Hotel. The sandwiches did very nicely, and I had just time to get a good lunch on getting to Euston.

I would rather that neither you nor Mary Anne[3] said anything of my going to see Lowe, especially as nothing is likely to come of it, but he was anything but disagreable* as Roscoe and Greenwood and others described him.

With best love to Mary Anne,
Ever your affectionate husband,
W. S. Jevons.

---

[1] i.e. Robert Lowe, the Chancellor of the Exchequer at this time. Robert Lowe, first Viscount Sherbrooke (1811–92), Fellow of Magdalen College, Oxford, 1835–6; emigrated to Australia, 1842; member of the legislative council of New South Wales, 1843–50; returned to England, 1850, and became M.P. for Kidderminster, 1852; Joint Secretary of the Board of Control, 1852–5; Vice-President of the Board of Trade, 1855–8; Vice-President of the Committee of the Privy Council on Education, 1859–64; M. P. for the University of London, 1868–80; Chancellor of the Exchequer, 1868–73; Home Secretary, 1873–4. See Vol. V, Letter 645, n. 3.

[2] Jevons had prepared for the Chancellor a report on the pressure of taxation, submitted on 13 March 1869, apparently at Lowe's request. This report seems to have influenced Lowe to abolish the nominal shilling duty on corn, and it appears that Jevons was Lowe's 'principal unofficial adviser' at this time. See Higgs's preface to Jevons's *The Principles of Economics* (1905) pp. XIV–XXII.

[3] Mary Anne Taylor (1840–1910), younger sister of Harriet Jevons. In February 1872 she married Jevons's cousin William Edgar Jevons. See Vol. I, p. 47, n. 4.

329.   W. S. JEVONS TO J. B. SMITH

Parsonage Road,
Withington,
Manchester.
24 April 70.[1]

J. B. Smith Esq., M.P.

My dear Sir,

It may perhaps be known to you that Mr. Frederick Hendriks[2] has lately been examined before the new Commission of Inquiry into the Monetary Question at Paris.[3] I have seen a report of his evidence and it seems to me so very able and so strongly demonstrative of the advantages of the Metrical System that I am very desirous of seeing it published in some way in England. I take the liberty of suggesting that you might perhaps ask Mr. Lowe to cause it to be laid before Parliament as a Parliamentary paper.[4] This would be advantageous in more than one way as if agreed to by Mr. Lowe it would show that he has not abandoned his ideas which I find many people here and abroad suppose to be the case though it certainly is not.

I am informed that the Coinage Committee of the U.S. Congress have decided in favour of assimilating the five dollar piece to the 25 franc piece which if true is decisive of the form of the future international Currency.[5]

Allow me to thank you for the admirable letter which I am told you almost forced the *Times* to print last autumn.[6] The coinage controversy

[1] The original manuscript of this letter is now in the J. B. Smith Papers, Central Reference Library, Manchester.

[2] Frederick Hendriks (1827–1909), actuary to various insurance companies, Vice-President of the Royal Statistical Society. Author of *Decimal Coinage: a plan for its immediate extension in England in connection with the International Coinage of France and other countries* (1866), described by Jevons as 'the excellent pamphlet . . . which first made the subject well known in England': *Money and the Mechanism of Exchange* (1878) p. 172.

[3] 'In 1870, a short time previous to the declaration of war with Germany, France summoned a fresh Imperial Commission, presided over by the Minister of Commerce and the Minister President of the Council of State (M. de Parieu), to take evidence from all sides on the various questions connected with the standard and its bearing upon international coinage. No less than thirty-seven witnesses were examined.' Jevons, *Money*, pp. 173–4.

[4] There is no evidence that J. B. Smith followed up this suggestion of Jevons's.

[5] There were at this time two rival schemes for assimilating the United States gold coinage to an international standard – the 'French' scheme, to reduce the value of a gold dollar to that of five francs of French gold coin, and the 'German' scheme to make the dollar consist of 1½ grams of pure gold, corresponding to a German crown. A bill (H.R. 1113, 41st Congress, 2nd session) incorporating the latter proposal had been introduced in Congress on 7 February 1870, read twice and referred to the Committee on Coinage, Weights and Measures, which, as Jevons reports, preferred the 'French' scheme. However, as this would have required a complete recoinage for the United States, the proposal was not carried into effect.

[6] *The Times*, 26 October 1869, p. 4. In this letter, written largely as an answer to the views of J. G. Hubbard, J. B. Smith had outlined the development of the movement for an international coinage and restated his reasons for supporting it.

which the Bank have lately reprinted is certainly the most unfair controversy that could be.[7]

Should you wish to see a copy of Mr. Hendriks evidence I shall be happy to let you see mine.

> Believe me,
> Yours faithfully,
> W. Stanley Jevons.

330.   W. S. JEVONS TO EDWARD ENFIELD[1]

address Withington

Blackpool
19 July 70.

Dear Mr. Enfield

After seeing you in London I made a second and more minute exam[n] of the books at Univ. Coll. and my account of them was communicated to the Trustees by Mr. Greenwood, together with the offer which you kindly made concerning them. The Trustees at once passed a Resolution enabling Mr. Greenwood & myself to accept them on behalf of the College and to make all requisite arrangements. As you will I suppose be in Scotland for some time nothing can probably be done just at present. Mr. Greenwood will also be away for a little time.

The books consist of more than 2000 volumes and excluding pamphlets or other things which you do not offer there are these principal portions   1. The Commons Journals   2. Several sets of Parliamentary Papers of various ages.   3. The Record Commissions Publications.

We should like to have all these as complete as possible but there will be a considerable number of Duplicate Parliamentary papers which we would select out & leave for Univ. Coll. to sell as waste paper.

It is certainly true that all the books you propose to give are at the Museum in the most perfect and accessible form – whereas if you carry out your proposal we shall have an accessible & extensive set of these official pub[s.] which will be of use to the Manchester people generally I hope as well as to our College circle. They will form a solid & heavy

---

[7] *Gold Coinage Controversy of 1869* (Bank of England, 1870). Cf. above, p. 211. Smith's letter of 26 October 1869 was reprinted in this volume, as also were Jevons's letters to *The Times* of 24 August and 10 September 1869.

[1] See Vol. II, Letter 35, n. 2, p. 64. Enfield was at this time a member of the Council of University College London and of its committee of management, posts he held from 1858 until his death; he became President of the Senate of the College, from 1878 until his death. He was also treasurer of University College Hospital from 1867 until his death and President of Manchester New College from 1878.

foundation to what will ultimately be as we may fairly hope a great library.[2]

We are here only for a few days longer.

Hoping that Harriet & yourself are enjoying Scotland

Yours very faithfully

W. Stanley Jevons

331.   W. S. JEVONS TO JOHN ROBSON[1]

Blackpool
24 July 1870.

John Robson Esqe
    University College

My dear Sir

The trustees of Owens College have been fully informed concerning the character & number of the books to which you allude. They are quite desirous of adding them to our library and have in fact passed a Resolution which will enable the Principal and myself to accept them should a formal offer, as I hope, be made. Mr. Greenwood & myself have in fact authority to do all that is requisite should the Council or Committee of U. C. L. wish to carry out the suggestion that has been made.

Although of little use in London so near the Museum they will in Manchester be by far the best collection of the sort, and will, I should think, be of use not only to those immediately connected with the College but to the public of Manchester.

Although there is every intention that they should be a permanent part of our future library, I think the Trustees would hardly like to bind themselves distinctly to preserve the books for ever. But if desired it might be understood that we should not part with them unless after placing

---

[2] The Minutes of Trustees of Owens College record that the offer of a gift of 'a large number of books' made by University College London, through W. S. Jevons, was accepted at the meeting held on 7 July 1870. A resolution of thanks for the 'valuable collection of blue books' given by University College was passed on 18 May 1871. The wording of the first resolution suggests some hesitation on the part of the Trustees to accept the collection without a careful inspection first. The Librarians of the time, James Holme Nicholson and James Taylor Kay, appear to have lacked enthusiasm over the gift and perhaps in consequence of this the volumes were never accessioned in the Owens College Library. The exact number of volumes accepted is therefore uncertain, although they can be identified by the University College London stamp. The early accessions registers show that throughout his career in Manchester Jevons was responsible for a large number of gifts to the Owens College Library.

[1] John Robson (1815–76), barrister, classical scholar; a master at University College School, 1840–54; Assistant Secretary, University College London, 1865; Secretary, 1867 until his death.

them again at the disposal of University College. It would doubtless be the object of the Council to preserve the books from the destruction to which they would probably go if sold, & we would gladly carry out this object as fully as possible.

We should of course like to have the sets of publications as complete as possible since their value would be much diminished by separation.

I am, my dear Sir

Yours faithfully

W. Stanley Jevons.

24th July 1870
W. S. Jevons

331A.   W. S. JEVONS TO W. B. HODGSON [1]

Owens College, Manchester,
August 11th, 1870. [2]

My Dear Sir,

Hearing that you are desirous of holding the new Chair of Economical Science and Commerce in the University of Edinburgh, I have much pleasure in expressing my strong hope that you may acquire a position which will aid you in your efforts to advance and spread a knowledge of Political Economy. It must be known to most persons how much you have done in prosecution of this aim by your lectures and publications. All your works, as I need hardly say, display a wide and intimate acquaintance with the literature of Economy, both foreign and English. Everyone who has enjoyed the pleasure and advantage of hearing your oral expositions must know how admirably and powerfully a scientific view of the subject in hand is set forth by you with a truly unrivalled fertility and aptness of illustration. To my mind, you always carry conviction of the truth and soundness of the opinions you advocate, and the power of your writings is increased by the fact that your strictly scientific investigations are combined with a wide knowledge of human nature. Thus, in your hands, theoretical views are applied and limited by an unusual acquaintance with all the practical conditions. I trust,

---

[1] William Ballantyne Hodgson (1815–80), Professor of Political Economy and Mercantile Law in the University of Edinburgh, 1871–80; Secretary of the Liverpool Mechanics' Institute, 1839, and afterwards Principal of the Institute School, where Jevons was one of his pupils. Cf. Vol. I, p. 13.

[2] Printed in *Testimonials in favour of W. B. Hodgson . . . Candidate for the Professorship of Political Economy and Mercantile Law in the University of Edinburgh* (1870) in the Jevons Collection, vol. 32, 491–541 (517–8), British Library of Political and Economic Science, London School of Economics.

therefore, that you may be elected to a post which will facilitate the prosecution of the objects you have in view.

I am, my dear Sir, yours faithfully,

W. Stanley Jevons.

W. B. Hodgson, Esq., LL.D.

332.   J. N. LOCKYER[1] TO W. S. JEVONS

Nature Office,
London.
Sept. 9. [1870]

My dear Sir,

May I have your address to print with Huxley's[2] next week? Nature will not reach Liverpool till Friday.[3]

Very faithfully yours,

J. N. Lockyer.

Professor Jevons.

333.   W. S. JEVONS TO SIR JOHN F. W. HERSCHEL
        [HLRS, 328]

Parsonage Road,
Withington,
Manchester,
29 Oct 1870.

My dear Sir,

It has been felt by several scientific men of Manchester – Mr. Joule,[1] Mr. Balfour Stewart,[2] Dr. Roscoe especially, that there is no sufficient

---

[1] Sir Joseph Norman Lockyer (1836–1920), astronomer, discoverer of helium. Lecturer in Astronomy at South Kensington, 1870; Professor of Astronomical Physics and Director of the Solar Physics Laboratory, Royal College of Science, 1890–1913. Lockyer became the founding editor of *Nature* in 1869. See A. J. Meadows, *Science and Controversy, a biography of Sir Norman Lockyer* (1972).

[2] Thomas Henry Huxley (1825–95), zoologist and champion of Darwin's theory; Hunterian professor at the Royal College of Surgeons, 1863–9; Fullerian professor at the Royal Institution, 1863–6; President of the Royal Society, 1883–5.

[3] Lockyer was hoping to publish the text of Jevons's proposed Presidential address to the Economic Section of the British Association in *Nature*, to coincide with the meeting which was to take place in Liverpool the following week. Huxley had complied with a similar request, as was acknowledged in the preamble to his address, published in full in *Nature*, 15 September 1870, pp. 399–406. Lockyer evidently intended to reassure Jevons that as *Nature* appeared on Thursdays, the text would not be available until after the presentation of his address. Jevons does not appear to have complied with this request, however, as only H. E. Roscoe's address as President of the Chemical Section appeared with Huxley's. A report of Jevons's address, together with those of the other Presidents of Sections, was published a week later, *Nature*, 22 September 1870, pp. 416–28 (428).

[1] See Vol. II, Letter 35, n. 13, p. 66.

[2] Balfour Stewart (1829–87), Professor of Natural Philosophy at Owens College, Manchester, 1870–87; well known for his research on radiant heat and pioneer work in spectrum analysis.

influence possessed by men of science in national affairs, and that the total want of common action in matters relating to Government is the cause of this. They, therefore, wish to ascertain how far it would be possible to draw together the influence which properly belongs to leading scientific men, so as to enable the majority of those who may unite together to attempt to carry out with some prospect of success any measures which they may decide upon. The Society is not intended to be in any way a Manchester undertaking, but when once started will be in the hands of the members. It is not intended to make it public until many of the leading men of science have agreed to join, and we hope that we may have your concurrence among the first. I do not remember to have seen any distinct opinion expressed by you on the subject of Government support to science but if you at all approve of the general feeling in favour of a more liberal use of the public money for scientific purposes we should venture to ask your name and influence in the matter. The enclosed paper[3] will in other respects explain itself.

> Believe me, my dear Sir,
> Yours faithfully,
> W. Stanley Jevons.

Sir J. Herschel Bart &c &c

334. SIR JOHN F. W. HERSCHEL TO W. S. JEVONS

> Collingwood,
> Nov. 10/70.

My dear Sir,

I did not reply immediately to yours of Oct 29 being unwilling to reply hastily to a proposal of the kind so marked. After giving it my best consideration however, I cannot say that I feel at all disposed to take a part in the intended movement. I think that we have already too many Leagues, Unions, Associations, and Combinations having for their object an organised agitation to influence the Government for special ends, and that the interests of Science as a great element of National and Universal well being may quite as well be trusted to the general wisdom of our Lords & Commons as those other great interests to which the circular

---

[3] The paper, which presumably set out the objects of the proposed society, is no longer with the original manuscript of the letter.

The whole question of the relations of the state to science was the subject of widespread discussion at this time. As a result of the report of a Committee of the Council of the British Association received at its Exeter meeting in 1869, a deputation had met Earl de Grey on 4 February 1870 to request the issue of a Royal Commission on this subject. The Commission was established, with the Duke of Devonshire as its chairman, and its final report appeared in 1872 – Scientific Instruction and the Advancement of Science, *Parl. Papers*, 1872 [C. 536] xxv.

accompanying your letter refers (Commerce, Manufacturers, Agriculture, Railways, Religion, Navigation, and War) and which seem to me to call for no *Parties* in either house for their advocacy, maintenance and improvement – but to rest more fitly (as I think Science may properly do) on their intrinsic and universally recognised importance to mankind.

Neither am I at all convinced that such a league or organised association would be likely permanently to confine its action to subjects purely within the limits of its own proper scope. I have seen with regret the British Association going beyond its proper sphere and in the steps taken and taking to procure the legislative introduction into this country of the metric system of weights and measures – a project encroaching on the habits, feeling, and convenience of the whole community and involving an amount of social disturbance infinitely beyond its alleged scientific importance even were that importance conceded. [1] Again I see at present the Society of Arts showing strong symptoms of entering into an agitation for a "spelling reform" [2] to be enforced in the National Schools by legislation or at all events by administrative *authority* in other words a project for the abolition of the etymological element of our language (a strictly scientific matter) etc. etc.

I will therefore trust that you will hold me excused for not complying with your suggestion that I should give in my adhesion to your circular.

Believe me,

My dear sir,

Yours very truly,

J. F. W. Herschel

---

[1] At the meeting of the British Association in 1870 a 'Report on the best means of providing for a uniformity of Weights and Measures with reference to the Interests of Science' had been presented by a committee under the chairmanship of Sir John Bowring. The report strongly advocated the universal adoption of the metric system. See *Report of the Fortieth Meeting of the British Association . . . held at Liverpool in September 1870*, p. 153.

[2] A paper by Alexander J. Ellis entitled 'On a Practical Method of meeting the Spelling Difficulty in School and in Life' had been read before the Royal Society of Arts on 20 April 1870 and gave rise to considerable subsequent discussion. The Council of the Royal Society of Arts, according to Edwin Chadwick, 'expressed their belief that the three R[s] might be taught in probably half the time now occupied in teaching them', but this point was not specifically pressed in the various submissions which the Society made to Parliament at this time in connection with the Elementary Education Bill. Cf. *Journal of the Society of Arts*, 18 (1870) 488–501.

335. F. BOWEN[1] TO W. S. JEVONS

Harvard College,
Cambridge – Nov. 23, '70.

My dear Sir,

The very day after receiving the "Elementary Logic" which you were kind enough to send me, I carried it into my Class-room, and have used it ever since as an aid in teaching the young men. It is much the best textbook for instruction that has yet appeared, though a crowd of "Logics" have been recently published in England, and a few in this country. I have examined most of these, and have thrown them aside as superficial and poorly executed. Your questions, exercises, and examples are excellent – just what was wanted. I wish that competent persons, really acquainted with the latest developments of science, and able to add to them by their own efforts, would oftener stoop to this humble task of preparing good textbooks; for we, whose vocation it is to teach the moral sciences need them sorely. I am glad that you have incorporated into this little work so much of the important matter in your two independent treatises on Similars and the Logic of Quality. You have thus popularized your own improvements.

In Pol. Economy it seems that we do not think alike so much as in Logic. And yet I do not think the dissidence is great, and the progress of events is likely to bring us still nearer together. I am only a moderate Protectionist, and dislike the excessive and unreasonable Tariff which has here been established as much as any one can. On the other hand, you must excuse me for believing that England has been fanatical on the subject of Free Trade for the last quarter of a century, and that her manufacturers and laboring classes are just beginning to find out their mistake. After the cheap labor of Belgium and Germany has displaced a little more of her industry, and caused some more distress among her artisans, perhaps Parliament may be induced to look a little to the other side of the shield, and Pol. Economists to revise some of their conclusions. In the present state of the relations between Labor and Capital, I cannot think it wise or just to tax heavily tea, coffee, sugar, beer, and tobacco, – the luxuries of the poor and to allow fine cutlery, silks and other costly manufactures, the luxuries of the rich, to go wholly untaxed. This may seem a democratic argument; but on this point, I suspect, you are at least as good a democrat as I am.[2]

---

[1] Francis Bowen (1811–90), Alvord Professor of Natural Religion, Moral Philosophy and Civil Polity at Harvard University, 1853–89; editor and proprietor of the *North American Review*, 1843–54. Bowen was well known for the moderate protectionist views which he professes in this letter.

[2] The concluding sheet of the original letter is missing.

336.   W. S. JEVONS TO A. MACMILLAN
        [MA]

Parsonage Road,
Withington
Manchester
28 March 1871

My dear Sir,

I send by book post a MS which I have just finished of a small work on Political Economy. I should be glad to have it published without delay, [1] and I daresay it will sell rather better than my little logical books. It is far from being a popular book, but there is a greater number of readers interested in any economical subject than in a logical or metaphysical one. [2]

If you have no objection I should like to have the "Theory of Political Economy" uniform with the Coal Question – It will then have a handsome readable type. I think it will not make more than about 240 pages of the same size as the Coal Question. No preface or index will be needed, but possibly an appendix of a few pages may have to be added. [3]

If you consent to undertake it, will you name the terms which I suppose will be the usual ones.

I hope in a few weeks to finish the articles on Mill's Logic which I propose to offer you for the magazine.

I have not begun the small schoolbook on political economy having my doubts on the ease of doing it. I am inclined to think that an "Elementary treatise on Political Economy and Monetary Science" if carefully put together and made interesting and impartial might sell very well. Professor Fawcett's Manual is very good but far too much an abstract of Mill. It has not a sufficient variety of information. What do you think of such an Elementary treatise or Elements?

Yours faithfully,
W. Stanley Jevons

A. Macmillan Esq.

---

[1] The *Theory of Political Economy* was in fact published in October 1871.

[2] This judgement by Jevons was in a sense correct, if applied to his monographs rather than his textbooks. According to Keynes, by 1936 the *Theory of Political Economy* had sold 7000 copies as against 1000 copies of Jevons's *Pure Logic* (1863), but on the other hand his *Primer of Logic* (1876) had sold 148,000 copies and his *Primer of Political Economy* (1878) 98,000 copies. Cf. *Essays in Biography, Collected Writings* x, 142, 145.

[3] As eventually printed, the first edition contained 267 pages of text, a preface of 11 pages, and no appendix or index.

337.   W. S. JEVONS TO A. MACMILLAN
       [MA]

Parsonage Road,
Withington
30 March 1871

My dear Sir,

The terms you name half profits and no risk – will suit me well. That is what we had I think with the Coal Question. I do not anticipate at all a large sale of the 'Theory' but should hope to sell one edition beyond doubt. You know best about the precise form in which you will put it – but I should like it to be of the same external size as the Coal Question.

I cannot have made plain what I said about an Elementary Treatise or Elements of Pol. Econ. I meant that one or other of these names might suit it. The book would be of a totally different kind from Mrs. Fawcetts' with which I am perfectly acquainted as I use it in one of my classes. The book I mean would be more like Professor Fawcetts' Manual, but larger rather than smaller being a sort of compendium or handbook of the science of Pol. Econ. The idea was suggested to me by Garnier's "Traité d'Économie Politique" which has gone through five or more editions in France, and is a very useful book.[1]

Professor Fawcetts' Manual is as it seems to me entirely good from his point of view, but too exclusively a reflection of Mill's opinions. My elements would be an impartial statement of all the more important views – with abundance of useful information interspersed.

But I do not need to trouble you about the matter until the book is done supposing I try to carry out the idea.[2]

I suppose you are sending the 'Theory' to a printer who will do the mathematical symbols, which occur here and there, in the best style.

I sent with the MS a drawing for 13 wood cuts – I should like these to be well cut and on a light or dark ground as you think best.

Yours faithfully,
W. Stanley Jevons.

---

[1] Joseph Garnier, *Traité d'économie politique, exposé didactique des principes et des applications de cette science et de l'organisation économique de la société*, sixth edition (1868).

Joseph-Clement Garnier (1813–82) was Professor of Political Economy at the Ecole des Ponts et Chaussées; co-founder, with Charles Guillaumin, of the Société d'économie politique, and principal editor of the *Journal des Economistes* at various dates from 1845 onwards.

[2] The book envisaged seems to have been something between the very brief introductory *Political Economy* which Jevons wrote for the Science Primers series in 1878 and the comprehensive *Principles of Economics* which he left unfinished at his death, but the proposal was not carried into effect.

338.   R. D. BAXTER[1] TO W. S. JEVONS

6 Victoria Street,
Westminster Abbey, S.W.
19 April 1871.

My dear Sir,

I send you a copy of my paper[2] on National Debts at the reading of which you presided and which has now grown into a book. I hope you will find that it is now tolerably complete.

I have been obliged to resort to estimates of income in order to ascertain the burden of the debt. I hope that you will think them not extravagant. The great difficulty was to bring all the calculations of income to one scale.

The French and United States incomes are calculated on a much more liberal not to say exaggerated basis than the English, while the Russian Austrian and Prussian were almost as much in error the other way. Hence it was no easy task to consider the corrections to be made and to make them without giving offence to the authors of the estimates.

The calculations about France have been confirmed since they were printed by Mr. Goschens French figures[3] in which he gives the rise in value of French real estate between 1836 and 1867 as from £85,000,000 to £160,000,000 sterling a proportion which very much bears out my calculation of the increase of the total income, and is a greater increase than the English which between 1841 and 1868 was from £85,000,000 to £144,000,000 in Schedule A.

A writer in the Economist[4] (said to be a distinguished French Economist probably M. Wolowsky [sic][5] states the income of France at £800,000,000.

We had a Meeting last night at the Statistical to hear the prize Essay read by Mr. Palgrave.[6] I was disappointed in it as it was more a compilation than an original work and it does not present its conclusions very clearly.

Have you considered Mr. Goschen's Local Taxation report?[7] We

---

[1] Robert Dudley Baxter (1827–75), pioneer in the statistical treatment of social and economic questions. His works included *The Budget and the Income Tax* (1860), *The National Income* (1868) and *The Political Progress of the Working Class* (1871).

[2] *National Debts, partly read before the British Association at Liverpool, September 1870* (1871).

[3] Goschen, *Report on . . . Local Taxation*, appendix A, part v, table vi, p. 171. For full reference to this report, see below, n. 7.

[4] *The Economist*, 15 April 1871, p. 441.

[5] Louis Wolowski (1810–76). See above, Letters 309 and 310, pp. 196 and 198.

[6] R. H. Inglis Palgrave, 'On the Local Taxation of Great Britain and Ireland', *JRSS*, 34 (1871) 111–235.

[7] Report of the Rt. Hon. G. J. Goschen, M. P. . . . on the Progressive Increase of Local Taxation, *Parl. Papers*, 1870 (470) LV. See also R. Dudley Baxter, *Local Government and Taxation and Mr. Goschen's Report* (1874).

debated it last night at a very long sitting. My objection to it is that he does not distinguish between burdens which are and are not Taxes, nor between taxes on personal and industrial property and general taxes on all three kinds of property so that he establishes no ratio of burden of the real taxation on each description of property.

His idea also of the burden having been transferred from the land seems to me foolish, since parishes are independent States for purposes of local taxation, and the increase has been in only a proportion of those States and not in the whole so that nothing has been transferred from one State to another or one kind of property to another so far as we have any data for determining.

Yours truly,
R. Dudley Baxter.

Professor Stanley Jevons.

339.   W. S. JEVONS TO H. CLARKE[1]
[LJN, 253]

13 Montague Street, Russel Square, W.C.,
24th June 1871

. . . I have only just received your note, forwarded from Manchester. The remarks[2] you mention are, I presume, those concerning the distribution of the Celtic population which prevailed towards the west and north-west. Isaac Taylor, in his interesting book, Words and Places,[3] gave, as perhaps you know, a good deal of information on the point, and I think you would find some correspondence with your own results concerning intellectual ability. I should think that the difference between the East and West of Scotland, remarked at the meeting, would be due to the same circumstances.

If there is time for you to add a note or paragraph to your paper, you had perhaps better verify independently what I have said, as it was only

---

[1] Hyde Clarke (1815–95), a civil engineer who wrote extensively on social and economic questions. Employed in the extension of railways and telegraphs in upper India, he became honorary agent for Darjeeling and the planters of eastern India. He was a Vice-President of the [Royal] Statistical Society, to whose proceedings he contributed five papers.

[2] Jevons, in his Opening Address as President of Section F of the British Association in September 1870, had commented on the higher mortality in cities of the north-west of England, and suggested that it might be connected with the higher proportion of Irish immigrants in these places. See *JRSS*, 33 (1870) 319–20, 323–6. Reprinted in *Methods*, pp. 194–216.

[3] Isaac Taylor, *Words and Places* (1865) chapter IX, 'The Celts'. Hyde Clarke, 'On the Geographical Distribution of Intellectual Qualities in England', *JRSS*, 34 (1871) 357–67.

just on the spur of the moment the remark occurred, and I should prefer not to be responsible for it.

The comparison of races is no doubt an invidious task, which might sometimes lead to trouble, but I do not see that in statistical inquiries you can suppress plain facts. I think that in legislation relating to different parts of the United Kingdom it is always well to be reminded that there may be distinctly different races to be dealt with, and the more mixture of races can be promoted the better. . . .

340.   W. S. JEVONS TO J. MILLS
        [TLJM, 337]

Owens College
October 17, 1871.

Dear Mr. Mills,

The Committee[1] have decided, as I may say, *nemine contradicente*, to propose you as President, and they desired me to arrange with you as to Inaugural Address in November.

I feel much pleasure at leaving the Society in your hands.[2]

Yours faithfully,
W. S. Jevons.

341.   W. L. SARGANT[1] TO W. S. JEVONS

Edgbaston
Oct. 29, 71.

Dear Sir,

I acknowledge at once your kind present,[2] not for the ordinary reason in favour of such haste, but because I am meditating an essay on one of the topics you treat.

Your treatment of it and mine will be as different as chalk from cheese. Still I had rather steer my boat clear of your vessel.

Our School board is mighty cantankerous, and as Chairman I have something to do to keep the peace.

---

[1] of the Manchester Statistical Society.

[2] W. S. Jevons was President of the Manchester Statistical Society from 1869 to 1871; John Mills from 1871 to 1873.

[1] William Lucas Sargant (1809–89); after graduating from Cambridge, entered his father's business of small-arms manufacture in Birmingham; Justice of the Peace, 1849; member and afterwards chairman of Birmingham School Board, 1870. Author of numerous economic works, including *The Science of Social Opulence* (1856), *Recent Political Economy* (1867) and *Essays of a Birmingham Manufacturer*, 4 vols (1868–72). See Vol. V, Letter 629.

[2] Evidently of a copy of the *Theory of Political Economy*, which was published in October 1871.

When I have read your book I will give you my opinions. I expect much novelty and gratification.

Yours faithfully,
W. L. Sargant.

342. R. LOWE TO W. S. JEVONS

11, Downing Street,
Whitehall.
[October 1871]

Dear Mr. Jevons,

I am much obliged to you for your work on political economy which I shall read without delay. I have always thought the subject of method has not received all the attention it deserves and that a little more attention to the workings of the human mind which lie at the root of all economical phenomena deserve more retention than they have received. [1] There are numberless things such as Light Heat Electricity of which we know nothing but in their effects and I dont see why the treatment which has nevertheless made them Sciences should not succeed in this case also.

Believe me,
Very truly yours
Robert Lowe

343. W. S. JEVONS TO J. E. CAIRNES

Parsonage Road
Withington
Manchester
14 Jany 72 [1]

My dear Sir

I have read with great interest your remarks in the Fortnightly review [2] and have thought them over for several days before writing you a few lines in reply.

As regards my observations on the too great influence of authority, it is not the writers but the readers and students which I referred to, as you will find evident in the last page of the book. The almost exclusive use of

---

[1] This sentence is reproduced exactly as in the original manuscript. It seems probable that Lowe was writing in haste, intended to put 'attention' where he wrote 'retention' and failed to notice that the end of the sentence was a partial repetition of the beginning.

[1] The original manuscript of this letter is in the Cairnes Papers, MS 8954, National Library of Ireland.

[2] J. E. Cairnes, 'New Theories in Political Economy', *Fortnightly Review*, New Series, 11 (1872) 72.

Mr Mills political Economy or that of Prof. Fawcett of which I have experience in the University of London examinations & elsewhere tends to force upon the present generation one set of opinions many of which I venture to think erroneous. Some writer who reviews Macdonell's Survey of P. E. in the last British Quarterly Review evidently has the same feeling and speaks of the Intellectual Tyranny associated with the name of Mr Mill. [3] This kind of tyranny exercised in logical and philosophical subjects by a well defined school of writers is equally irksome to me in my other branch of teaching work, and I feel sure that it is as requisite now as ever to protest against any exclusive tendencies of the kind

As regards the theory of value I have not made many express references to the differences of market & cost values by those names, but in reality the difference is implied in the chapters on Exchange & Labour. I did not use the names because I considered values to be always governed by the same general principles in each case. In the chapter on Exchange the dependence of value on supply and demand is treated wholly without regard to the mode of supply. It is when I pass in the next chapter to the question of labour as yielding supply that values are found to be limited in the long run by the costs of production, as fully stated in pp. 181–2. You will there find that I adduce the correspondence of my formulae with the usual view of the subject as affording a confirmation of the correction of the previous theories.

The fundamental objection which you make to my theory of exchange is that I define value by utility and then propose to use prices to measure the variation of utility. This seems a *vicious circle* – but I do not think you will find it to be so really, and the method seems to me exactly analogous to that employed in other theoretical subjects such as that of light, heat, electricity, &c. The properties of the basis of light undulations are entirely hypothetical. Scientific men assume those properties as they like, calculate what would happen on such conditions and then by comparison with facts ascertain whether they are correct. They have no means of measuring the properties of the ether except by arguing back from observation. So there is no means of measuring pleasure & pain directly, but as those feelings govern sales and purchases, the prices of the market are those facts from which one may argue back to the intensity of the pleasures concerned. Even gravity is known only in its effects; we cannot

[3] *British Quarterly Review*, 55 (1872) 243–4. The article, which is unsigned, reviews Jevons's *Theory* as well as John Macdonell's *A Survey of Political Economy* (Edinburgh, 1871), to which the major part of the review is devoted. In the passage mentioned by Jevons, the writer commented: 'The (apparently) established laws of the science [*of political economy*] had a close and fruitful application to our own economical state, partly because they were mainly generalizations from it; and these laws were discovered and enforced by a succession of eminent thinkers. . . . But the kind of intellectual tyranny which is associated in our own generation with the name of Mr. Mill is fast becoming an extinct tradition. . . .'

measure gravity itself and merely observe how rapidly it causes a body to fall. So we must measure the elements of the human mind by its concrete results as manifested in labour, & the amounts of commodity consumed and the relative values at which they are esteemed.

The criticisms on the theory which I have yet met do not at all shake my confidence in the general correctness of the way of viewing the subject, but they show that I have on many points very inadequately explained myself. If I could write the book again I should probably put many things in a clearer and simpler light and illustrate them more.

With sincere thanks for your kind attention to my speculations and the agreable* way in which you have written concerning it.

Believe me
Yours faithfully
W. Stanley Jevons.

344. A. B. HOPKINS[1] TO W. S. JEVONS

11 Brook Crescent
Philip Street, Aston,
Birmingham.
Ap. 11, 1872.

Sir,

In your intensely interesting book on the Theory of Political Economy, there is a point to which I take the liberty of calling your attention.

After laying down (pp. 53–61) in the most clear and convincing manner a symbolic expression for the total utility and the degree of utility of a commodity at any point in its consumption, you proceed (p. 62) to the General Law of the Variation of the final degree of Utility: viz. that "it varies with the quantity of commodity and finally decreases as that quantity increases."

It appears to me that this Law is amenable to the same kind of considerations as you employ in the preceding section, and that the same mathematical materials will furnish an expression which shall be, at least as far as theory goes perfectly precise. So obviously, indeed, does this expression seem to flow from the foregoing investigation, that I cannot help feeling somewhat surprised that you have not thought fit to insert it.

---

[1] In *White's Directory of Birmingham* for 1873 one John Hopkins is listed as living in Brook Crescent, Aston. A. B. Hopkins was presumably a member of the same family, but it has not proved possible to obtain any further information about him.

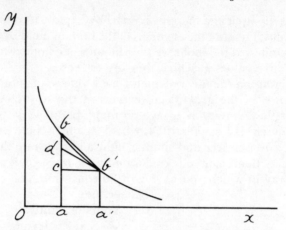

Draw b'c parallel to the axis of x, and draw the secant b'b.

You have shown that the degree of utility is $\dfrac{du}{dx}$ and is consequently a function of x. Let this degree of utility be represented by y, *so* that $y = \dfrac{du}{dx}$ $= \phi\,(x)$. Then $y - \triangle y = \phi\,(x + \triangle x)$ and $-\triangle y = \phi\,(x + \triangle x) - \phi\,(x)$. Now for the increment of commodity aa' we have the corresponding decrement of utility bc. These lines represent $\triangle x$ and $\triangle y$ respectively. Hence $\dfrac{\triangle y}{\triangle x} = -\dfrac{bc}{b'c} = -\tan bb'c$. Or, if we take x, y, the coordinates of b' and x', y' those of b, and consider the latter as current coordinates, we shall have an expression which will be always true. But this will be the equation to the secant b'b, which in the limit becomes the tangent b'd.

Hence $\dfrac{dy}{dx}$ $\left(\text{or } \dfrac{d^2u}{dx^2}\right) = -\tan db'c.$ [2]

The above process would of course require a more detailed treatment in a book than I have thought it necessary to give it here.

I am, Sir,

With great admiration and respect,

Yours obediently,

Albert B. Hopkins.

Professor Jevons.

P.S. In p. 100, line 1, should not $\dfrac{y}{x}$ be $\dfrac{x}{y}$? [3]

[2] Hopkins does not explicitly state an expression for the 'General Law of the Variation of the Final Degree of Utility', but his conclusion is essentially that which was economically stated by Marshall – 'Subject to the qualifications mentioned in the text $\dfrac{d^2u}{dx^2}$ is always negative' – *Principles of Economics*, Mathematical Appendix, ninth edition, vol. 1, p. 838. Jevons did not adopt Hopkins's suggested diagrammatic exposition in any subsequent edition of *T.P.E.*

[3] The passage in question reads: 'hence the utility per unit of beef must be $\dfrac{y}{x}$ times that of corn; or,

345. W. S. JEVONS TO HERBERT JEVONS
[LJN, 257]

Ludlow,
12th May 1872.

. . . Harriet and I are now on a visit here of a week or ten days.

I have been rather more ill than I like to think of. It commenced shortly after Christmas by indigestion and sleeplessness, and although I managed to carry on my college work until Easter, my doctor then ordered me to leave off all work whatever; I seem to have exhausted my nervous system by over-work, so that any exertion disarranges my digestion and heart, but after some sharp treatment, involving several weeks in bed, or in the house, I think I am coming all right again. I shall have to spend the next three or four months as a perfect holiday, and we have various plans as to what to do; not unlikely we shall go to Norway.

I am to be one of the fifteen new members of the Royal Society elected this year, and Harry Roscoe informs me that in the ballot by the council I came out at, or very near, the top of the list. . . .

346. W. S. JEVONS TO A. MACMILLAN
[MA]

Parsonage Road,
Withington,
Manchester.
13 Sept. 1872.

My dear Sir,

I mentioned to you some time since that I was engaged upon a rather large work on Logic. Although illness has interfered of late with its progress there is so much of the work completed that I am desirous of commencing the printing. Some 300 pages type are actually ready for the press and the remainder is mostly written and only wants copying out or correcting and completing here and there.

---

considering the increments as infinitely small, the degrees of utility will be inversely as the magnitudes of the increments.' In fact this was incorrect: Jevons had telescoped two steps in the argument into one. In the second and later editions the passage was altered to read: 'Now the increment of beef, $\triangle y$, is $\frac{y}{x}$ times as great as the increment of corn, $\triangle x$, so that, in order that their utilities shall be equal, the degree of utility of beef must be $\frac{x}{y}$ times as great as the utility of corn. Thus we arrive at the principle that *the degrees of utility of commodities exchanged will be in the inverse proportion of the magnitudes of the increments exchanged* . . .'(second edition, p. 99.)

The proposed title is as follows,
>"*The Principles of Science*
>A Treatise upon Logic and
>scientific method"

The earlier part consists of a statement of my formal logic put in as interesting a form as possible but at least two thirds of the work consists in an application of logical principles to physical science which will I hope prove interesting. There are many indications that a work of this kind is wanted at the present time.

I estimate the length of the book at 250,000 words which with a page containing 300 words will make two volumes of about 400 pages each. I think that you will from this be able to judge what kind of type to put it in, and before reaching the end of the first volume I shall be able to judge with considerable certainty as to the length of the whole.

I shall be glad if you will as soon as convenient state the terms upon which you will undertake the publication of such a work. The common arrangement of half profits and no risk would meet my expectations but at the same time I must say that I may want some time in bringing the whole to completion. My health is so far from being satisfactory that I could not engage to finish the proofs in any definite time and I wish to feel quite at liberty to take my own time about it.

I have already spent the greater part of seven years upon it and I should certainly hope to complete it in three years more at the utmost. I wish to know what kind of agreement you could propose which would leave me at perfect liberty in the printing so that I could forward portions of the copy just as I can finish them and yet would leave the publication in your hands supposing that I am able to do the work in any reasonable time. Were I in good health I have no doubt I could do it in nine months and have the work out in October 1873 but I want to have ample time for delays. Most parts of the book have already been written several times over and a very great amount of labour has been spent upon it. Indeed I consider it the most important book that I can ever hope to produce. Supposing that we should commence the printing *I do not wish anyone to know for the present of its being in the press.*

>Believe me,
>Yours faithfully,
>W. S. Jevons.

347. W. S. JEVONS TO J. E. CAIRNES

Parsonage Road
Withington
Manchester
5 Oct 72[1]

Dear Cairnes

You will probably have received the copy of the paper which I sent in accordance with your desire. I have now great pleasure in answering the rest of your letter as far as I am able.

The increased price of coal appears to me to be *mainly* due to increased demand. The consumption is growing with alarming rapidity. The two latest returns of the quantity raised are as follows

1870	110,431,000 tons
1871	117,439,000 "

The quantity raised during the present year will doubtless be greatly in excess of the last amount. Incidentally I may mention that the consumption is keeping up to the geometrical ratio of increase with remarkable exactness as at the assumed rate of 3½ per cent per annum the amount for 1871 was calculated from that of 1861 at 117,900,000. At present however the increase is exceptionally rapid and as the number of pits cannot be rapidly increased the coal owners are reaping a vast profit. Of course when there is time to increase the means of supply the price must become more moderate – but at the same time there must be increase in the cost of production to some extent and the price is not likely ever to be as low after one of these great advances as before. I think in short that it is during these active periods that the general tendency to increased consumption makes itself apparent and in this as in many other matters the progressive increase is complicated with the 10-yearly fluctuation.

With regard to the course of wages in the United States I have no information but such as is found in Wells's reports which are known to you.[2] If there is no great hurry I should be happy to ask my brother who is settled in New York and who takes interest in such questions whether he can find any independent information.

The question of prices in India is one of great difficulty. I have made some inquiry but have yet obtained no more information than what is contained in the paper of M[r] Ollerenshaw which I forward.[3] I have also

---

[1] The original manuscript of this letter is now the Cairnes Papers, MS 8954, National Library of Ireland.

[2] D. A. Wells produced four annual reports during his period of office, published from 1867 to 1870. See above, Letter 311, n. 2, p. 200.

[3] J. C. Ollerenshaw, 'Our Export Trade in Cotton Goods to India', *Transactions of the Manchester Statistical Society*, 1869–70, pp. 109–24. Ollerenshaw was not listed as a member of the Society and no

compared the prices of oriental produce as given in my pamphlet "Serious Fall &c" pp. 27–8 with the corresponding prices in the Economist of 29 April 1871. By taking a time some 18 months ago we avoid the interference of the recent speculative rise. The list which I enclose includes Chinese as well as Indian articles – and you will see that some of the principal articles have not risen such as rice, sago, Rum.

I have also given a few prices taken from the last Economist but which I have not by me to give fuller quotations from.

I hardly like myself to attempt to form any opinion on the matter without going into very much more inquiry. I have been so much occupied with logical questions for the last few years that I have given no proper attention to these statistical matters. If however you are not in any immediate hurry I will endeavour to get the opinions of Mr Ollerenshaw or other men who from the value of their trade are acquainted with prices of Indian articles.

Thanks for your inquiries concerning my health. I am sorry to say that though I have had a holyday* for 6 months I am only partially better & have to give up half my College work during this session. But I hope that by taking every thing very easily I may gradually recover my former strength for the most part.

I was much grieved to hear that you thought it desirable to resign your professorship on account of health. I am glad however to find that you think of republishing your essays.[4] I shall be happy to get all information I can upon any point and if I hear from you that there is sufficient time I will hope to be able to answer your present queries much more satisfactorily.

Believe me
Yours very faithfully
W. S. Jevons.

---

further information about him has been traced. The paper is no longer with the manuscript.

[4] Cairnes's *Essays in Political Economy Theoretical and Applied* were published by Macmillan in 1873. It seems probable that Cairnes had written to Jevons for information on price and wage movements in order to carry on the tables of such movements down to 1858 given in an appendix to the book – but the final words of that appendix are 'This intention the writer has been prevented from carrying into effect'.

348. W. S. JEVONS TO J. L. SHADWELL[1]
[LJN, 268–70]

Parsonage Road, Withington,
17th October 1872.

. . . More than six months ago you did me the favour to send me some critical remarks upon my *Theory of Political Economy*. I was then, as I informed you at the time, prevented from giving any attention to the subject by the advice of my physician, and after being absent from home nearly the whole of the summer, it is only within the last few weeks that I have ventured to attempt any work again. You will therefore, perhaps, excuse my long delay in answering your letter, which was, nevertheless, of much interest to me.

You desire to retain Adam Smith's sense of the word value, and to use as a measure of value the length of time which a man will labour in order to obtain any given commodity. Now, you will find that in page 181 I show my view of the matter to be in accordance with the doctrine of labour *measuring* value, so far as it is true. Articles do exchange in quantities proportional to the products of equal quantities of labour.[2] But the subject requires to be much more carefully analysed, for, as I point out in chap. v., labour is excessively variable in painfulness, and the length of time is not sufficient to measure the amount of labour. It is true that equal quantities of labour are of equal value to the labourer, using the term value to express esteem or amount of pleasure and pain involved, but equal periods of labour do not necessarily represent equal amounts.

You object again that I have given no measure of happiness, but you will observe that there are many things which we cannot measure except by their effects. For instance, gravity cannot be measured except by the velocity which it produces in a body in a given time. All the other physical forces, such as light, heat, electricity, are incapable of being measured like water or timber, and it is by their effects that we estimate them. So pleasure must be estimated by its effects; and, though I did not go into the point, labour might undoubtedly be used as one of these effects. The average pain which a common labourer undergoes during, say, a quarter

---

[1] John Lancelot Shadwell was Prizeman in the Senior Class of Political Economy at University College London in 1870 and 1871. In 1877 he published *A System of Political Economy* in which he upheld Adam Smith's concept of labour as a measure of value. He was also the author of *Political Economy for the People* (reprinted from the *Labour News*, 1880) and *The Depression of Trade* (1885).

[2] *T.P.E.*, chapter v, 'Theory of Labour', section entitled 'Relation of the Theories of Labour and Exchange': 'thus we have proved that commodities will exchange in any market in the ratio of the quantities produced by the same quantity of labour'.

For some comment on this neglected part of *T.P.E.*, see R. D. Collison Black, Introduction to the Pelican Classics Edition (1970) pp. 24–5.

of an hour's work after he has been ten hours at work, would measure the utility to him of his last increments of wages – but the pain of this quarter of an hour is greater than that of any of the previous quarters.

Then, again, the pleasure may be defined by the amount of commodity producing it. Then the ordinary or average good occasioned to a man by an ounce of bread *after $\frac{3}{4}$ lb. of bread have already been eaten* might be taken as a unit of pleasure, remembering of course that the pleasure derived from any commodity is not proportional to that commodity. Then, as I have pointed out, pp. 12–14, all commercial statistics form data, which, if rendered more complete, would enable us to assign numerical values to our formulae. Prices express the relative esteem for commodities, and enable us to compare the pleasure produced by the final increments of the commodities. Had we complete tables of prices compared with quantities consumed, we could determine the numerical laws of variation of utility.

I believe I was not sufficiently careful to point out the process by which we might (with perfect statistics) turn all the formulae into numerical expressions, but I only attempted the first step, which was to get the formulae correctly, and the main point of difference from Adam Smith was the distinguishing of the *degree of utility from the total amount of utility.*

With regard to the relative variation of value of gold and silver, I was aware of what was stated about the increased production of silver, but I am not aware that this increase is nearly so great as that of the increase of gold. And I think that it entirely fails to account for the gold price of silver never varying more than about 3 per cent, and generally much less. . . .

349.   W. S. JEVONS TO J. L. SHADWELL
        [LJN, 270–1]

Parsonage Road,
Withington,
5th December, 1872

. . . I have been intending, day after day, to thank you for sending me the copy of the *Westminster Review*[1] containing your article on the 'Theory of Wages'. I particularly remarked the article at the time of its appearance, but not being in good health, set it down for reading at a future time. I have now read it more than once, and carefully considered it, and so far as I can pretend to judge, I think you have put forth the truth very clearly and soundly. I feel sure that the general proposition which you put forth,

[1] J. L. Shadwell, 'A Theory of Wages', *Westminster Review*, 97 (1872) 184–203.

that wages are ultimately governed by efficiency of labour, will some day or other be recognised as true, and though Mr. Hearn, myself, and perhaps some previous writers, have had some notions to the same effect, yet I think that you have stated the truth more roundly and fully. I am especially pleased with your protest against the effort to procure *cheap labour* as a means of promoting the prosperity of a country. I have often felt inclined to view the matter much in the same light, that cheap labour means a low reward for the main mass of the population, and the good chiefly of landed proprietors, but I do not remember this truth as being anywhere stated so clearly before.

I think that you are perfectly correct in taking *dear labour* to be the test of prosperity of a people, the dearness being, in fact, the measure of efficiency. It is only in the details of your argument that I should be inclined to criticise at all. I cannot concur in what you say on p. 202 of over-population resulting only from fluctuations of commerce.[2] Surely there is always over-population when people are improvident, and unable, or careless, to provide for the inevitable vicissitudes of the seasons. Ireland has furnished the clearest possible case of over-population, and I think that the same may be said of the whole agricultural population of the United Kingdom, which has only been to a certain extent saved by the extension of manufactures, as I tried to show in the chapters on population in my *Coal Question*.

Again, do you not sometimes ignore the variation in the value of money which on several occasions has produced an apparent rise of wages? I entertain no doubt that such is the case at present, and that it lies at the basis of all these strikes.

A more important point which I should dissent from is your adoption of a general average of wages and a treatment of the higher rates of pay to skilled mechanics and others as exceptional cases. In my Theory I have attempted to show that every one who works for pay will ultimately be paid according to what he contributes to the general industry. I think that it is the very essence of wages to vary with the skill and efficiency of the labourer, and you will readily see that this follows from your own theory. It is a convenient simplification of the subject to pass over this question of the difference of wages; but you so far detract from the consistency and value of your theory.

May I express a wish that you will not rest contented with having printed so concise an essay on the subject, but will develop your views more fully? I think there is great need in political economy of keeping independence of thought alive.

---

[2] 'What is called "over population" results rather from the fluctuations of commerce, which so frequently deprive men of the employment to which they are accustomed, than from any imprudence on the part of parents' (loc. cit., p. 202).

For myself, I am able to do so little work at present, and have such hard tasks of a different sort on hand, that I have little hope of writing anything more on political economy for some time to come. . . .

350.   HENRY AND ROBERT LANGTON TO W. S. JEVONS

Manchester & Salford District Provident Society
Manchester. 17th December 1872

Dear Sir,

In making our annual appeal on behalf of the Sick Relief Department of the District Provident Society, we wish to draw the attention of our Subscribers to the following facts:—Not only has the actual cost of living increased since last year, but the price of every necessary is doubled, and in some cases trebled.[1] Savings which previously might have tided over a temporary season of distress, are now quickly swallowed up, and the pressure upon the funds of the Society is sooner felt, and assistance more urgently needed than during previous seasons. To put this more forcibly before you, we give in a tabular form the difference between the present cost of living of a family of eight persons, and what it was in January last year.

	Requirements of a family of 8 persons per week	Price 1871	Price 1872	January 1871	December 1872	Excess
2 2 2						
	2 cwt. of Coals	7d cwt	1/1	− 1 2	− 2 2	− 1 −
3	10 4-lbs Loaves Bread	6d.	8d.	− 5 0	− 6 8	− 1 8
3	4 lbs Meat, Bacon, &c	7d.	9d.	− 2 4	− 3 −	− − 8
4	30 lbs Potatoes	1/2	1/8	− 1 9	− 2 6	− − 9
3	House Rent	4/-	4/6	− 4 −	− 4 6	− − 6
1	Milk & Sundries	−	−	− 1 −	− 2 −	− 1 −
0	Total £			− 15 3	1 − 10	− 5 7

---

¹ Jevons's response to this letter is not recorded, but the facts and ideas in it must have run counter to his own views and knowledge on two subjects – charity and prices. In his Inaugural Address to the Manchester Statistical Society on 10 November 1869 Jevons had referred to 'the tendency of medical charities . . . to nourish the spirit of pauperism' and felt himself bound to 'call in question the policy of the whole of our medical charities . . . and a large part of the vast amount of private charity' – *Methods*, pp. 188–9.

Jevons's own price index number covers only the period 1785–1865, but was linked with Sauerbeck's index by Walter Layton in *An Introduction to the Study of Prices* (1912). This index shows a rise from 133 in 1871 to 145 in 1872 (1900 = 100). For the same years Sauerbeck's index of food prices (average of 1867–77 = 100) rose from 98 to 102 (loc. cit., pp. 150–1). Hence more general indexes did not show, any more than the tabular statement in the letter, that 'the price of every necessary is doubled'.

We again mention the two points in our system of relief, which we think specially worthy of your attention:

1.   That relief is administered by the officers of the Society *only*, no personal application being on any account permitted.

2.   That our cases, with but few exceptions, are the recommendations of Medical Men, Sick-Nurses, and others whose vocation brings them most into contact with poverty and misfortune.

Since November last year 800 families numbering 4000 persons have been assisted by the Society, at a cost of about £500 – besides which 39 persons were sent to Southport and 370 families were supplied with clothing, bedding &c. Donations or Subscriptions may be paid to Messrs. Heywood Bros. St. Ann's Street, or to Mr. James Smith, 6 Queen Street, Albert Square, to the credit of the Sick Relief Fund of the District Provident Society – The Sums subscribed to this department are kept distinct from the general account, and are wholly devoted to the object for which they are given.

We remain,

Yours truly,

Henry Langton) Hon Secs.
Robert   )